The Princeton Review®

AP® COMPUTER SCIENCE A

PREP

2021 Edition

The Staff of The Princeton Review

PrincetonReview.com

Penguin
Random
House

The Princeton Review
110 East 42nd St, 7th Floor
New York, NY 10017
Email: editorialsupport@review.com

Published in the United States by Penguin Random House LLC, New York, and in Canada by Random House of Canada, a division of Penguin Random House Ltd., Toronto.

ISBN: 978-0-525-56949-7
ISSN: 2690-5345

Editor: Selena Coppock
Production Editors: Liz Dacey, Emma Parker
Production Artist: Jennifer Chapman
Content Developers: Ann Heltzel, Deepa Muralidhar, Derek Miller

Printed in the United States of America.

10 9 8 7 6 5 4 3 2 1

2021 Edition

Editorial

Rob Franek, Editor-in-Chief
Deborah Weber, Director of Production
Gabriel Berlin, Production Design Manager
Selena Coppock, Managing Editor
Aaron Riccio, Senior Editor
Meave Shelton, Senior Editor
Chris Chimera, Editor
Eleanor Green, Editor
Orion McBean, Editor
Brian Saladino, Editor
Patricia Murphy, Editorial Assistant

Random House Publishing Team

Tom Russell, VP, Publisher
Alison Stoltzfus, Publishing Director
Amanda Yee, Associate Managing Editor
Ellen L. Reed, Production Manager
Suzanne Lee, Designer

ACKNOWLEDGMENTS

Special thanks to Ann Heltzel, Deepa Muralidhar, and Derek Miller for their content development work on the 2021 edition of this book. Additionally, The Princeton Review would like to thank Jennifer Chapman, Liz Dacey, and Emma Parker for their contributions to this title.

Contents

Get More
(Free) Content
at **PrincetonReview.com/prep**

As easy as **1·2·3**

1 Go to PrincetonReview.com/prep and enter the following ISBN for your book:
9780525569497

2 Answer a few simple questions to set up an exclusive Princeton Review account. *(If you already have one, you can just log in.)*

3 Enjoy access to your **FREE** content!

Once you've registered, you can...

- Take a full-length practice SAT and ACT

- Access Practice Test 4 plus detailed Answers and Explanations

- Get valuable advice about the college application process, including tips for writing a great essay and where to apply for financial aid

- If you're still choosing between colleges, use our searchable rankings of *The Best 386 Colleges* to find out more information about your dream school

- Access comprehensive study guides and a variety of printable resources including AP Score Conversion charts, Key Terms lists, and the Glossary

- Check to see if there have been any corrections or updates to this edition

- Get our take on any recent or pending updates to the AP Computer Science A Exam

Need to report a potential **content** issue?

Contact **EditorialSupport@review.com** and include:

- full title of the book
- ISBN
- page number

Need to report a **technical** issue?

Contact **TPRStudentTech@review.com** and provide:

- your full name
- email address used to register the book
- full book title and ISBN
- Operating system (Mac/PC) and browser (Firefox, Safari, etc.)

Look For These Icons Throughout The Book

 PROVEN TECHNIQUES

 APPLIED STRATEGIES

 STUDY BREAK

 OTHER REFERENCES

 ONLINE ARTICLES

Part I
Using This
Book to Improve
Your AP Score

- Preview: Your Knowledge, Your Expectations
- Your Guide to Using This Book
- How to Begin

PREVIEW: YOUR KNOWLEDGE, YOUR EXPECTATIONS

Your route to a high score on the AP Computer Science A Exam depends a lot on how you plan to use this book. Start thinking about your plan by responding to the following questions.

1. Rate your level of confidence in your knowledge of the content tested by the AP Computer Science A Exam:

   A. Very confident—I know it all
   B. I'm pretty confident, but there are topics for which I could use help
   C. Not confident—I need quite a bit of support
   D. I'm not sure.

2. If you have a goal score in mind, circle your goal score for the AP Computer Science A Exam:

   5   4   3   2   1   I'm not sure yet

3. What do you expect to learn from this book? Circle all that apply to you.

   A. A general overview of the test and what to expect
   B. Strategies for how to approach the test
   C. The content tested by this exam
   D. I'm not sure yet.

YOUR GUIDE TO USING THIS BOOK

This book is organized to provide as much—or as little—support as you need, so you can use this book in whatever way will be most helpful to improving your score on the AP Computer Science A Exam.

- The remainder of **Part I** will provide guidance on how to use this book and help you determine your strengths and weaknesses.

- **Part II** of this book contains Practice Test 1, its answers and explanations, and a scoring guide. We recommend that you take this test before going any further in order to realistically determine:
  o your starting point right now
  o which question types you're ready for and which you might need to practice
  o which content topics you are familiar with and which you will want to carefully review

It's Bubble Time
Bubble sheets for the tests in this book can be found in the back of the book and are available online—you can print them out from your online student tools. We highly recommend that you do so before taking a practice test, as learning how to transfer your answers to a bubble sheet is an important part of preparing for the test.

Note that the answer key for Practice Test 1 has been specifically designed to help you self-diagnose any potential areas of weakness, so that you can best focus your test preparation and be efficient with your time.

- **Part III** of this book will:
  - o provide information about the structure, scoring, and content of the AP Computer Science A Exam
  - o help you to make a study plan
  - o point you toward additional resources

- **Part IV** of this book will explore various strategies:
  - o how to attack multiple-choice questions (MCQs)
  - o how to effectively answer free-response questions (FRQs)
  - o how to manage your time to maximize the number of points available to you

- **Part V** of this book covers the content you need for the AP Computer Science A Exam.

- **Part VI** of this book contains Practice Tests 2 and 3, plus their answer and explanations, and a scoring guide. (Practice Test 4 and answers and explanations can be found online.) We recommend that you pepper in Practice Tests as you study for your exam. Don't take all Practice Tests in a row or even in rapid succession: start with Practice Test 1 to get a sense of where you are, then as you complete your content review, take a Practice Test every so often to see how you are doing and if you are improving or need to review certain topics.

You may choose to use some parts of this book over others, or you may work through the entire book. Your approach will depend on your needs and how much time you have. Now let's look at how to make this determination.

HOW TO BEGIN

1. **Take Practice Test 1**

   Before you can decide how to use this book, you need to take a practice test. Doing so will give you insight into your strengths and weaknesses, and the test will also help you make an effective study plan. If you're feeling test-phobic, remind yourself that a practice test is a tool for diagnosing yourself—it's not how well you do that matters but how you use information gleaned from your performance to guide your preparation.

   So, before you read further, take Practice Test 1 starting on page 9 of this book. Be sure to finish it in one sitting, following the instructions that appear before the test.

2. **Check Your Answers**

Using the answer key on page 52, count the number of multiple-choice questions you answered correctly and the number you missed. Don't worry about the explanations for now, and don't worry about why you missed questions. We'll get to that soon.

3. **Reflect on the Test**

After you take your first test, respond to the following questions:

- How much time did you spend on the multiple-choice questions?

- How much time did you spend on each free-response question?

- How many multiple-choice questions did you miss?

- Do you feel you had the knowledge to address the subject matter of the free-response questions?

4. **Read Part III of this Book and Complete the Self-Evaluation**

Part III will provide information on how the test is structured and scored. It will also set out areas of content that are tested.

As you read Part III, re-evaluate your answers to the questions above. At the end of Part III, you will revisit and refine those questions. You will then be able to make a study plan, based on your needs and available time, that will allow you to use this book most effectively.

5. Engage with Parts IV and V as Needed

Notice the word *engage*. You'll get more out of this book if you use it intentionally than if you read it passively, hoping for an improved score through osmosis.

Strategy chapters will help you think about your approach to the question types on this exam. Part IV will open with a reminder to think about how you approach questions now and then close with a reflection section asking you to think about how or whether you will change your approach in the future.

The content chapters in Part V are designed to provide a review of the content tested on the AP Computer Science A Exam, including the level of detail you need to know and how the content is tested. In addition, the content chapters are broken up to exactly match the 10 Unit structure of the AP Computer Science A course, as outlined by the College Board. You will have the opportunity to assess your mastery of the content of each chapter through test-appropriate questions and a reflection section.

6. Take Practice Tests 2, 3, 4 and Assess Your Performance

Once you feel you have developed the strategies you need and gained the knowledge you lacked, you should take Practice Test 2, which starts on page 275 of this book. You should do so in one sitting, following the instructions at the beginning of the test.

When you are finished, check your answers to the multiple-choice sections. See if a teacher or friend will read your free-response answers and provide feedback, and go over them with you.

Once you have taken the test, reflect on the areas on which you still need work, and revisit the chapters in this book that address those deficiencies. Then go back and take Practice Test 3 and do the same, then Practice Test 4. You've got 4 practice tests with this book—be sure to make use of all of them! (Note that Practice Test 4 is an online PDF found in your Student Tools. Go back a few pages for step-by-step directions on how to register your book and access all of your online resources.)

7. Keep Working

As mentioned earlier, there are other resources available to you, including a wealth of information on the AP Students website (apstudent.collegeboard. org/apcourse/ap-computer-science-a). On this site, you can continue to explore areas that you could improve upon and engage in those areas right up until the day of the test. You should use a mix of web resources and book review to solidify your understanding of any question subjects that you keep getting wrong.

Need Some Guidance?
If you're looking for a way to get the most out of your studying, check out our free study guide for this exam, which you can access via your online student tools. See the "Get More (Free) Content" page for details on accessing this great resource and more.

Part II
Practice Test

Practice Test 1

AP® Computer Science A Exam

SECTION I: Multiple-Choice Questions

DO NOT OPEN THIS BOOKLET UNTIL YOU ARE TOLD TO DO SO.

At a Glance

Total Time
1 hour 30 minutes
Number of Questions
40
Percent of Total Score
50%
Writing Instrument
Pencil required

Instructions

Section I of this examination contains 40 multiple-choice questions. Fill in only the ovals for numbers 1 through 40 on your answer sheet.

Indicate all of your answers to the multiple-choice questions on the answer sheet. No credit will be given for anything written in this exam booklet, but you may use the booklet for notes or scratch work. After you have decided which of the suggested answers is best, completely fill in the corresponding oval on the answer sheet. Give only one answer to each question. If you change an answer, be sure that the previous mark is erased completely. Here is a sample question and answer.

Sample Question   Sample Answer

Chicago is a
(A) state
(B) city
(C) country
(D) continent
(E) county

Use your time effectively, working as quickly as you can without losing accuracy. Do not spend too much time on any one question. Go on to other questions and come back to the ones you have not answered if you have time. It is not expected that everyone will know the answers to all the multiple-choice questions.

About Guessing

Many candidates wonder whether or not to guess the answers to questions about which they are not certain. Multiple-choice scores are based on the number of questions answered correctly. Points are not deducted for incorrect answers, and no points are awarded for unanswered questions. Because points are not deducted for incorrect answers, you are encouraged to answer all multiple-choice questions. On any questions you do not know the answer to, you should eliminate as many choices as you can, and then select the best answer among the remaining choices.

GO ON TO THE NEXT PAGE.

Java Quick Reference

Class Constructors and Methods	Explanation
String Class	
`String(String str)`	Constructs a new `String` object that represents the same sequence of characters as `str`
`int length()`	Returns the number of characters in a `String` object
`String substring(int from, int to)`	Returns the substring beginning at index `from` and ending at index `to - 1`
`String substring(int from)`	Returns `substring(from, length())`
`int indexOf(String str)`	Returns the index of the first occurrence of `str`; returns `-1` if not found
`boolean equals(String other)`	Returns `true` if `this` is equal to `other`; returns `false` otherwise
`int compareTo(String other)`	Returns a value <0 if `this` is less than `other`; returns zero if `this` is equal to `other`; returns a value of >0 if `this` is greater than `other`
Integer Class	
`Integer(int value)`	Constructs a new `Integer` object that represents the specified `int` value
`Integer.MIN_VALUE`	The minimum value represented by an `int` or `Integer`
`Integer.MAX_VALUE`	The maximum value represented by an `int` or `Integer`
`int intValue()`	Returns the value of this `Integer` as an `int`
Double Class	
`Double(double value)`	Constructs a new `Double` object that represents the specified `double` value
`double doubleValue()`	Returns the value of this `Double` as a `double`
Math Class	
`static int abs(int x)`	Returns the absolute value of an `int` value
`static double abs(double x)`	Returns the absolute value of a `double` value
`static double pow(double base, double exponent)`	Returns the value of the first parameter raised to the power of the second parameter
`static double sqrt(double x)`	Returns the positive square root of a `double` value
`static double random()`	Returns a `double` value greater than or equal to `0.0` and less than `1.0`
ArrayList Class	
`int size()`	Returns the number of elements in the list
`boolean add(E obj)`	Appends `obj` to end of list; returns `true`
`void add(int index, E obj)`	Inserts `obj` at position index (`0 <= index <= size`), moving elements at position `index` and higher to the right (adds 1 to their indices) and adds 1 to size
`E get(int index)`	Returns the element at position index in the list
`E set(int index, E obj)`	Replaces the element at position index with `obj`; returns the element formerly at position index
`E remove(int index)`	Removes the element at position index, moving elements at position `index + 1` and higher to the left (subtracts 1 from their indices) and subtracts 1 from size; returns the element formerly at position index
Object Class	
`boolean equals(Object other)`	
`String toString()`	

GO ON TO THE NEXT PAGE.

COMPUTER SCIENCE A

SECTION I

Time—1 hour and 30 minutes

Number of Questions—40

Percent of total exam grade—50%

Directions: Determine the answer to each of the following questions or incomplete statements, using the available space for any necessary scratchwork. Then decide which is the best of the choices given and fill in the corresponding oval on the answer sheet. No credit will be given for anything written in the examination booklet. Do not spend too much time on any one problem.

Notes:
- Assume that the classes listed in the Quick Reference have been imported where appropriate.
- Assume that declarations of variables and methods appear within the context of an enclosing class.
- Assume that method calls that are not prefixed with an object or class name and are not shown within a complete class definition appear within the context of an enclosing class.
- Unless otherwise noted in the question, assume that parameters in the method calls are not `null` and that methods are called only when their preconditions are satisfied.

1. Evaluate the following expression: 4 + 6 % 12 / 4?

    (A) 1
    (B) 2
    (C) 4
    (D) 4.5
    (E) 5

2. Which of the following expressions does **not** evaluate to 0.2?

    (A) `(1.0 * 2) / (1.0 * 10)`
    (B) `2.0 / 10`
    (C) `(double) 2 / 10`
    (D) `(double)(2 / 10)`
    (E) `Math.sqrt(4) / Math.sqrt(100)`

3. Choose the code used to print the following:

    ```
            "Friends"
    ```
    (A) `System.out.print(""Friends"");`
    (B) `System.out.print("//"Friends//"");`
    (C) `System.out.print("/"Friends/"");`
    (D) `System.out.print("\"Friends\"");`
    (E) `System.out.print("\\"Friends \\"");`

GO ON TO THE NEXT PAGE.

4. Determine the output of the following code.

```
String animal1 = "elephant";
String animal2 = "lion";
swap(animal1, animal2);
animal1.toUpperCase();
animal2.toLowerCase();

System.out.println(animal1 + "    " + animal2);

public static void swap(String a1, String a2) {
    String hold = a1;
    a1 = a2;
    a2 = hold;
}
```

(A) elephant   lion
(B) ELEPHANT   lion
(C) lion   elephant
(D) LION   elephant
(E) LION   ELEPHANT

Questions 5–6 refer to the `Constellation` class below.

```
public class Constellation {
    private String name;
    private String month;
    private int northernLatitude;
    private int southernLatitude;

    Constellation(String n, String m)
    {
        name = n;
        month = m;
        northernLatitude = 0;
        southernLatitude = 0;
    }

    Constellation(String n, String m, int nLat, int sLat)
    {
        name = n;
        month = m;
        northernLatitude = nLat;
        southernLatitude = sLat;
    }
    public void chgMonth(String m)
    {
        String month = m;
    }
```

GO ON TO THE NEXT PAGE.

5. Using the `Constellation class`, which of the following will cause a compiler error?

(A) `Constellation c1 = new Constellation("Hercules", "July");`
(B) `Constellation c2 = new Constellation("Pisces", "Nov", 90, 65);`
(C) `Constellation c3 = new Constellation("Aquarius", "Oct", 65.0, 90.0);`
(D) `Constellation c4 = new Constellation("Leo", "4", 0, 0);`
(E) `Constellation c5 = new Constellation("Phoenix", "Nov", 32, 90);`

6. A programmer has attempted to add three mutator methods to the `Constellation` class.

```
I.  public void chgLatitude(String direction, int latitude)
    {
        if (direction.toUpperCase().equals("N"))
            northernLatitude = latitude;
        else if (direction.toUpperCase().equals("S"))
            southernLatitude = latitude;
    }

II. public void chgLatitude(int nLatitude, int sLatitude)
    {
        northernLatitude = nLatitude;
        southernLatitude = sLatitude;
    }

III. public void chgLatitude(double nLatitude, double sLatitude)
    {
        northernLatitude = (int) nLatitude;
        southernLatitude = (int) sLatitude;
    }
}
```

Which of the three will compile without a compiler error?

(A) I only
(B) II only
(C) III only
(D) I and II only
(E) I, II, and III

GO ON TO THE NEXT PAGE.

7. Determine the output of the following code.

```
int x = 10;
int y = 5;

if (x == 10)
{
    if (y <= 5)
            y++;
    else if (y < 4)
                    x=3;
            else
                    y+=6;
}
if (y > 5)
{
    if (x != 10)
    {
            x = 0;
            y = 0;
    }
    else
            x = -5;
}
```

(A) x = 0, y = 0
(B) x = -5, y = 6
(C) x = 10, y = 5
(D) x = 3, y = 5
(E) None of the above

GO ON TO THE NEXT PAGE.

8. A programmer intended to write code to print three words in ascending lexicographical order. Follow the code and determine the printed output.

```
1    String word1 = "frog";
2    String word2 = "dog";
3    String word3 = "cat";
4
5    if (word1.compareTo(word2) < 0)
6       if (word2.compareTo(word3) < 0)
7        System.out.println(word1 + " " + word2 + " " + word3);
8      else
9        System.out.println(word1 + " " + word3 + " " + word2);
10   else
11      if (word1.compareTo(word2) > 0)
12         if (word2.compareTo(word3) < 0)
13           System.out.println(word1 + " " + word2 + " " + word3);
14         else
15           System.out.println(word1 + " " + word3 + " " + word2);
16       else
17         if (word2.equals(word3))
18           System.out.println( "all the words are the same");
19         else
20           System.out.println( "word1 and word2 are duplicates");
```

(A) frog   cat   dog
(B) cat   dog   frog
(C) dog   frog   cat
(D) frog   dog   cat
(E) dog   cat   frog

9. Using the following variable declarations, determine which of the following would evaluate to true.

```
int temp = 90;
boolean cloudy = false;
```

I.   if (temp >= 90 && !cloudy)
II. if (!(temp > 90 || cloudy))
III. if (!(temp > 90 && !cloudy))

(A) I only
(B) II only
(C) III only
(D) Two of the above will evaluate to true.
(E) All the above will evaluate to true.

GO ON TO THE NEXT PAGE.

10. Consider the following code:

```
1    String dog1 = new String("Poodle");
2    String dog2 = new String("Beagle");
3    dog1 = dog2;
4    String dog3 = new String("Beagle");
5
6    if (dog1 == dog2)
7        System.out.println("dog1 and dog2 are one and the same dog");
8    else
9        System.out.println("dog1 and dog2 are not the same dog");
10
11   if (dog1 == dog3)
12       System.out.println("dog1 and dog3 are one and the same dog");
13   else
14       System.out.println("dog1 and dog3 are not the same dog");
15
16   if (dog1.equals(dog3))
17       System.out.println("dog1 and dog3 are the same breed");
18   else
19       System.out.println("dog1 and dog3 are not the same breed");
```

Which of the following represents the output that will be produced by the code?

(A) dog1 and dog2 are one and the same dog
     dog1 and dog3 are one and the same dog
     dog1 and dog3 are the same breed

(B) dog1 and dog2 are one and the same dog
     dog1 and dog3 are one and the same dog
     dog1 and dog3 are not the same breed

(C) dog1 and dog2 are one and the same dog
     dog1 and dog3 are not the same dog
     dog1 and dog3 are the same breed

(D) dog1 and dog2 are one and the same dog
     dog1 and dog3 are not the same dog
     dog1 and dog3 are not the same breed

(E) dog1 and dog2 are not the same dog
     dog1 and dog3 are not the same dog
     dog1 and dog3 are the same breed

GO ON TO THE NEXT PAGE.

11. Choose the correct option to complete lines 3 and 4 such that `str2` will contain the letters of str1 in reverse order.

```
1   String str1 = "banana";
2   String str2 = "";
3   // missing code
4   // missing code
5   {
6       str2 += str1.substring(i, i+1);
7       i--;
8   }
```

(A) `int i = 0;`
    `while (i < str1.length)`

(B) `int i = str1.length();`
    `while (i >= 0)`

(C) `int i = str1.length()-1;`
    `while (i >= 0)`

(D) `int i = str1.length();`
    `while (i > 0)`

(E) `int i = str1.length()-1;`
    `while (i > 0)`

12. Consider the following code excerpt :

```
9    int n = // some integer greater than zero
10   int count = 0;
11   int p = 0;
12   int q = 0;
13   for (p=1; p < n; p++)
14       for (q=1; q <= n; q++)
15           count ++;
```

What will be the final value of count?

(A) n^n

(B) $n^2 - 1$

(C) $(n-1)^2$

(D) $n(n-1)$

(E) n^2

13. Given the following code excerpt, determine the output.

```
1   int x = 0;
2   for (int j = 1; j < 4; j++)
3   {
4     if (x !=0 && j / x > 0)
5       System.out.print(j / x + " ");
6     else
7       System.out.print(j * x + " ");
8   }
```

(A) 0 0 0

(B) 0 0 0 0

(C) 1 2 3

(D) 1 0 2 0 3 0

(E) ArithmeticException: Divide by Zero

GO ON TO THE NEXT PAGE.

14. Consider the following code:

```
1    String space = " ";
2    String symbol = "*";
3    int num = 5;
4    for (int i = 1; i <= num; i++)
5    {
6            System.out.print(symbol);
7    }
8    System.out.print("\n");
9    for (int i = 1; i <= num; i++)
10   {
11       for (int j = num - i; j > 0; j--)
12       {
13               System.out.print(space);
14       }
15       System.out.println(symbol);
16   }
17   for (int i = 1; i <= num; i++)
18   {
19           System.out.print(symbol);
20   }
```

Which of the following represents the output?

(A)	*****	(D)	*****
	****		*
	***		*
	**		*
	*		*
	*****		*****

(B)	*****	(E)	*****
	****		*
	***		**
	**		***
	*		****
	*****		*****

(C)	*****		
	*		
	*		
	*		
	*		
	*****		

GO ON TO THE NEXT PAGE.

15. What will be printed as a result of the following code excerpt?

```
int sum = 0;
for (int i = 1; i < 2; i++)
  for (int j = 1; j <= 3; j++)
    for (int k = 1; k < 4; k++)
      sum += (i * j * k);

System.out.println(sum);
```

(A) 18
(B) 36
(C) 45
(D) 60
(E) 108

16. Consider the following code:

```
1    int j = 0;
2    String s = "map ";
3    while ( j < s.length())
4    {
5       int k = s.length()
6       while ( k > j )
7       {
8          System.out.println(s.substring(j, k));
9          k--;
10      }
11      j++;
12   }
```

Which of the following represents the output?

(A) map	(D) m
ma	ma
m	map
ap	a
a	ap
	p
(B) map	(E) p
ma	ap
m	p
ap	map
a	ma
p	m
(C) map	
ap	
p	
ap	
p	
p	

GO ON TO THE NEXT PAGE.

17. A factorial is shown by an exclamation point(!) following a number. The factorial of 5 or 5! is calculated by (5)(4)(3)(2)(1) = 120.

Assuming n is an integer greater than 1, Choose the method that will return n!

I.	```public static int f(int n) { int factorial = 1; for (int i = n; i > 0 ; i--) { factorial *= n; } return factorial; }```
II.	```public static int f(int n) { int factorial = 1; int j = 1; while (j <= n) { factorial *= j; j++; } return factorial; }```
III.	```public static int f(int n) { if (n==1) return n; return n * f(n-1); }```

(A) I only

(B) II only

(C) III only

(D) II and III only

(E) I, II, and III

GO ON TO THE NEXT PAGE.

18. Given the following code excerpt for the Tile Class:

```
1    public class Tile
2    {
3      private int styleNumber;
4      private String color;
5      private double width;
6      private double height;
7      private String material;
8      private double price;

9      Tile(int style, String col)
10     {
11       styleNumber = style;
12       color = col;
13     }
14     Tile(int style, String col, double w, double h, String mat, double price)
15     {
16       styleNumber = style;
17       color = col;
18       width = w;
19       height = h;
20       material = mat;
21       price = price;
22     }
23     Tile(int style, String col, String mat, double price)
24     {
25         styleNumber = style;
26         color = col;
27         material = mat;
28         price = price;
29     }
30     public void chgMaterial(String mat)
31     {
32       String material = mat;
33     }
34     public String toString()
35     {
36       return (styleNumber + " " + color + " " + width + " " + height + " " +
37              material + " " + price);
38     }
39   }
```

What is the output after the following client code is executed?

```
Tile t1 = new Tile(785, "grey", "ceramic", 6.95);
   t1.chgMaterial("marble");
   System.out.print(t1.toString());
```

(A) Tile@5ccd43c2
(B) 785 grey 0.0 0.0 marble 0.0
(C) 785 grey 0.0 0.0 ceramic 0.0
(D) 785 grey 0.0 0.0 ceramic 6.95
(E) 785 grey 0.0 0.0 marble 6.95

GO ON TO THE NEXT PAGE.

19. What is the output after the following client code is executed?

```
Tile t2 = new Tile(101, "blue");
System.out.print(t2);
```

(A) Tile@5ccd43c2
(B) 101 blue 0.0 0.0 null 0.0
(C) Type mismatch error
(D) NullPointerException
(E) There will be no output; the program will not compile.

20. The Tile Class is going to be used for an application built for a small independent tile store. The owner wants the programmer to add a field for the number of unopened boxes of tile he has for each style of tile he has in stock and a method to change the value. What would be the proper declaration for this field?

(A) `public static int inventory;`
(B) `private static double inventory;`
(C) `final int inventory;`
(D) `private int inventory;`
(E) `private int [] inventory;`

21. Given the following code excerpt:

```
9   int[] nums = {11, 22, 33, 44, 55, 66};
10
11  for (int i = 0; i < nums.length; i++)
12      nums[nums[i] / 11] = nums[i];
```

Determine the final contents of **nums**.

(A) 1, 2, 3, 4, 5, 6
(B) 11, 11, 33, 33, 55, 55
(C) 11, 11, 22, 33, 44, 55
(D) 11, 22, 22, 33, 33, 55
(E) 11, 22, 33, 44, 55, 66

GO ON TO THE NEXT PAGE.

22. Given the following code excerpt:

```
13  int[] arr1 = {1, 2, 3, 4, 5, 6};
14  int[] arr2 = arr1;
15  int last = arr1.length -1;
16
17  for (int i = 0; i < arr1.length; i++)
18      arr2[i] = arr1[last-i];
19
20  for (int i = 0; i < arr1.length; i++)
21      System.out.print(arr1[i] + "  ");
22
23  System.out.println(" ");
24
25  for (int i = 0; i < arr2.length; i++)
26      System.out.print(arr2[i] + "  ");
```

Determine the statement below that reflects the resulting output.

(A) 1 2 3 4 5 6
     1 2 3 4 5 6

(B) 1 2 3 4 5 6
     6 5 4 4 5 6

(C) 6 5 4 3 2 1
     6 5 4 4 5 6

(D) 6 5 4 4 5 6
     1 2 3 4 5 6

(E) 6 5 4 4 5 6
     6 5 4 4 5 6

GO ON TO THE NEXT PAGE.

23. Given the following code excerpt:

```
27  int[] arr3 = {1, 2, 3, 4, 5, 6};
28
29  for (int element : arr3)
30  {
31      element *= 2;
32      System.out.print(element + "  ");
33  }
34  System.out.println(" ");
35
36  for (int element : arr3)
37      System.out.print(element + "  ");
```

Determine the statement below that reflects the resulting output.

(A) 1 2 3 4 5 6
     1 2 3 4 5 6

(B) 2 4 6 8 10 12
     1 2 3 4 5 6

(C) 2 4 6 8 10 12
     2 4 6 8 10 12

(D) A compiler error will occur.
(E) A run-time exception will occur.

GO ON TO THE NEXT PAGE.

24. Given an array **numbers** containing a variety of integers and the following code excerpt:

```
38  int holdSmallest = Integer.MAX_VALUE;
39  int holdLargest = 0;
40  int a = 0;
41  int b = 0;
42  for (int i = 0; i < numbers.length; i++)
43  {
44    if (numbers[i] <= holdSmallest)
45    {
46        holdSmallest = numbers[i];
47        a = i;
48    }
49    if (numbers[i] >= holdLargest)
50    {
51        holdLargest = numbers[i];
52        b = i;
53    }
54  }
55  System.out.println(a + " " + b);
```

Determine the statement below that reflects the most successful outcome.

(A) The code will print the smallest and largest values in the numbers array.

(B) The code will print the locations of the smallest and largest values in the numbers array.

(C) The code will print the locations of the smallest and largest non-negative values in the numbers array.

(D) The code will print the location of the smallest value in the numbers array and the largest non-negative value in the numbers array.

(E) The code will print the location of the smallest non-negative value in the numbers array and the largest value in the numbers array.

GO ON TO THE NEXT PAGE.

25. Choose the missing code below that will accurately find the average of the values in the sales array.

```
56  double avg = 0;
57  int i = 0;
58  int sum = 0;
59  for (int element : sales)
60
61     //Missing code
62
63
```

(A)	``` { sum += element; } double avg = (double) sum / sales.length; ```
(B)	``` { sum += sales[i]; } double avg = (double) sum / sales.length; ```
(C)	``` { sum += sales; } double avg = (double)sum / sales.length; ```
(D)	``` { sum += sales[element]; } double avg = (double)sum / sales.length; ```
(E)	``` { sum += element[sales]; } double avg = (double)sum / sales.length; ```

26. A programmer has written two different methods for a client program to swap the elements of one array with those of another array.

```
11      public static void swap1(int[] a1, int[] a2)
12      {
13        for (int i = 0; i < a1.length; i++)
14        {
15         int arrhold = a1[i];
16         a1[i] = a2[i];
17         a2[i] = arrhold;
18        }
19      }
```

```
20
21  public static void swap2(int[] a1, int[] a2) {
22              int [] arrhold= a1;
23              a1 = a2;
24              a2 = arrhold;
25        }
```

Which of the following statements best reflects the outcome of the two methods?

(A) Both methods will swap the contents of the two arrays correctly in all cases.

(B) swap1 will swap the contents of the two arrays correctly **only** if both arrays have the same number of elements, whereas swap2 will work correctly for all cases.

(C) swap1 will only swap the contents of the two arrays correctly if both arrays have the same number of elements, whereas swap2 will **never** work correctly.

(D) swap1 will only swap the contents of the two arrays correctly if both arrays have the same number of elements or a2 has more elements, whereas swap2 will work correctly for all cases.

(E) Neither method will swap the contents of the two arrays correctly under any conditions.

27. Which code has declared and properly populated the given ArrayList?

I.	ArrayList <String> alist1 = new ArrayList<String>(); alist1.add("4.5");
II.	ArrayList <Integer> alist2 = new ArrayList<Integer>(); alist1.add((int) 4.5);

III.	ArrayList <Double> alist3 ;
	alist3 = new ArrayList<Double>();
	alist3.add(4.5);

(A) I only
(B) I and II
(C) I and III
(D) II and III
(E) I, II, and III

GO ON TO THE NEXT PAGE.

28. Given the following code excerpt:

```
ArrayList <Integer> alist1 = new ArrayList<Integer>();
int [] a1 = {2, 4, 6, 7, 8, 10, 11};
for (int a: a1) {
   alist1.add(a);
}
for (int i = 0; i < alist1.size(); i++) {
   if (alist1.get(i) % 2 == 0){
     alist1.remove(i);
   }
}
System.out.println(alist1);
```

Determine the output.

(A) [4, 7, 10, 11]
(B) [2, 4, 7, 10, 11]]
(C) [2, 7, 10, 11]
(D) [7, 11]
(E) An IndexOutOfBoundsException will occur

Questions 29–30 refer to the following code excerpt.

```
2   ArrayList <Integer> alist5 = new ArrayList<Integer>();
3   int [] a1 = {21, 6, 2, 8, 1};
4   for (int a: a1)
5   {
6       alist5.add(a);
7   }
8   for (int k = 0; k < alist5.size()-1; k++)
9   {
10      for (int i = 0; i < alist5.size()-2; i++)
11      {
12          if (alist5.get(i) > alist5.get(i + 1) )
13          {
14              int hold = alist5.remove(i);
15              alist5.add(i+1, hold );
16          }
17      }
18  }
19  System.out.println(alist5);
```

29. How many times will line 12 be executed?

(A) 6 times
(B) 12 times
(C) 15 times
(D) 16 times
(E) 20 times

30. What will be the final output after the code executes?

(A) [21, 8, 6, 2, 1]
(B) [6, 21, 2, 8, 1]
(C) [6, 2, 8, 21, 1]
(D) [2, 6, 8, 21, 1]
(E) [1, 2, 6, 8, 21]

GO ON TO THE NEXT PAGE.

31. Given **nums**—a rectanglular, but not necessarily square, two-dimensional array of integers, choose the code to correctly print the array:

```
4    int [][] arr2d = {{1, 2, 3, 4},{ 5, 6, 7, 8}};
5    String s= "";
6    for (int a = 0; a < arr2d[0].length; a++)
7    {
8        for (int b = 0; b < arr2d.length; b++)
9        {
10           s +=arr2d [b][a] + " ";
11       }
12       s += "\n";
13   }
14   System.out.print(s);
```

Determine the resulting output.

(A) 1   2   3   4
     5   6   7   8

(B) 1   5   2   6
     3   7   4   8

(C) 1   2
     3   4
     5   6
     7   8

(D) 1   5
     2   6
     3   7
     4   8

(E) 1
     2
     3
     4
     5
     6
     7
     8

32. Given **nums**—a rectangular, two-dimensional array of integers, choose the code to print the entire array.

| I. | ```
for (int r = 0; r < nums.length; r++ )
{
    for (int c = 0; c < nums[0].length; c++)
    {
        System.out.print(nums[r][c]);
    }
    System.out.print("\n");
}
``` |
|---|---|
| II. | ```
for (int [] row: nums)
{
    for (int col: row)
    {
        System.out.print(col + " ");
    }
    System.out.println("");
}
``` |
| III. | ```
for (int r = 0; r < nums[0].length; r++)
{
    for (int c = 0; c < nums.length; c++ )
    {
        System.out.print(nums[r][c] + " ");
    }
        System.out.print("\n");
}
``` |

(A) I only
(B) I and II only
(C) I and III only
(D) II and III only
(E) I, II, and III

GO ON TO THE NEXT PAGE.
```

Questions 33–34 refer to the `Percussion` and `Xylophone` class below.

```
public class Percussion {
    private String name;
    private double weight;
    Percussion() {
    }
    Percussion(String n, double w)
    {
        name = n;
        weight = w;
    }
    public String getName()
    {
        return name;
    }
    public double getWeight()
    {
        return weight;
    }
}
public class Drums extends Percussion
{
}
public class Xylophone extends Percussion {
    private int numberOfKeys;

    Xylophone(String name, double weight, int numberOfKeys){

        <missing code>

    }
    public int getNumKeys()
    {
        return numberOfKeys;
    }
}
```

33. Which of the following is the most appropriate replacement for `<missing code>` in the Xylophone constructor?

(A)	`this.numberOfKeys = numberOfKeys;` `super(name, weight);`
(B)	`super(name, weight);` `this.numberOfKeys = numberOfKeys;`
(C)	`super(name, weight);` `numberOfKeys = this.numberOfKeys;`
(D)	`this.numberOfKeys = numberOfKeys;`
(E)	`numberOfKeys = this.numberOfKeys;`

GO ON TO THE NEXT PAGE.

34. Assuming the above classes compile correctly, which of the following will not compile within a client program?

(A) `Xylophone [] xylophones = new Xylophone[5];`

(B) `Percussion [] xylophones = new Xylophone[5];`

(C) `Xylophone x1 = new Xylophone ("xylophone", 65, 32);`
`System.out.println(x1.getNumKeys());`

(D) `Xylophone x1 = new Xylophone ("xylophone", 65, 32);`
`System.out.println(x1.numberOfKeys);`

(E) `Drums [] drums;`

35. A client program wishes to compare the two xylophone objects as follows:

```
Xylophone x2 = new Xylophone ("xylophone", 80, 32);
Xylophone x3 = new Xylophone ("xylophone", 65, 32);
```

The two objects should be considered "equally heavy" if and only if they have the same weight. Which of the following code excerpts accomplishes that task?

(A)	`if (x2.weight==x3.weight)`
	`    System.out.println("equally heavy");`
	`else`
	`    System.out.println("not equally heavy");`

(B)	`if (x2.weight()==x3.weight())`
	`    System.out.println("equally heavy");`
	`else`
	`    System.out.println("not equally heavy");`

(C)	`if (x2.getWeight()==x3.getWeight())`
	`    System.out.println("equally heavy");`
	`else`
	`    System.out.println("not equally heavy");`

(D)	`if (x2.weight.equals(x3.weight)`
	`    System.out.println("equally heavy");`
	`else`
	`    System.out.println("not equally heavy");`

(E)	The weight of each object cannot be compared.

GO ON TO THE NEXT PAGE.

Questions 36–37 refer to the following classes.

```
public class Dog {
    private int height;
    private String size;
    private String color;
    Dog (int iheight, int iweight, String icolor)
    {
        height = iheight;
        color = icolor;
        if (iweight >= 65)
            size = "large";
        else
            size = "medium";
    }
    public int getheight() {return height;}
    public String getSize() {return size;}
    public String getColor() {return color;}
    public String toString() {return "    color is: " + color;}
}

public class SportingDog extends Dog {
    private String purpose;
    SportingDog(int h, int w, String c)
        {
        super(h, w, c);
        purpose = "hunting";
    }
    public String getPurpose()
    {
        return purpose;
    }
}

public class Retriever extends SportingDog{
    private String type;

    Retriever(String itype, String icolor, int iweight)
    {
        super(24, iweight, icolor);
        type = itype;
    }
    public String toString() {return "    type: " + type + super.toString();}
}
```

36. Which of the following declarations will not compile?

(A) `Dog d1 = new SportingDog(30, 74, "Black");`
(B) `Dog d2 = new Retriever("Labrador", "yellow", 75);`
(C) `SportingDog d3 = new Retriever("Golden", "Red", 70);`
(D) `SportingDog d4 = new Dog(25, 80, "Red");`
(E) `Retriever d5 = new Retriever("Golden", "Blonde", 60);`

GO ON TO THE NEXT PAGE.

37. What is the output after the execution of the following code in the client program:

```
Dog mason = new Retriever("Labrador", "chocolate", 85);
System.out.println(mason.toString());
```

(A) type: Labrador

(B) type: Labrador   color is: chocolate   purpose: hunting

(C) color is: chocolate   type: Labrador

(D) type: Labrador   purpose: hunting   color is: chocolate

(E) type: Labrador   color is: chocolate

38. The following pow method was written to return b raised to the xth power where x > 0, but it does not work properly. Choose the changes to the method below to work properly.

```
1    public double pow(double b, int x)
2    {
3    if (x==0)
4      return 0;
5    else
6        return b + pow (b, x-1);
7    }
```

(A) Change lines 3 and 4 to:
```
3        if (x==1)
4            return 1;
```
(B) Change lines 3 and 4 to:
```
3        if (x==1)
4            return b;
```
(C) Change line 6 to:
```
6      return b * mystery(b, x-1);
```
(D) Both (A) and (C)

(E) Both (B) and (C)

39. What is output given the following code excerpt?

```
System.out.println(f(8765));
public static int f(int n)
{
    if (n == 0)
        return 0;
    else
        return f(n/10) + n % 10;
}
```

(A) 5678

(B) 8765

(C) 58

(D) 26

(E) A run-time error

GO ON TO THE NEXT PAGE.

40. Choose the best solution to complete the missing code such that the code will implement a binary search to find the variable number in `arr`.

```
int number = <some number in arr>;
System.out.println(search(arr, 0, arr.length - 1, number));

public int search(int[] a, int first, int last, int sought) {
    int mid = (first + last)/2;

    if (<missing code>) {
        last = mid - 1;
        return search(a, first, last, sought);
    }
    else if (<missing code>)) {
        first = mid + 1;
        return search(a, first, last, sought);
    }

    return mid;

}
```

(A) a[mid] > sought   a[mid] < sought
(B) a[mid] + 1 > sought   a[mid] < sought
(C) a[mid] > sought   a[mid] - 1 < sought
(D) a[mid] + 1 > sought   a[mid] - 1 < sought
(E) a[mid] = sought   a[mid] = sought

END OF SECTION I

**IF YOU FINISH BEFORE TIME IS CALLED,
YOU MAY CHECK YOUR WORK ON THIS SECTION.**

DO NOT GO ON TO SECTION II UNTIL YOU ARE TOLD TO DO SO.

COMPUTER SCIENCE A

SECTION II

Time—1 hour and 30 minutes

Number of Questions—4

Percent of Total Grade—50%

<u>Directions</u>: SHOW ALL YOUR WORK. REMEMBER THAT PROGRAM SEGMENTS ARE TO BE WRITTEN IN JAVA™.

<u>Notes:</u>

- Assume that the classes listed in the Java Quick Reference have been imported where appropriate.

- Unless otherwise noted in the question, assume that parameters in method calls are not null and that methods are called only when their preconditions are satisfied.

- In writing solutions for each question, you may use any of the accessible methods that are listed in classes defined in that question. Writing significant amounts of code that can be replaced by a call to one of these methods will not receive full credit.

FREE-RESPONSE QUESTIONS

1. This question involves the implementation of a simulation rolling two dice. A client program will specify the number of rolls of the sample size and the number of faces on each of the two dice. A method will return the percentage of times the roll results in a double. Double in this case means when two dice match or have the same value (not a data type).

You will write two of the methods in this class.

```java
public class DiceSimulation {

    /** Sample size of simulation          */
    private int numSampleSize;

    /** Number of faces on the die          */
    private int numFaces;

    /** Constructs a DiceSimulation where sampleSize is the number of rolls to be simulated and
     *  faces is the number of faces on the die (some die have many more or less than 6 faces)
     */
    public DiceSimulation(int numSamples, int faces) {
        numSampleSize = numSamples;
        numFaces = faces;
    }

    /** Returns an integer from 1 to the number of faces to simulate a die roll */
    public int roll() {
                        implemented in part (a)
    }

    /** Simulates rolling two die with the number faces given, for the number of sample size
     *  rolls. Returns the percentage of matches that were rolled
     *  as an integer (eg. 0.50 would be 50)
     */
    public int runSimulation() {
                        implemented in part (b)



    }
}
```

GO ON TO THE NEXT PAGE.

The following table contains sample code and the expected results.

Statements and Expressions	Value Returned / Comment
`DiceSimulation s1 = new DiceSimulation(10, 6)`	(no value returned) A DiceSimulation d1 is declared and instantiated.
`s1.runSimulation()`	10 rolls are simulated, only the percentage of matches is displayed. See further explanation below.

```
The 10 rolls might look like this (nothing is printed at this time)
Die1:  3      Die2:  4
Die1:  1      Die2:  5
Die1:  2      Die2:  2
Die1:  3      Die2:  4
Die1:  6      Die2:  6
Die1:  3      Die2:  4
Die1:  3      Die2:  3
Die1:  6      Die2:  4
Die1:  3      Die2:  1
Die1:  5      Die2:  5
The percentage the method would return is 40.
```

(a) Write the `roll` method to simulate the roll of one die.

Class information for this question

<u>public class DiceSimulation</u>

```
private int numSampleSize;
private int numFaces;

public DiceSimulation (int numSamples, int faces)
public int roll()
public int runSimulation()
```

WRITE YOUR SOLUTION BELOW

```
/** Returns an integer from 1 to number of faces to simulate a die roll */
public int roll() {
```

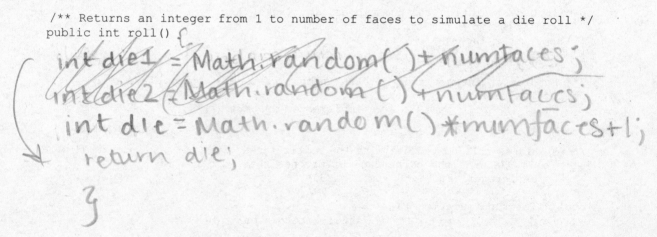

```
    int die1 = Math.random() + numFaces;
    int die2 = Math.random() + numFaces;
    int die = Math.random() * numfaces+1;
    return die;
}
```

GO ON TO THE NEXT PAGE.

(b) Write the runSimulation method.

```
public int runSimulation(){
    int countDouble =0;
    for (int i=0 ; i <= numSamples; i++){
        int die1 = roll();
        int die2 = roll();
        if (die1 == die2){
            countDouble++;
        }
    int percent = (countDouble/numSamples) * 100;
    return percent;
}
```

GO ON TO THE NEXT PAGE.

2. This question involves the implementation of a calorie counter system that is represented by the CalorieCount class. A CalorieCount object is created with 5 parameters:

- Daily Calories limit—the recommended number of calories per day

- Daily Calories intake—the number of calories a person has eaten in a day

- Grams of protein per day

- Grams of Carbohydrate per day

- Grams of Fat per day

The CalorieCount class provides a constructor and the following methods:

- addMeal—takes in calories, grams of protein, grams of carbs, and grams of fat from a meal and updates corresponding instance fields

- getProteinPercentage—returns the percent of protein in a given day (4 * grams protein / daily calorie intake)

- onTrack—returns true if the calorie intake does not exceed the daily calories limit, otherwise returns false

The following table contains a sample code and the expected results.

Statements and Expressions	Value Returned (blank if no value)	Comment
`CalorieCount sunday = new CalorieCount(1500);`		Creates an instance with a 1500 calorie limit.
`sunday.addMeal(716, 38, 38, 45);`		Adds 716 calories, 38 grams protein, 38 grams of carbs, 45 grams of fat to the appropriate instance fields
`sunday.addMeal(230, 16, 8, 16);`		Adds 230 calories, 16 grams protein, 8 grams of carbs, 16 grams of fat to the appropriate instance fields
`sunday.addMeal(568, 38, 50, 24);`		Adds 568 calories, 38 grams protein, 50 grams of carbs, 24 grams of fat to the appropriate instance fields
`onTrack()`	False	Returns true if calorie intake does not exceed calorie limit
`getProteinPercentage()`	.24	Multiplies grams of protein by 4 then divides by calorie intake

GO ON TO THE NEXT PAGE.

Write the entire CalorieCount class. Your implementation must meet all specifications and conform to all examples.

```
class CalorieCount {
private int dailyCalorieLimit;
private int dailyCalorieIntake;
private int gramsOfProtein;
private int gramsOfCarbohydrates;
private int gramsOfFat;

    CalorieCount (int calLimit) {
        dailyCalorieLimit = calLimit;

    }
    public addMeal (int c, int p, int ca, int f)
    {

        dailyCalorieIntake = c;
        gramsOfProtein = p;
        gramsOfCarbohydrates = ca;
        gramsOfFat = f;

    }

    get ProteinPercentage () {
        return (gramsOfProtein * 4) / dailyCalorieIntake
    }

}
```

GO ON TO THE NEXT PAGE.

3. This question involves the implementation of a Travel Planner system that is represented by the TravelPlan and Tour classes. A client will create Tour objects that will represent tours or activities of interest. Each Tour object is made up of an activity date, start time, end time, and name of the activity. The client will also create a TravelPlan object comprised of a destination and an arraylist of Tours. You will write three methods of the TravelPlan class.

A partial declaration of the Tour class is shown below.

```
public class Tour {
    private int actDate;   // date is in mmddyyyy format
    private int startTime; // times are represented in military format
    private int endTime;   // 1430 for 2:30 pm
    private String activity;

/**  Constructs a Tour
 *    All instance fields are initialized
 */
    Tour(int actDate, int startTime, int endTime, String activity)
    {
    /*  implementation not shown
    }
    public int getActDate() {      return actDate; }
    public int getStartTime() { return startTime; }
    public int getEndTime() {      return endTime; }
    public String getActivity() { return activity; }
```

A partial declaration of the TravelPlan class is shown below.

```
    import java.util.ArrayList;

    public class TravelPlan {
        private String destination;
        private ArrayList <Tour> plans;

/**  Constructs a Tour
 *    Instance fields: destination and plans are initialized
 */
        TravelPlan(String destination)
        {
        /*  to be implemented in part (a)  */
        }

/**  Returns true if the timeframe in t overlaps with another Tour in plans;
 */  otherwise false
        public boolean checkForConflicts(Tour t)
        {
        /*  to be implemented in part (b)  */
        }

/**  Must call checkForConflicts for full credit, if checkForConflicts returns false
 */  (the timeframe does not overlap), adds t to plans.  Returns true if
 */   t was added, otherwise returns false
 */
        public boolean addTour(Tour t)
        {
        /*  to be implemented in part (c)  */
        }
```

GO ON TO THE NEXT PAGE.

The following table contains sample code and the expected results.

Statements and Expressions	Value Returned (blank if no value)	Comment
`TravelPlan p1 = new TravelPlan("Capetown");`		Creates an instance with a destination "CapeTown" and an empty arraylist of type Tour
`Tours t1 = new Tours(12132020, 800, 1230, "Bungee jumping");`		Create a Tour instance with date, start time, end time, and activity
`Tours t2 = new Tours(12132020, 900, 1430, "Body surfing");`		Create a Tour instance with date, start time, end time, and activity
`p1.addtour(t1)`	true	Checks for conflicts in `plans`, since there are none, adds the Tour object, returns true
`p1.addtour(t2)`	false	Checks for conflicts in `plans`, since there is a conflict, returns false
`Tours t3 = new Tours(12132020, 1400, 1700, "Shark cage diving");`		Create a Tour instance with date, start time, end time, and activity
`p1.addtour(t3)`	true	Checks for conflicts in `plans`, since there are none, adds the Tour object, returns true
`Tours t4 = new Tours(1222020, 800, 1700, "Deep Sea Fishing");`		Create a Tour instance with date, start time, end time, and activity
`p1.addtour(t4)`	true	Checks for conflicts in `plans`, since there are none, adds the Tour object, returns true

GO ON TO THE NEXT PAGE.

(a) Write the `TravelPlan` constructor.

Class information for this question

```
public class Tour
private int actDate
private int startTime
private int endTime
private String activity

Tour(int actDate, int startTime, int endTime, String activity)
public int getActDate()
public int getStartTime()
public int getEndTime()
public String getActivity()

public class TravelPlan
private String destination;
private ArrayList <Tour> plans;

public TravelPlan(String destination)
public boolean checkForConflicts(Tour t)
public boolean addTour(Tour t)
```

GO ON TO THE NEXT PAGE.

(b) Write the `TravelPlan checkForConflicts` method.

GO ON TO THE NEXT PAGE.

(c) Write the `TravelPlan addTour` method.

GO ON TO THE NEXT PAGE.

4. This question involves the implementation of a class Seating Chart. A seating chart object will represent a two-dimensional String array. The number of rows and columns for the array will be sent as parameters, as well as a one-dimensional array of type Name. You may assume there will be enough rows and columns to accommodate all the entries from the array.

The declaration of the Name class is shown.

```
public class Name
{
    private String lastName;
    private String firstName;

    Name(String lName, String fName){<implementation not shown>}
    public String getLastName() {return lastName;}
    public String getFirstName() {return firstName;}
}
```

A partial declaration of the SeatingChart class is shown below.

```
public class SeatingChart {
    private String [][] chart;

/**  Constructs a SeatingChart having r rows and c columns. All elements contained in the
 *   names array should be placed randomly in the chart array using the format: last
 *   Name, firstName
 *   (e.g. Johlie, Angelina).  Any locations not used in the chart should be
 *   initialized to the empty string.
 */
    SeatingChart(Name[] names, int rows, int cols){

        /*  to be implemented in part (a)  */

    }

/**  Returns a string containing all elements of the chart array in row-major order.
 *   The method should return
 *   a string containing all the elements in the chart array.  The method
 *   padWithSpaces should be called on each
 *   element of chart before it is added to the string to ensure each name will be
 *   printed with the same
 *   length.  Each row of the chart should be separated by a line break.
 */
    public String toString() {

        /*  to be implemented in part (b)  */

    }

/**  Pads a string with spaces to ensure each string is exactly 35 characters long. */

    private String padWithSpaces(String s) {
        String str = s;
        for (int a = s.length(); a < 35; a++) {
            str += " ";
        }
        return str;
    }
}
```

GO ON TO THE NEXT PAGE.

The following table contains sample code and the expected results.

Statements and Expressions	Value Returned / Comment
`SeatingChart msJones = new SeatingChart(theNames,4,3);`	(no value returned) A two dimensional array is initialized with 4 rows and 3 columns. Every element in `theNames` is placed randomly in chart in the following format: lastname, firstname e.g., Washington, George. Empty string is placed in any unused locations.
`System.out.println(msJones.toString);`	Prints the names in chart in row-major order. See example below:

```
Miller,Minnie        Fitzgerald,Fred        Dade,Ali
Indigo,Inde          Banner,Boris           Lane,Lois

Titon,Tim            Robilard,Robbie
Georgian,Greg

Brne,Jane
```

GO ON TO THE NEXT PAGE.

(a) Write the `SeatingChart` constructor.

```
Class information for this question

public class Name
    private String lastName;
    private String firstName;

    Name(String lName, String fName)
    public String getLastName() {return lastName;}
    public String getFirstName() {return firstName;}

public class SeatingChart
    private String [][] chart;

    SeatingChart(Name[] names, int rows, int cols)
    public String toString()
    private String padWithSpaces(String s)
```

GO ON TO THE NEXT PAGE.

(b) Write the `SeatingChart toString()` method.

STOP

END OF EXAM

Practice Test 1:
Answers and
Explanations

PRACTICE TEST 1 ANSWER KEY

1.	E		21.	B
2.	D		22.	E
3.	D		23.	B
4.	A		24.	D
5.	C		25.	A
6.	E		26.	C
7.	B		27.	E
8.	A		28.	A
9.	E		29.	B
10.	C		30.	D
11.	C		31.	D
12.	D		32.	B
13.	A		33.	B
14.	C		34.	D
15.	B		35.	C
16.	B		36.	D
17.	D		37.	E
18.	C		38.	E
19.	B		39.	D
20.	D		40.	A

PRACTICE TEST 1 EXPLANATIONS

Section I: Multiple-Choice Questions

1. **E**   Modulus division and division have the same order of precedence. Going from left to right, Modulus (%) is first: 6 % 12 is 6. Division (/) is next and will be handled as integer division since both sides of the operation are integers: 6/4 is 1. Finally using addition: 4 + 1 = 5. The correct answer is (E).

2. **D**   Anytime a double data type is used in an operation, the result will yield a double. In (A) (1.0 * 2), (B) (2.0), and (C) ((double) 2), the numerator is 2.0. Choice (E) also yields 2.0 since the Math.sqrt method returns a double. Choice (D) attempts to cast to double too late. The parenthesis (2/10) yields 0 before it can be cast to a double.

3. **D**   First off, every string literal will be enclosed in quotation marks (""). Next, to print a character that serves as a control character with specific meanings in java, characters like \, ", or n to indicate a new line, each character will have to be preceded by its own \. Thus, to print "Friends", each " will require its own \. Choices (A), (B), and (C) are missing the backslash. Choice (E) has too many backslashes and will give compiler error. Choice (D) is the correct answer because a backslash is used to indicate a control break.

4. **A**   The fields animal1 and animal2 are unchanged because there is no assignment statement and swap does not return any data. The results from method toUpperCase() and toLowerCase() are not assigned to animal1 (such as animal1 = animal1.toUpperCase()) thus not changing animal1 at all. Choice (A) is the correct answer as strings are immutable.

5. **C**   Choices (B), (D), and (E) all pass a String, String, int, int as arguments to the second Constellation constructor. Choice (A) passes two Strings to the first constructor. Choice (C) is the correct answer as a double cannot be passed to a parameter of type int because there may be a loss of precision.

6. **E**   Options i and ii will use an int parameter to update the instance field(s) of type int. Option iii will cast the double to int before update the instance field of type int. There may be a loss of precision, but it would be a logic error, not a compiler error. The correct answer is (E), as all options will comply correctly.

7. **B**

```
int x = 10;
int y = 5;

if (x == 10)            x is 10 so follow this branch
{
    if (y <= 5)         y is 5 so follow this branch, add 1 to y, it is now 6
        y++;
    else if (y < 4)
            x=3;
        else
            y+=6;
}                        the first if statement is complete
if (y > 5)               y is 6, so follow this branch
{
    if (x != 10)        x is 10 so skip to the else
    {
        x = 0;
        y = 0;
    }
    else                 follow this branch, assign -5 to x
        x = -5;
}
                        Thus, x = -5 and y = 6
```

The correct answer is (B).

8. **A**   The rules of compareTo are as follows: if string1.compareTo(string2) < 0, then the strings are in lexicographical order, whereas, if string1.compareTo(string2) > 0, then the strings are in reversed order.

```
1   String word1 = "frog";
2   String word2 = "dog";
3   String word3 = "cat";
4
5   if (word1.compareTo(word2) < 0)   frog does not come before dog, skip to the else
6       if (word2.compareTo(word3) < 0)
7       System.out.println(word1 + " " + word2 + " " + word3);
8       else
9   System.out.println(word1 + " " + word3 + " " + word2);
10  else                                skip to here
11      if (word1.compareTo(word2) > 0) frog comes after dog, so follow this branch
12      if (word2.compareTo(word3) < 0)   dog does not precede cat, skip to the else
13          System.out.println(word1 + " " + word2 + " " + word3);
14      else
15          System.out.println(word1 + " " + word3 + " " + word2);   frog  cat  dog
16      else
17              if (word2.equals(word3))
18          System.out.println( "all the words are the same");
19          else
20          System.out.println( "word1 and word2 are duplicates");
```

The correct answer is (A).

9. **E** The following is given: **temp = 90**   **cloudy = false.** Option i is evaluated as true: temp is >= 90 (true) && cloudy(true). Both sides of the && are true, so the entire condition is true. Option ii is evaluated as true: DeMorgan's Law can be used to simplify the !( ). The simplified version is temp <= 90 && !cloudy—which are both true, so the entire condition is true. Option iii is also evaluated as true. Again, DeMorgan's Law can be used to simplify the !( ). The simplified version is temp <=90 || cloudy. Since the temp is 90, the first condition is true. By short circuit, the entire condition is true. The correct answer is (E).

10. **C** Line 3 assigns dog2's object reference to dog1. These two object variables are now pointing at the same object, the contents of which is "Beagle". Thus, the results of if(dog1 == dog2) on line 6 is true. Line 4 creates another object whose contents are "Beagle". Thus, the results of if(dog1 == dog3) on line 11 is false. The == is comparing whether the variables refer to the same object, not whether the content of the objects is the same. The results of if (dog1.equals(dog3)) on line 16 are true. The method .equals compares the contents of the two objects: they both contain "Beagle". The correct answer is (C).

11. **C** Choice (A) starts at 0 and will decrement to a negative index, causing an out of bounds exception. Choices (B) and (D) start the index at str1.length, which is out of bounds. The last character in a string should be referenced by length-1. Choice (E) correctly starts at length-1, however, the loop only continues while the index is greater than 0, missing the first character of str1. The correct answer is (C).

12. **D** Analytical problems of this type are more easily solved by selecting a value and testing the results. In this case, substitute a small number such as "3" for n, then trace the code. The outer loop executes from 1 to 2, which is 2 times. The inner loop will execute from 1 to 3, which is 3 times. The code inside the loops is simply counting by 1. The inner loop will be executed (2 times 3) 6 times, thereby adding 6 to count.

Now, substitute 3 for n in all the possible answers.

	Expression	result
(A)	3^3	27
(B)	3^2-1	8
(C)	$(3-1)^2$	4
(D)	$3(3-1)$	6
(E)	3^2	9

Thus, the answer to this problem is (D), n(n-1). Analytically, you could have looked at the first loop processing from 1 to n-1, the second loop processing from 1 to n, and made the same assessment.

13.   **A**   Choice (E) is eliminated with short circuit. Line 4 looks to determine if x !=0, but it IS 0, so logic immediately branches to the else statement on line 7. Variable x is initialized to 0, and j is initialized to 1, so line 7 multiplies j(1) times x(0) = 0 and prints the result. This eliminates (C) and (D). Both (A) and (B) are all zeroes, so the question becomes, how many 0s will be printed? Line 2 specifies j will start at 1 and end at 3, thus printing three 0's. The correct answer is (A).

14.   **C**   The loop located at lines 4–7: prints symbol(*) 5 times.
      Line 8 is a control break to the next line
      The loop located at lines 9–16 is executed 5 times. The loop within at lines 11–14 prints 5—j spaces, so the first time through it will print 4 spaces, next time 3 spaces, and so on. (Note: this eliminates all answers except for (C).) After the spaces are printed on each line, a single symbol(*) is printed with println (which will then move to the next line).
      The loop at 17–19 is the same as the first loop, printing symbol (*) 5 times. The correct answer is (C).

15.   **B**   i will only have the value 1, j will range from 1 to 3, and k will range from 1 to 3. The three variables will be multiplied by each other, then added to the sum. The results will look like this:
      i * j * k
      1 * 1 * 1 = 1
      1 * 1 * 2 = 2
      1 * 1 * 3 = 3
      1 * 2 * 1 = 2
      1 * 2 * 2 = 4
      1 * 2 * 3 = 6
      1 * 3 * 1 = 3
      1 * 3 * 2 = 6
      1 * 3 * 3 = 9   The sum of which is 36
      The correct answer is (B).

16.   **B**   The substring() method has two parameters. The first specifies where to start, the second how far to go (up to but NOT including).
      The outer loop at lines 3–11 is controlled by j. j starts off at 0, eventually ending at 2.
      The inner loop at lines 5–10 is controlled by k. k starts off at 3 and will execute as long as it is greater than j.
      The first time through the outer loop the following will be printed:

```
s.substring(0, 3)        prints map
s.substring(0,2)         prints ma
s.substring (0,1)        prints m
```

      The second time through the outer loop the following will be printed:

```
s.substring(1, 3)        prints ap
s.substring(1,2)         prints a
```

      The final time through the outer loop the following will be printed:

```
s.substring(2, 3)        prints p
```

      The correct answer is (B).

17. **D** Once again, it is helpful to choose a value for n to analyze the code. Choosing 3 for n, analyze the code.

Option I—Each time through the loop, factorial will be multiplied by 3. This does not follow the definition of a factorial.

Option II—The loop is controlled by j, which will range from 1 to n, in this case 3. Each time through the loop, factorial is multiplied by j, thereby producing a result of $1 \times 2 \times 3$, which is correct.

Option III—A recursive solution that sends n(3) to the function.

First pass is	f(3) -> 3 * f(2)	
Second pass is	f(2) -> 2 * f(1)	
Final pass is	f(1) -> 1	$3 \times 2 \times 1$ will yield 6 as expected.

The correct answer is (D), as only options ii and iii will work.

18. **C** When a local variable is created, it is used instead of the instance variable. When the constructor is invoked, line 28 does not update the instance variable price. Without specifying this.price = price, the local parameter is assigned the same value it already holds. Thus, (D) and (E) are eliminated. Choice (A) is eliminated because the toString method has been defined in the Tile Class to print the instance variables (not the object reference). The chgMaterial(mat) method at line 30 also updates a local variable rather than the instance variable, eliminating (B). The correct answer is (C).

19. **B** If a print statement is passed an object, its toString() method will be invoked. This eliminates all answers except (B), which is the correct answer.

20. **D** A static variable would be used for something that would belong to the entire class. Since inventory needs to exist for each style, it cannot be static, but it must be an instance of the class, eliminating (A) and (B). Choice (C) is eliminated because the keyword final is only used for constants that do not change value, but the owner has also asked for a method to change the value. Since styleNumber is an instance field, it implies there is a separate instance is created for each style. Thus an array is not needed, eliminating choice (E). The correct answer is (D).

21. **B** The array is initialized as {11, 22, 33, 44, 55, 66};

First pass: nums[nums[0] / 11] = nums[0];
             nums[11 / 11] = nums[0];
             nums[1] = nums[0];   The array is now: {11, 11, 33, 44, 55, 66};

Second pass: nums[nums[1] / 11] = nums[1];
             nums[11 / 11] = nums[1];
             nums[1] = nums[1];   The array is unchanged: {11, 11, 33, 44, 55, 66};

Third pass: nums[nums[2] / 11] = nums[2];
             nums[33 / 11] = nums[2];
             nums[3] = nums[2];   The array is now: {11, 11, 33, 33, 55, 66};

Fourth pass: nums[nums[3] / 11] = nums[3];
             nums[33 / 11] = nums[3];
             nums[3] = nums[3];   The array is unchanged: {11, 11, 33, 33, 55, 66};

Fifth pass: nums[nums[4] / 11] = nums[4];
             nums[55 / 11] = nums[4];
             nums[5] = nums[4];   The array is now: {11, 11, 33, 33, 55, 55};

Fifth pass: nums[nums[5] / 11] = nums[5];
             nums[55 / 11] = nums[5];
             nums[5] = nums[5];   The array is unchanged: {11, 11, 33, 33, 55, 55};

The correct answer is (B).

22. **E** Line 2 assigns the arr1 object reference to arr2 object reference. Thus, both variables are now pointing to the exact same array in memory.

The loop at lines 17-18 is the only code that modifies the array.

both arr1 and arr2: {1, 2, 3, 4, 5, 6};   last = 5

                 arr2[i] = arr1[last-i];
first pass: arr2[0] = arr1[5-0];   {6, 2, 3, 4, 5, 6}
second pass: arr2[1] = arr1[5-1];   {6, 5, 3, 4, 2, 6}
third pass: arr2[2] = arr1[5-2];   {6, 5, 4, 3, 2, 6}
fourth pass: arr2[3] = arr1[5-3];   {6, 5, 4, 4, 2, 6}
fifth pass: arr2[4] = arr1[5-4];   {6, 5, 4, 4, 5, 6}
last pass: arr2[5] = arr1[5-5];   {6, 5, 4, 4, 5, 6}

The correct answer is (E).

23. **B** The `for` loop on line 2 creates a local variable named element which will hold each value of arr3 without having to use an index. Modifying this local variable does not modify the individual contents within the array. The loop multiplies each element by 2, printing it as it does so.

2, 4, 6, 8, 10, 12

The loop at line 36 prints the contents of the array that remain unchanged:

1, 2, 3, 4, 5, 6

The correct answer is (B).

24. **D** Since index i is assigned to variables a and b, it is a location that is being printed. This eliminates (A). Scanning the remaining answers, it would be helpful if we could derive a chart to understand the possibilities.

	Location of:	Location of:
(B)	Smallest integer	Largest integer
(C)	Smallest positive(non-negative) integer	Largest(non-negative) integer
(D)	Smallest integer	Largest(non-negative) integer
(E)	Smallest positive(non-negative) integer	Largest integer

The variable `holdSmallest` is initialized with `Integer.MAX_VALUE`, which is the largest integer an `int` field may hold. Thus, the code will work to find the smallest number in the array even if it is a negative number. This eliminates (C) and (E). The variable `holdLargest` is initialized to 0, so when looking for a larger integer, it will only be replaced if it is larger than 0, or in other words, a non-negative integer. This eliminates (B). The correct answer is (D).

25. **A** Choice (B) is eliminated because there is no increment to variable i. Choice (C) is eliminated because without an index, it implies the entire array (not each element) is being added to sum over and over. Choice (D) cannot use `element`, because it will contain the contents of a location within the array, rather than a location. Choice (E) uses the variable name of the array as the index. Choice (A) is correct because it uses the temporary variable `element`, which will actually hold the contents of each location within the array.

26. **C** Examining the code of `swap1`, it will only work if the arrays are the same length. There is no accommodation for one array being longer than the other. In fact if array 1 is longer, there will be an out of bounds error on the second array. This eliminates (A), (D), and (E). The code of `swap2` does not work. Array variables hold a reference to the array, not the actual elements. This eliminates (B). The correct answer is (C).

27. **E** Option I declares an arraylist of type string then adds "4.5", which is a `string`. It is correct.
Option II declares an arraylist of type Integer then casts `4.5` to an `int` before adding it to the arraylist, which is acceptable. It is correct.
Option III declares an arraylist variable, then completes the declaration of the arraylist as type Double on the next line. It then adds a double to the arraylist which is correct.
The correct answer is (E).

28. **A** The first loop loads the contents of the array into the arraylist. The next loop begins to remove the elements if the element is even. The loop will continue to run until it reaches the size of the arraylist. As elements of the arraylist are removed, the size will decrease, so there is no risk of going out of bounds. However, the index i will occasionally skip elements because of the re-numbering that takes place.

{2, 4, 6, 7, 8, 10, 11};

i=0, The 2 is even, so it is removed; the array is now

{4, 6, 7, 8, 10, 11};

i=1, Notice, the 4 will now be skipped. The 6 is even, so it is removed; the array is now

{4, 7, 8, 10, 11};

i=2 The 8 is even, so it is removed; the array is now

{4, 7, 10, 11};

i=3 The 11 is odd, so the array stays the same:

{4, 7, 10, 11};

The correct answer is (A).

29. **B** Size of the array is 5, so size−1 is 4. Outer loop executes 0 – 3 (4 times).
Size −2 is 3. Inner loop executes 0 – 2 (3 times).
Since line 12 is executed every time the inner loop is executed, it will be executed (4)(3) = 12 times.
The correct answer is (B).

30. **D** The inner loop does not go far enough to process the entire array. Size is 5, and size −1 is 4, so the index can only be less than 4, stopping at index 3. The last entry in the arraylist will never be sorted. The sort makes 4 passes through the array list, but it never reaches the last entry of the arraylist. The passes will look as follows:

```
0    [6, 21, 2, 8, 1]

1    [6, 2, 21, 8, 1]

2    [6, 2, 8, 21, 1]

3    [2, 6, 8, 21, 1]
```

The correct answer is (D).

31. **D** The array is printed in column major order. The outer loop runs from 0 to row length—1 (the number of columns). The inner loop runs from 0 to the length of the array (which means the number of rows).

The original array is

1 2 3 4

5 6 7 8

The outer loop starts with column 0, prints (0,0) 1   (1,0) 5

The outer loop increments to column 1   (0,1) 2   (1,1) 6

The outer loop increments to column 2   (0,2) 3   (1,2) 7

The outer loop increments to column 3   (0,3) 4   (1,3) 8

The correct answer is (D).

32. **B** Option iii will go out of bounds. The r (rows) will iterate as many times as there are columns. If there are less rows than columns, the index will go out of bounds. The correct answer is (B).

33. **B** Since name and weight are instance variables in the Percussion class, values for those variables should be passed while calling super. The call to super must be the first line in a method. Thus, (A), (D), and (E) are eliminated. The assignment statement of numberOfKeys is reversed in (C). The local variable is being initialized by the instance field. The correct answer is (B).

34. **D** The variable numberOfKeys is not visible outside the Xylophone class. Choices (A) and (B) are simply creating arrays of Xylophone objects. Choice (C) creates a xylophone object then uses the proper accessor method to print the number of keys. Choice (E) declares a variable for an array of type Drums. Choice (D) attempts to print a private instance variable without using an accessor method. It will not compile so the correct answer is (D).

35. **C** The accessor method getWeight() will return the weight of each instance so that they can be compared. Choice (A) is incorrect because the weight field is not visible. Choice (B) is not correct because weight() is not a defined method. Choice (D) is not correct because not only is weight not visible, but .equals is not used to compare primitive types. Choice (E) is incorrect because (C) compares the fields correctly. The correct answer is (C).

36. **D** Use the Is-a relationship to check the solutions
A—SportingDog is a Dog

B—Retriever is a Dog

C—Retriever is a Sporting Dog

D—Dog is a Sporting Dog (no, the relationship is the opposite: not all dogs are sporting dogs)

E—Retriever is a Retriever

The correct answer is (D).

37.　**E**　The Retriever toString() method is invoked first, returning `type: Labrador + super.toString()`. No toString() method is found in SportingDog, but a toString() method is found in Dog, adding `color is: chocolate` to the print line.

The correct answer is (E).

38.　**E**　Try substituting numbers for the variables. Try finding 3^2 by making `x=3, n=2`. The solution is found by 3 x 3.

The base case will be 3 (when the exponent is 1). This should infer that the `if` statement at line 3 should be

```
if (n==1)  return x
```

There is another error on line 6. Line 6 is using addition when raising to a power is multiplying the base x times. Thus, the + sign should be changed to addition.

After making the changes in the code, it is advisable to test it to ensure it works:

```
                  x=3, n=2
1    public double pow(double x, int n)
2    {
3    if (n==1)
4         return x;
5    else
6         return x * pow (x, n-1);
7    }
```

```
f(3,2)
  |
3 * pow(3,1)
  |
  3

3 * 3 = 9
```

The correct answer is (E).

39.　**D**　It is best to walk the code.

```
System.out.println(f(8765));
public static int f(int n)
{
      if (n == 0)
            return 0;
      else
            return f(n/10) + n % 10;
}
```

```
        f(8765)
          |
        f(876) + 5
          |
      f(87) + 6
        |
f(8) + 7
  |
0 + 8

8 + 7 + 6 + 5
```

The correct answer is (D).

40.　**A**　If `sought` is less than the element at index mid, the beginning of the array should be searched. The location of the middle of the array, `mid - 1`, should be assigned to `last`. If `sought` is greater than the element at index `mid`, `mid + 1` should be assigned to `first` so that the latter half of the array can be searched. This process should be repeated until `sought` is found. The correct answer is (A).

Section II: Free-Response Questions

1. (a) DiceSimulation Canonical Solution

```java
public int roll() {
  return (int)(Math.random() * numFaces + 1);
}
```

    (b)

```java
public int runSimulation()
{
int die1 = 0;
int die2 = 0;
int countDouble = 0;
for (int i = 0; i < numSampleSize; i++) {
     die1 = roll();
     die2 = roll();
     if (die1 == die2) {
          countDouble++;
     }
}
return (int)((1.0 * countDouble/numSampleSize ) * 100);
}
```

2.   CalorieCount—Canonical Code

```
public class CalorieCount {
  private int numCaloriesLimit;
  private int numCaloriesIntake;
  private int gramsProtein;
  private int gramsCarbohydrate;
  private int gramsFat;

  public CalorieCount (int numCal) {
     numCaloriesLimit = numCal;
     numCaloriesIntake = 0;
     gramsProtein = 0;
     gramsCarbohydrate = 0;
     gramsFat = 0;
  }
  public void addMeal(int calories, int protein, int carbs, int fat) {
     numCaloriesIntake += calories;
     gramsProtein += protein;
     gramsCarbohydrate += carbs;
     gramsFat +=fat;
  }
  public double getProteinPercentage() {
     return 4.0 * gramsProtein / numCaloriesIntake;
  }
  public boolean onTrack() {
     return numCaloriesIntake <= numCaloriesLimit;
  }
}
```

3. (a)

```
/**   Constructs a TravelPlan.
 *    Instance fields: destination and plans are initialized.
 */

TravelPlan (String destination)
```

(b)

```
/**   Returns true if the timeframe in t overlaps with another Tour in plans;
 */   otherwise false.

public boolean checkForConflicts(Tour t)
```

(c)

```
/**   Must call checkForConflicts for full credit, if checkForConflicts returns false
 */   (the timeframe does not overlap), adds t to plans.  Returns true if
 */    t was added, otherwise returns false.
 */

public boolean addTour(Tour t)
```

4. (a)   SeatingChart Canonical Solution

```
SeatingChart(Name[] names, int r, int c)
{
   chart = new String[r][c];
   for (int i = 0; i < chart.length; i++)
   {
       for (int j = 0; j < chart[0].length; j++)
       {
            chart[i][j] = "";
       }
   }
   int count = 0;
   int i = (int) (Math.random() * names.length );
   int row = i / c;
   int col = i % c;
   while (count < names.length) {
       while (!chart[row][col].equals(""))
       {
            i = (int) (Math.random() * names.length);
            row = i / c;
            col = i % c;
       }
       chart[row][col]= names[count].getLastName() + ", " +
names[count].getFirstName();
       count ++;
       }
   }
```

(b)

```
public String toString()
{
    String str = "";
    for (int a = 0; a < chart.length; a++) {
        for (int b= 0; b < chart[a].length; b++) {
            str += padWithSpaces(chart[a][b]);
        }
        str += "\n";
    }
    return str;
}

}
```

GRADING RUBRICS

1. DiceSimulation Rubric

Part (a)

+3   `roll` method

         +1   Math.random() or the Random class is used

         +1   multiplied by numFaces + 1

         +1   result of computation is cast to int appropriately and returned

Part (b)

+6   `runSimulation` method

         +1   local variables are declared and initialized for the two dice

         +1   roll is used to give the dice values

         +1   a loop is used to execute sample size times (no more, no less)

         +1   the value of die1 and die2 is compared with = = , doubles are counted appropriately

         +1   the percentage of doubles is calculated (avoiding integer division), multiplied by 100

         +1   percentage is returned as an int

2. CalorieCount Rubric

+1   Declares all appropriate `private` instance variables

+2   Constructor

      +1   Declares header: `public CalorieCount (int `*`calorieLimit`*`)`

      +1   Uses parameter and appropriate values to initialize instance variables

+2   `addMeal` method

      +1   Declares header: `public void addMeal(int calories, int protein, int carbs, int fat)`

      +1   updates instance variables appropriately

+2   `getProteinPercentage` method

      +1   Declares header: `public double getProteinPercentage()`

      +1   calculation and return: `return 4.0 * gramsProtein / numCaloriesIntake;`

+2   `onTrack` method

      +1   Declares header: `public boolean onTrack()`

      +1   correctly returns `true` or `false`

                    e.g., `return numCaloriesIntake <= numCaloriesLimit;`

3. TravelPlan Rubric

Part (a)

+3	Constructor	
	+1	Constructor uses class name `TravelPlan`
	+1	Updates destination instance field appropriately (uses `this.`)
	+1	Creates array list appropriately

Part (b)

+4	`checkForConflicts` method	
	+1	uses a loop to traverse every item in the arraylist (no bounds errors)
	+1	uses .get(index) to access the object in the arraylist
	+1	uses getStartTime() and getEndTime() to access the private fields in the Tour object
	+1	uses appropriate logic to determine whether there is a time conflict on the same day, returns true if there is a conflict, false otherwise

Part (c)

+2	`addTour` method	
	+1	calls checkForConflict method to determine if there is a conflict (loses this point if instead, writes the logic to determine if there is a conflict in this method), adds Tour if there is no conflict
	+1	returns `true` if tour is added, or `false` if the tour is not added

4. SeatingChart Rubric

Part (a)

+6		Constructor
	+1	chart is initialized using rows and columns passed in parameters
	+1	random numbers are generated in the correct range
	+1	a unique random number is used each time to place the name in the 2D array (duplicate names are avoided) and all names are placed (none are skipped)
	+1	row and column in the seating chart are derived properly from the random number
	+1	The name is stored in chart as a string(last name, (comma), firstname; e.g., Washington, George)
	+1	Any unused spaces left in the array should be initialized to the empty string (not null)

Part (b)

+3		toString method
	+1	builds a single string with all names from the 2D array, calling padWithSpaces to make all names an equal length
	+1	"\n" creates a line break after each row
	+1	returns a string

Part III
About the AP Computer Science A Exam

- The Structure of the AP Computer Science A Exam
- How AP Exams Are Used
- Other Resources
- Have You Heard About AP Computer Science Principles?
- In Conclusion

THE STRUCTURE OF THE AP COMPUTER SCIENCE A EXAM

The AP Computer Science A Exam is a two-part test. The chart below illustrates the test's structure:

Section	Question Type	Number of Questions	Time Allowed	Percent of Final Grade
I	**Multiple Choice**	40	90 min.	50%
II	**Free Response**	4	90 min.	50%
	Question 1: Methods and Control Structures (9 points)			12.5%
	Question 2: Class (9 points)			12.5%
	Question 3: Array/ArrayList (9 points)			12.5%
	Question 4: 2D Array (9 points)			12.5%

The AP Computer Science A course and exam require that potential solutions of problems be written in the Java programming language. You should be able to perform the following tasks:

- design, implement, and analyze solutions to problems
- use and implement commonly used algorithms
- use standard data structures
- develop and select appropriate algorithms and data structures to solve new problems
- write solutions fluently in an object-oriented paradigm
- write, run, test, and debug solutions in the Java programming language, utilizing standard Java library classes from the AP Java subset
- read and understand programs consisting of several classes and interacting objects
- read and understand a description of the design and development process leading to such a program (examples of such solutions can be found in the AP Computer Science Labs)
- understand the ethical and social implications of computer use

The following table shows the classification categories and how they are represented in the multiple-choice section of the exam. Because questions can be classified as being in more than one category, the total of the percentages is greater than 100%.

Units	Exam Weighting
Unit 1: Primitive Types	2.5-5%
Unit 2: Using Objects	5–7.5%
Unit 3: Boolean Expressions and if Statements	15–17.5%
Unit 4: Iteration	17.5–22.5%
Unit 5: Writing Classes	5–7.5%
Unit 6: Array	10–15%
Unit 7: ArrayList	2.5–7.5%
Unit 8: 2D Array	7.5–10%
Unit 9: Inheritance	5–10%
Unit 10: Recursion	5–7.5%

Have You Noticed?
You may notice that our Part V content chapters align exactly with these units. You're welcome :)

In addition to the multiple-choice questions, there are four mandatory free-response questions. You'll have a total of 90 minutes to answer all four of them. You should spend approximately 22 minutes per question, but be aware that you must manage your own time. Additional time spent on one question will reduce the time that you have left to answer another.

The multiple-choice questions are scored by machine, while the free-response questions are scored by thousands of college faculty and expert AP teachers at the annual AP Reading. Scores on the free-response questions are weighted and combined with the weighted results of the multiple-choice questions. These composite, weighted raw scores are then converted into the reported AP Exam scores of 5, 4, 3, 2, and 1.

Score (Meaning)	Percentage of test-takers receiving this score	Equivalent grade in a first-year college course	Credit granted for this score?
5 (Extremely well qualified)	27.0%	A	Most schools
4 (well qualified)	22.1%	A-, B+, B	Most schools
3 (qualified)	20.8%	B-, C+, C	Some do, but some don't
2 (possibly qualified)	11.8%	C-	Very few do
1 (no recommendation)	18.3%	D	No

The data above is based on the May 2019 administration of the AP Exam.

To score your multiple-choice questions, award yourself one point for every correct answer and credit 0 points to your score for every question that you left blank.

Free-Response Questions

Section II of the AP Computer Science A Exam is the free-response section. Free-response questions are scored from 0 to 9.

Unfortunately, we can't give you a ton of black and white rules about free-response question scoring—the actual scoring for each question is all based on the questions themselves. There is no one-size-fits-all way to score a Computer Science A free-response question. The College Board does map out some penalties, though, and they're in this handy list.

1-Point Penalty

- Extraneous code that causes a side effect or prevents earning points in the rubric (e.g., *information written to output*)
- Local variables used but none declared
- Destruction of persistent data (e.g., *changing value referenced by parameter*)
- Void method or constructor that returns a value

No Penalty

- Extraneous code that causes no side effect
- Extraneous code that is unreachable and would not have earned points in rubric
- Spelling/case discrepancies where there is no ambiguity
- Local variable not declared, provided that other variables are declared in some part
- `private` qualifier on local variable
- Missing `public` qualifier on class or constructor header
- Keyword used as an identifier
- Common mathematical symbols used for operators ($\times$ • $\div$ $\leq$ $\geq$ $<$ $>$ $\neq$)
- [] vs. () vs. <>
- = instead of == (and vice versa)
- Array/collection element access confusion ([] vs. set for r-values)
- Array/collection element modification confusion ([] vs. set for l-values)
- Length/size confusion for array, `String`, and `ArrayList`, with or without ()
- Extraneous [] when referencing entire array
- [i,j] instead of [i][j]
- Extraneous size in array declaration, (e.g., `int[size] nums = new int[size];`)
- Missing ; provided that line breaks and indentation clearly convey intent
- Missing { } where indentation clearly conveys intent and { } are used elsewhere
- Missing ( ) on parameter-less method or constructor invocations
- Missing ( ) around `if`/`while` conditions
- Use of local variable outside declared scope (must be within same method body)
- Failure to cast object retrieved from nongeneric collection

HOW AP EXAMS ARE USED

Different colleges use AP Exams in different ways, so it is important that you visit a particular college's website in order to determine how it accepts AP Exam scores. The three items below represent the main ways in which AP Exam scores can be used.

- **College Credit.** Some colleges will give you college credit if you receive a high score on an AP Exam. These credits count toward your graduation requirements, meaning that you can take fewer courses while in college. Given the cost of college, this could be quite a benefit, indeed.

- **Satisfy Requirements.** Some colleges will allow you to "place out" of certain requirements if you do well on an AP Exam, even if they do not give you actual college credits. For example, you might not need to take an introductory-level course, or perhaps you might not need to take a class in a certain discipline at all.

- **Admissions Plus.** Even if your AP Exam will not result in college credit or even allow you to place out of certain courses, most colleges will respect your decision to push yourself by taking an AP course. In addition, if you take an AP Exam outside of an AP course, they will likely respect that drive too. A high score on an AP Exam shows mastery of more difficult content than is typically taught in high school courses, and colleges may take that into account during the admissions process.

How Will I Know?
Your dream college's website may explain how it uses the AP Exam scores, or you can contact the school's admissions department to verify AP Exam score acceptance information.

Some people think that AP courses are reserved for high school seniors, but that is not the case. Don't be afraid to see about being placed into an AP course during your junior or even sophomore year. A good AP Exam score looks fantastic on a college application and can set you apart from other candidates.

More Great Books

The Princeton Review writes tons of books to guide you through test preparation and college admissions. If you're thinking about college, check out our wildly popular book *The Best 386 Colleges* and visit our website PrincetonReview.com for gobs of college rankings and ratings.

OTHER RESOURCES

There are many resources available to help you improve your score on the AP Computer Science A Exam, not the least of which are your teachers. If you are taking an AP course, you may be able to get extra attention from your teacher, such as feedback on your essays. If you are not in an AP course, you can reach out to a teacher who teaches AP Computer Science A and ask if he or she will review your free-response questions or otherwise help you master the content.

Another wonderful resource is AP Students, the official website of the AP Exams (part of the College Board's website). The scope of information available on AP Central is quite broad and includes the following:

- course descriptions, which include further details on what content is covered by the exam
- sample questions from the AP Computer Science A Exam
- free-response question prompts and multiple-choice questions from previous years

The AP Students home page address is apstudent.collegeboard.org/exploreap.

For up-to-date information about the AP Computer Science A Exam, please visit apstudent.collegeboard.org/apcourse/ap-computer-science-a.

Finally, The Princeton Review offers tutoring and small group instruction. Our expert instructors can help you refine your strategic approach and enhance your content knowledge. For more information, call 1-800-2REVIEW.

HAVE YOU HEARD OF AP COMPUTER SCIENCE PRINCIPLES?

In the fall of 2017, the College Board rolled out a new AP course and exam, AP Computer Science Principles. As the College Board puts it, "AP Computer Science Principles introduces students to the central ideas of computer science, instilling the ideas and practices of computational thinking, and inviting students to understand how computing changes the world. Students develop innovative computational artifacts using the same creative processes artists, writers, computer scientists, and engineers use to bring ideas to life."

This course is a great on-ramp into computer science, a world that has historically been quite daunting to many people. But "comp sci" as they call it, is more bark than bite: computer science is a program in which you learn how to "speak" (code) a language, just as you might learn French or Spanish or Mandarin. And learning a language probably doesn't seem quite as intimidating as learning computer science, now does it?

You are probably enrolled in an AP Computer Science A course if you bought this book, but we wanted to tell you a bit more about AP Comp Sci Principles for your edification. It's useful to know more about this new course so that if a friend ever says to you, "I don't think that I could handle computer science," you can say, "Friend! Yes you can! Do you know how to use creative processes or think about patterns or study languages? Computer Science is for everyone! [stares off into the sunset to let inspiring speech sink in]" Well maybe not THAT, but this is just good stuff to know.

The College Board recently announced some changes to AP Computer Science Principles Conceptual Framework, for 2020–2021 implementation. They have changed the course from covering 7 Big Ideas to covering 5 Big Ideas. Those are:

- Big Idea 1: Creative Development (CRD)
- Big Idea 2: Data (DAT)
- Big Idea 3: Algorithms and Programming (AAP)
- Big Idea 4: Computing Systems and Networks (CSN)
- Big Idea 5: Impact of Computing (IOC)

The College Board isn't kidding—these are some BIG ideas!

Computational Thinking Practices

The College Board drills down this course into computational thinking practices. Those items are:

PRACTICE 1: COMPUTATIONAL SOLUTION DESIGN
Design and evaluate solutions for a purpose.

Students are expected to:

- investigate the situation, context, or task
- determine and design an appropriate method or approach to achieve the purpose
- explain how collaboration affects the development of a solution
- evaluate solution options

PRACTICE 2: ALGORITHMS AND PROGRAM DEVELOPMENT
Develop and implement algorithms.

Students are expected to:

- represent algorithmic processes without using a programming language
- implement an algorithm in a program

PRACTICE 3: ABSTRACTION IN PROGRAM DEVELOPMENT
Develop programs that incorporate abstractions.

Students are expected to:

- generalize data sources through variables
- use abstraction to manage complexity in a program
- explain how abstraction manages complexity

PRACTICE 4: CODE ANALYSIS
Evaluate and test algorithms and programs.

Students are expected to:

- explain how a code segment or program functions
- determine the result of code segments
- identify and correct errors in algorithms and programs, including error discovery through testing

PRACTICE 5: COMPUTING INNOVATIONS
Investigate computing innovations.

Students are expected to:

- explain how computing systems work
- explain how knowledge can be generated from data
- describe the impact of a computing innovation
- describe the impact of gathering data
- evaluate the use of computing based on legal and ethical factors

PRACTICE 6: RESPONSIBLE COMPUTING
Contribute to an inclusive, safe, collaborative, and ethical computing culture.

Students are expected to:

- collaborate in the development of solutions
- use safe and secure methods when using computing devices
- acknowledge the intellectual property of others

Your AP Computer Science Principles teacher has quite a bit of room for interpretation and choice in how she/he can teach these things, so each course will be unique. The Exam, though, is somewhat cut and dried. The College Board maps out the Exam as this:

Section I: Performance Tasks

2 Tasks | 40% of Score

- Performance Task 1: Create—Applications from Ideas. Students will develop a computer program of their choice
- Performance Task 2: Explore—Impact of Computing Innovations. Students will identify a computing innovation, explore its impact, and create a related digital artifact

Section II: End-of-Course Exam

~74 Multiple-Choice Questions | 2 Hours | 60% of Score

- Single-select multiple-choice: Select 1 answer from among 4 options
- Multiple-select multiple-choice: Select 2 answers from among 4 options

Please note that the College Board rolled out changes to AP Computer Science Principles very recently and this is the most up-to-date information. This information is for the 2020–2021 school year, so please look at the College Board's website for any additional information. This is what was available at the time this book went to print.

For the sake of sharing information, let's do a side by side comparison of Comp Sci A versus Principles. Check out the differences below.

	Computer Science A	Computer Science Principles
What it's about	The fundamentals of programming and problem solving using the JAVA language	The fundamentals of computing, including problem solving, working with data, understanding the Internet, cybersecurity, and programming
Goals	Developing skills for future study or a career in computer science or other STEM fields	Broadening your understanding of computer science for use in a diversity of majors and careers
The Exam	• One end-of-year exam: multiple choice and free response	• Two projects during the course • One end-of-year exam: multiple choice

IN CONCLUSION

AP Computer Science Principles (APCSP) can be a great course to get comfortable in the computer science space. If you have already signed up for AP Computer Science A (APCS-A) (which you likely have, since you have purchased this book), then we assume that you are already comfortable with the Big Ideas of Comp Sci. So we'll dive into APCS-A in just a moment—first, let's quickly think about how you might wish to use your AP Exam score.

Although many schools award credit for both exams, *each exam has a different course equivalent*; for example, AP Comp Science A might replace a STEM major programming course, while AP Comp Science Principles replaces a more applied and/or general education requirement course. Consult the school's website for further clarification.

Here's an assortment of schools to give you a sense of who accepts what (or anything!). More information can be found online.

School	APCS-A Score Accepted	Credits Awarded	APCSP Score Accepted	Credits Awarded
Boston University	4 or 5	4	4 or 5	4 (both)
Rutgers University	4 or 5	4	4 or 5	3
West Chester University	3 or higher	3	4 or higher	3
The Ohio State University	3 or higher	3 for a 3; 6 for a 4 or 5	3 or higher	3
University of Alabama	4 or higher	4	3 or higher	3
Yale University	None!	None!	We wish!	Nice try!
UCLA	3 or higher	8	3 or higher	8
Duke University	4 or 5	200-level placement	5	100-level placement
Howard University	None!	None!!	None!!!	None!!!!
University of Miami	4 or 5	4	4 or 5	3
Wesleyan University	4 or 5	1	Not listed	n/a

- Note: The colleges state on their websites that these figures are "subject to change"…what a surprise!

As is true for everything college-related, there is no clear-cut decision that can be made here. In many cases, AP Comp Science A is the best bang-for-the-buck regarding credits; however, a 3 is accepted for AP Comp Science Principles more often than for Comp Science A. AP Computer Science A will often satisfy a major Comp Sci programming requirement, but the Principles course will not. Then again, if you're not embarking on a STEM journey, why not "AP out" of a general education course to bang out a requirement? Decisions, decisions, decisions!

For more information, hit up Google and search for your college name followed by "ap credits."

Part IV
Test-Taking Strategies for the AP Computer Science A Exam

PREVIEW

Review your Practice Test 1 results and then respond to the following questions:

- How many multiple-choice questions did you miss even though you knew the answer?

- On how many multiple-choice questions did you guess blindly?

- How many multiple-choice questions did you miss after eliminating some answers and guessing based on the remaining answers?

- Did you find any of the free-response questions easier or harder than others—and, if so, why?

HOW TO USE THE CHAPTERS IN THIS PART

Before reading the following strategy chapters, think about what you are doing now. As you read and engage in the directed practice, be sure to think critically about the ways you can change your approach.

Chapter 1
How to Approach
Multiple-Choice
Questions

THE BASICS

The directions for the multiple-choice section of the AP Computer Science A Exam are pretty simple. They read as follows:

Directions: Determine the answer to each of the following questions or incomplete statements, using the available space for any necessary scratchwork. Then decide which is the best of the choices given and fill in the corresponding oval on the answer sheet. No credit will be given for anything written in the examination booklet. Do not spend too much time on any one problem.

In short, you're being asked to do what you've done on many other multiple-choice exams: pick the best answer and then fill in the corresponding bubble on a separate sheet of paper. You will not be given credit for answers you record in your test booklet (by circling them, for example) but do not fill in on your answer sheet. The section consists of 40 questions and you will be given 90 minutes to complete it.

The College Board also provides a breakdown of the general subject matter covered on the exam. This breakdown will not appear in your test booklet; it comes from the preparatory material that the College Board publishes. Here again is the chart we showed you in Part III:

Units	Exam Weighting
Unit 1: Primitive Types	2.5-5%
Unit 2: Using Objects	5–7.5%
Unit 3: Boolean Expressions and if Statements	15–17.5%
Unit 4: Iteration	17.5–22.5%
Unit 5: Writing Classes	5–7.5%
Unit 6: Array	10–15%
Unit 7: ArrayList	2.5–7.5%
Unit 8: 2D Array	7.5–10%
Unit 9: Inheritance	5–10%
Unit 10: Recursion	5–7.5%

A few important notes about the AP Computer Science A Exam directly from the College Board:

- Assume that the classes listed in the Java Quick Reference have been imported where appropriate.
- Assume that declarations of variables and methods appear within the context of an enclosing class.
- Assume that method calls that are not prefixed with an object or class name and are not shown within a complete class definition appear within the context of an enclosing class.
- Unless otherwise noted in the question, assume that parameters in method calls are not null and that methods are called only when their preconditions are satisfied.

MULTIPLE-CHOICE STRATEGIES

Process of Elimination (POE)

As you work through the multiple-choice section, always keep in mind that you are not graded on your thinking process or scratchwork. All that ultimately matters is that you indicate the correct answer. Even if you aren't sure how to answer a question in a methodically "correct" way, see if you can eliminate any answers based on common sense and then take a guess.

Throughout the book, we will point out areas where you can use common sense to eliminate answers.

Although we all like to be able to solve problems the "correct" way, using a Process of Elimination (POE) and guessing aggressively can help earn you a few more points. It may be these points that make the difference between a 3 and a 4 or push you from a 4 to a 5.

Don't Be Afraid to Guess

If you don't know the answer, guess! There is no penalty for a wrong answer, so there is no reason to leave an answer blank. Obviously, the more incorrect answers you can eliminate, the better your odds of guessing the correct answer.

Be Strategic About Long Questions

Some multiple-choice questions require a page or two of reading to answer the question. Skip any questions that will either take a long time to read or a long time to calculate. Circle the questions and come back to them after you've completed the rest of the section.

Don't Turn a Question into a Crusade!

Most people don't run out of time on standardized tests because they work too slowly. Instead, they run out of time because they spend half of the test wrestling with two or three particular questions.

You should never spend more than a minute or two on any question. If a question doesn't involve calculation, then you know the answer, you can take an educated guess at the answer, or you don't know the answer. Figure out where you stand on a question, make a decision, and move on.

Any question that requires more than two minutes' worth of calculations probably isn't worth doing. Remember, skipping a question early in the section is a good thing if it means that you'll have time to get two right later on.

Watch for Special Cases in Algorithm Descriptions

On the exam, you may know that the average run-time for finding an element in a binary search tree is $O(n \log n)$. Watch out if the question casually mentions that the data is inserted in the tree in sorted order. Now the run-time deteriorates into the worst case, $O(n)$. These special occasions may pop up on the AP Computer Science A Exam, so watch out.

Remember the Base Case in Recursive Algorithms

Recursive methods without a base case run forever. Be sure that a base case exists and is the correct base case. For example, a factorial function whose base case is

```
if (n == 1){
    return 0;
}
```

is incorrect because 1! = 1.

Watch for < vs. <= and > vs. >=

The difference between < and <= or between > and >= can be huge, especially in loops. You can bet that this discrepancy will appear in multiple-choice questions!

Know How to Use the AP Computer Science Java Subset

This chapter offers strategies that will help make you a better test-taker and, hopefully, a better scorer on the AP Computer Science A exam. However, there are some things you just have to know. Although you'll have a Quick Reference for the AP Computer Science Java Subset as part of the exam, review the AP Computer Science Java Subset classes beforehand and know what methods are available, what they do, and how to use them. The Quick Reference will help, but it won't substitute for knowing the classes.

Preconditions and Postconditions

Read these carefully when given. They may provide the clue needed to answer the question. For instance, a precondition may state that the array passed to a method is in sorted order.

Parameter Passing

Remember that arguments passed to methods do not keep changes made to them inside the method. For instance, it is impossible to write a method that swaps the value of two integer primitives. Don't confuse this, however, with changing the contents (attributes) of an object that is passed to a method.

Client Program vs. Method

There is likely to be at least one question that defines a class and asks you to choose among different implementations for a method. Pay close attention to whether the method is a "client program" or a method of the class. If it's a client program, the implementation of the method may not access any private data fields or private methods of the class directly. If it's a method of the class, the implementation is free to access both private data fields and private methods.

Boolean Short-Circuiting

Conditionals in if statements and while statements "short-circuit." For example,

```
if ((a != 0) && (b / a == 5))
```

is *not* the same as

```
if ((b / a == 5) && (a != 0))
```

since Java will stop evaluating a compound boolean statement once the truth value is determined. (More on this later.)

Memorize DeMorgan's Laws

There will be at least one question on the exam for which these laws will be useful.

```
!(p || q) is equivalent to !p && !q
!(p && q) is equivalent to !p || !q
```

Find Data in a Class

Watch out for answer choices that have code segments that attempt to change a data field declared final. This is illegal code.

Mixing double and int in an Expression

In operations that have both an int variable and a double variable, unless explicitly cast otherwise, the int is converted to a double and the result of the operation is a double.

Trial and Error

If a question asks about the result of a code segment based on the value of variables, pick simple values for the variables, and determine the results based on those values. Eliminate any choice that is inconsistent with that result. This is often easier than determining the results in more general terms.

Chapter 2
How to Approach
Free-Response
Questions

FREE-RESPONSE STRATEGIES

Write Java Code, Not Pseudocode

Only Java code is graded; pseudocode is not graded. Don't waste time writing pseudocode if you don't know how to code the solution to a problem. (On the other hand, write pseudocode as a starting point to writing your Java code if it helps you to do so.)

Don't Comment on Your Code

Unless you write some code that is extremely tricky (and see below for whether or not you should do that!), there's no need to write comments. It just takes time (that you don't have a lot of), and the comments will be largely ignored by the graders anyway (you won't get points if your comment is correct but your code is wrong). You also run the risk of misleading the grader if your code is correct but your comments are incorrect.

Write Legibly

This seems obvious, but if a grader can't read your code, you won't get any points.

Don't Erase Large Chunks of Code

If you make extensive changes to the code you're writing, it's better to put a big "X" through the bad code rather than erase it. It saves you time and makes it easier for the graders to read.

Don't Write More Than One Solution to a Problem

Graders will grade the first solution they see. If you rewrite a solution, be sure to cross out the old one.

Don't Leave any Problem Blank

You don't get any points if you don't write anything down. Even if you're unsure how to answer a particular problem (or part of a problem), analyze the problem and code the method's "infrastructure."

For instance, if the method signature indicates that it creates and returns an `ArrayList`, writing

```
ArrayList returnedList = new ArrayList( );
return returnedList;
```

is likely to get you at least partial credit—even if you don't know how to fill the `ArrayList` with the correct objects.

KISS (Keep It Simple, Student)

The free-response problems are designed to make the solutions relatively straight-forward. If your solution is getting complicated, there's probably an easier or better way to solve the problem. At the same time, don't try for seemingly elegant but unreadable code. Remember that graders must read hundreds of exams in a week—they may not be able to figure out all of the nuances of your code. KEEP IT SIMPLE!

Write Standard Solutions

Use AP-style variable, class, and method names and follow the indentation style of the AP sample code (even if you don't like their style!). Although graders always try to be fair and accurate, they are human and do make mistakes. The closer your answer adheres to the sample solution given to the graders, the easier it will be for them to grade.

Wherever possible, use clear and intuitive nomenclature. For example, use r and c or row and col for looping through the rows and columns of a two-dimensional array, don't use x and y or a and b or *jack* and *jill*. This ensures that graders can easily follow the flow of your code.

If the Pseudocode for an Algorithm is Given, Use it!

Sometimes you will have to create your own algorithm for a method. Often though, the pseudocode for the algorithm or method is given to you as part of the problem; all you need to do is implement the algorithm. In that case, use the pseudocode that's given to you! Don't make it harder on yourself by trying to re-create the algorithm or implement your own special version. Furthermore, you can often write the code for a method based on given pseudocode even if you don't understand the underlying algorithm.

Answer Part (c) to a Problem Even If You Can't Do Parts (a) and (b)

Many parts of free-response problems build on previous parts. For example, the question in part (c) may use the methods you wrote in parts (a) and (b). However, you do not need to have answered parts (a) and (b) correctly in order to get full credit for part (c). In fact, part (c) is sometimes easier than either part (a) or (b). If part (c) states that you should use parts (a) and (b), use them!

Don't Make Easy-to-Avoid Mistakes

Students often lose points on the free-response section because they make common errors. Here are some things you can do to avoid these mistakes.

- Unless the problem *explicitly* asks you to output something (using System.out.print), *never* output anything in a method you write.
- Watch method signatures. Be sure to call methods with the correct name and correct number and type of parameters. If the method is not void, be sure that the method you write returns a value with the correct type as specified in the signature.
- Use the objectName.methodName() syntax when calling methods of a given object; use the ClassName.methodName() syntax when calling static methods such as the random method of the Math class.
- Be sure to declare any variables you use (and give them descriptive names).
- Don't create objects when you don't need to. For instance, if a method you call returns an ArrayList, declare it as

  ```
  ArrayList returnedList;
  returnedList = obj.getList( );
  ```
  and
  ```
  ArrayList returnedList = new ArrayList( );
  returnedList = obj.getList( );
  ```

- Use proper indentation. Even if you use curly brackets for all of your conditionals and loops, the indentation will demonstrate your intent should you forget, for example, a closing curly brace.

Design Question

One problem in the free-response section is likely to be a design problem for which you will be given a description of a class and asked to write an interface (code) for it. You may also be asked to implement selected methods in your class. Be sure to use appropriate class, method, and private data field names. For example, "method1" is not likely to be a good name for a method that returns the total price of an object; "totalPrice" is a more appropriate name. Be sure to include all methods, private data fields, and *all* of the constructors (including the default constructor) asked for in the problem. If you are asked to implement a method, be sure to use the correct class, method, and private data field names *as you defined them* in the design part.

Arrays and ArrayLists

At least one problem (probably more) on the exam is likely to involve walking through arrays and/or ArrayLists. Know the differences between the two types of structures and how to loop through elements in the array or an ArrayList. Know how to use iterators and how to work with two-dimensional arrays.

GENERAL STRATEGIES

The following strategies apply to both the multiple-choice and free-response sections of the exam.

Write in the Test Booklet

Don't try to do the questions in your head. Write things down! Take notes on the question. In addition to making the problem easier to solve, having notes in the test booklet will make it easier to go back and check your work if you have time at the end of the test.

Underline Key Words in Questions

Words like *client program, sorted, ordered, constant, positive, never, always,* and *must* all specify conditions to a problem. On both the multiple-choice and free-response sections, underline these key words as you read the question to reinforce their importance to the problem.

Don't Do More Work Than You Need to

You are not graded for your work at all on the multiple-choice section, and you are not given extra credit for clever or well-documented answers on the free-response section. Keep it simple and strive to get the answer right rather than impress the graders.

Look Through the Exam First—Use the Two-Pass System

Keep in mind that all of the multiple-choice questions are worth the same number of points, and each free-response question is worth the same number of points as the other free-response questions. There is no need to do them in order. Instead use a two-pass system.

Go through each section twice. The first time, do all the questions that you can get answers to immediately—that is, the questions with little or no analysis or the questions on computer science topics in which you are well-versed.

On the first round, skip the questions in the topics that make you uncomfortable. Also, you might want to skip the ones that look like number crunchers (you might still be expected to crunch a few numbers—even without a calculator). Circle the questions that you skip in your test booklet so you can find them easily during the second pass.

Once you've done all the questions that come easily to you, go back and pick out the tough ones that you have the best shot at.

That's why the two-pass system is so handy. By using it, you make sure that you get to see all the questions that you can get right, instead of running out of time because you got bogged down on questions you couldn't do earlier in the test.

A word of caution though, if you skip a multiple-choice question, be sure that you take extra care in marking your answer sheet. Always be sure that the answer you bubble in on the answer sheet is for the correct question number. In addition, don't forget to circle the skipped question in the multiple-choice booklet so that you remember to come back to it if you have time at the end of the test.

Pace Yourself and Keep Track of Time

On the multiple-choice section, you should take an average of 2 minutes per problem. This will give you 3 minutes to look over the test at the beginning and 7 minutes for a final check at the end. As a comparison, if you take 3 minutes per problem, you're going to answer only 30 questions; if you take 5 minutes per problem, you're going to answer only 18 questions. Bear in mind, however, that 2 per minutes per question is an average. Some questions will not require this much time, so it's okay if a few questions take you longer than 2 minutes. After the first pass, reevaluate your pacing goal based on the number of questions and amount of time you have remaining.

On the free-response section, you should pace yourself at a rate of 20 minutes per complete problem. This will give you roughly 2 minutes per problem to check your answer and a minute at the beginning to look over the problems.

Finally...

Don't panic. If you've prepared, the test is easier than it looks at first glance. Take your time, approach each question calmly and logically, remember the tips in this chapter, and you'll be fine.

Get Ready to Move On...

Now that you have the hints, strategies, and background information locked in, it's time to move on to the serious business at hand...the subject review (Part V). Read over the following chapters, take notes, and compare them to your textbook and class notes as preparation to take Practice Test 2 in the back of the book. Once you've mastered what's in this book and learned from your mistakes on the practice tests, you'll be ready to ace the real AP Exam.

REFLECT

Think about what you learned in Part IV, and respond to the following questions:

- How much time will you spend on multiple-choice questions?

- How will you change your approach to multiple-choice questions?

- What is your multiple-choice guessing strategy?

- How much time will you spend on free-response questions?

- How will you change your approach to the free-response questions?

- Will you seek further help, outside of this book (such as a teacher, tutor, or AP Students), on how to approach multiple-choice questions, free-response questions, or a pacing strategy?

Part V
Content Review for the AP Computer Science A Exam

Chapter 3
Primitive Types

Computer Science (CS) is a fancy title used for many aspects of computing, usually on the developing end; its areas include computer programming, which is exactly what we will be doing in AP Computer Science A (APCS). APCS focuses on the language of Java and its components, and in many cases, you will be the programmer. Although the person using your program (the user) will typically see only the end result of your program, CS gives you the tools to write statements (code) that will ideally make the user's experience both functional and enjoyable.

PROGRAMMING STYLE

Computer programming is similar to a foreign language; it has nouns, verbs, and other parts of speech, and it has different forms of style, just like speaking languages. Just as you might use different words and ways of speaking—tone, expressions, etc.—with your family versus your friends, CS has many different languages and, within each language, its own ways of getting the job done. In both the CS world and the APCS world, a particular **programming style** is expected in order to show fluency in the language. A company that might hire you for a CS job will likely expect you to conform to its own unique programming style; similarly, the College Board will expect you to conform to its accepted programming style based on its research of CS styles accepted at universities around the world.

Comments, Identifiers, White Space

Commenting is an extremely vital style technique in the programming world. Comments do not actually cause the program to behave any differently, whether absent or present; however, comments serve many purposes including:

- allowing the programmer to make "notes" within the program that she or he may want to reference later
- allowing the person reading and/or using the program ("the reader" and/or "the user") to understand the code in a less cryptic way, when applicable
- revealing to the programmer/reader/user aspects of the program that are required to make the program operate as intended and/or are produced as a result of the program's execution

There are two types of **commenting** in Java. **In-line,** or **short, comments** appear after or near a statement and are preceded by two forward slashes ("//") followed by the comment. **Long comments** that extend beyond a single line of code are surrounded by special characters; they begin with ("/*") and end with ("*/").

For example,

```
//   This is a short comment
/*   This is a
     long comment */
```

Identifiers are names that are given to represent data stored in the memory of the computer during the program's execution. Rather than using a nonsensical memory address code to reference data, Java allows the programmer to name an identifier to perform this job. When we name identifiers in Java, there are guidelines that we *must* use and guidelines that the College Board *expects* us to use:

- An identifier may contain any combination of letters, numbers, and underscore ("_"), but *must* begin with a letter and may not contain any other characters, including spaces.
- An identifier *should* be a logical name that corresponds to the data it is associated with; for example, an identifier associated with the side of a triangle would be more useful as *side1* instead of *s*.
- An identifier *should* begin with a lowercase letter and, if it is composed of several words, should denote each subsequent word with a capital letter. If we decided to create an identifier associated with our triangle's number of sides, `numberOfSides` or `numOfSides` would conform to this style; `NumberOfSides` and `numofsides` would not.

White space is another element of style that does not affect the overall functionality of the program. Rather, it enhances the readability of the program by allowing the programmer to space out the code to separate specific statements or tasks from others. Much like a book may leave empty space at the end of a chapter and begin the next chapter on the next page without affecting the overall story, white space has a similar effect.

Compiling & Errors

When the programmer writes Java code, statements are written that are understood within a Java development environment. The computer, however, does not understand this language, much like you would likely not understand a foreign language spoken in its native environment. Therefore, an **interpreter** is used within the developer environment, enabling the computer to understand the Java code. A computer only operates using code written in **binary** (zeroes and ones, literally!), and so the interpreter "translates" your Java code into binary. This process is called **compiling**. As a result, in most instances as well as on the AP Exam, modern computer programmers do not need to understand binary code directly.

When an interactive development environment ("IDE") is used to compile your code, the code will be automatically checked for basic programming errors. If an error is found within the code, the compiling is halted and an error message is produced (this feedback is where the "interactive" part comes in); this situation is called a **compile-time error**. Although the error message/code is not always helpful in a direct way, it does allow the programmer to troubleshoot the issue in a more directed way. Unfortunately, since the AP Exam is a pencil-and-paper test, you will have access to neither a computer nor a compiler. Your code must be absent of errors in order to receive full credit for the response (or any credit if it's a multiple-choice question).

A **logical error** is more difficult to troubleshoot; rather than a problem with the syntax of the Java code itself, a logical error lies in the desired output/purpose of the program. Similar to ordering dinner and receiving a perfectly prepared dessert instead, you are getting a good result, but it is not appropriate for the desired task.

A **run-time error** is an error that is not caught by the compiler, yet produces an error during the execution of the program. In many ways, this is the worst (and most embarrassing) error for the programmer, because it is not realized until the task is supposedly "done." An analog to this situation is a crash that occurs when you are editing your favorite image in a graphics program. It's frustrating for the user and annoying for the programmer when you leave negative feedback on the company's website!

---

1. Assuming all other statements in the program are correct, each of the following statements will allow the program to compile EXCEPT

   (A) // This is a comment
   (B) /* This is a comment */
   (C) // myName is a good identifier name
   (D) // myname is a good identifier name
   (E) All of the above statements will compile.

Here's How to Crack It

Choices (A), (B), and (C) are all valid comments in Java, regardless of their contents and the fact that (B) is not actually any longer than a single line. Choice (D) uses a poor identifier name, not a good one, but neither of these situations will result in a non-compiling program. Therefore, (E) is correct.

OBJECTS & PRIMITIVE DATA

Output (and some input)

In order for your program to "do anything" from the user's perspective (at this level, anyway!), it must produce output to the screen. A program may produce output to many devices, including storage drives and printers, but APCS requires us to produce output only to the screen.

There are two similar statements that we use to produce output to the screen in this course:

```
System.out.print(…);
System.out.println(…);
```

The ellipses in these statements will contain the data and/or identifiers that will be displayed on the screen. We will see the difference between these statements in a minute.

For example, if a triangle has a side length of 2 stored in the memory using the identifier side1 and we wanted to output that information to the screen, we could use one of the following two commands:

```
System.out.print(2);
System.out.print(side1);
```

Since both 2 and side1 represent numerical values, they can be outputted to the screen in this way. If the programmer wanted to display non-numerical data, however, he or she would use a **string literal** (or simply a **string**) to accomplish this task. A string literal is simply one or more characters combined into a single unit. The previous sentence, and this sentence, can be considered as string literals. In a Java program, string literals must be surrounded by double quotes ("") to avoid a compile error. In our triangle example, we can use a string literal to make the output more user-friendly:

```
System.out.println("The length of side 1 is:");
System.out.print(side1);
// side1 may be simply substituted with 2, in this case
```

Note the usage of the println statement rather than the print statement, which will output the string literal and then put the cursor at the beginning of the next line for further output, rather than displaying the next output on the same line. Note, also, that the statement

```
System.out.print(side1);
```

will display the *value* stored using the side1 identifier, 2. In contrast, the statement

```
System.out.print("side1");
```

will literally display

```
side1
```

because the double quotes create a string literal here. The College Board loves to ask multiple-choice questions that determine whether you understand these differences.

If quotation marks are how the programmer signals the beginning and end of a string literal, how would he or she display quotation marks? For example, what if an instructional program was intended to display

```
Be sure to display the value of side1 not "side 1".
```

The command below might seem like an appropriate solution but would actually cause a compile time error.

```
System.out.print("Be sure to display the value of side1 not
"side 1".");
```

The complier will interpret the quotation mark in front of side1 as the close of the string and will not know what to do with the rest of it. To display a quotation mark, the programmer must use an **escape sequence**. Escape sequences are small pieces of coding beginning with a backslash (\) used to indicate specific characters. To successfully display the above live, use the command

```
System.out.print("Be sure to print the value of side1 not
\"side1\".");
```

Similarly, the escape sequence \n can be used to create a line break in the middle of a string. For example the command

```
System.out.print("The first line\nThe second line");
```

will display

```
The first line

The second line
```

So if a backslash indicates an escape sequence, how does a programmer print a backslash? This is done using another escape sequence, \\. The following command

```
System.out.println("Use \\n to indicate a new line.")
```

will display

```
Use \n to indicate a new line.
```

There are other escape sequences in Java, but only these three appear on the AP Computer Science A Exam.

---

2. Assuming all other statements in the program are correct, each of the following statements will allow the program to compile EXCEPT

   (A) `System.out.print(1);`
   (B) `System.out.print("1");`
   (C) `System.out.print(side1);`
   (D) `System.out.print("side1");`
   (E) All of the above statements will compile.

Here's How to Crack It

Choices (A) and (B) will both display 1, although (A) is numerical and (B) is a string literal. Choice (D) will display the string literal `side1`. Since there is no indication in the question that `side1` has been associated with any data, (C) will generate an error because Java does not know what to display. Therefore, (C) is the answer. Be very careful when choosing "all of the above" or "none of the above" answer choices!

As you might imagine, input is also important in programming. Although you may learn some techniques of getting user input (the Scanner class, for example), the AP Exam will not test any input methods or classes. Instead, the input will be assumed and given as a comment in the coding. It may be similar to this.

```
int k = ..., //read user input
```

You will not be asked to prompt the user for input, unless there is pre-existing code in the task that does it for you. Nice.

Variables & Assignment

Let's put those identifiers to work.

In order to actually "create" an identifier, we need to **assign** a data value to that identifier. This task is done by writing an assignment statement.

The syntax of an assignment statement is

type identifier = data;

Continuing with our triangle example, if we wanted to actually assign the data value of 2 to a new identifier called `side1`, we could use this statement:

```
int side1 = 2;
```

This statement tells the compiler that (1) our identifier is called `side1`, (2) the data assigned to that identifier should be 2, and (3) our data is an integer (more on this in the next section). The equals sign ("=") is called an **assignment operator** and is required by Java. The semicolon, which we also saw in the output statements above, denotes that the statement is finished. Note that an assignment statement does NOT produce any output to the screen.

When data is associated with an identifier, the identifier is called a **variable**. The reason we use this term is because, like in math, the value of the variable can be changed; it can *vary*! Look at the following code:

```
int myFavoriteNumber = 22;
myFavoriteNumber = 78;
System.out.print ("My favorite number is " +
myFavoriteNumber);
```

Can you predict the output? The variable myFavoriteNumber is first assigned the value of 22, but it is then reassigned to the value 78. Therefore, the original value is no longer stored in the computer's memory and the 78 remains. The output would be

```
My favorite number is 78
```

A few items to note in this example:

- Once a variable is given a type (again, more on this later), its type should not be restated. This fact explains why the second assignment statement is missing `int`.
- The string literal is outputted as written, but the variable's *value*, not its name, is outputted.
- In order to output a string literal and a numerical value using the same output statement, use the **concatenation operator** between the two items. Although this operator looks like a typical + sign, it does not "add" the values in the traditional sense; instead, it simply outputs the two values next to each other. For example, two plus two equals four in the mathematical sense, but two concatenated with two produces 22.

---

3. Assuming all other statements in the program are correct, each of the following statements will allow the program to compile EXCEPT

(A) `System.out.print("Ilove Java");`
(B) `System.out.println("Ilove" + "Java");`
(C) `System.out.print(1 + "love" + Java");`
(D) `System.out.println(1 + "love" + "Java");`
(E) `System.out.print("I love" + " " + "Java");`

Here's How to Crack It

Choices (A) and (B), although their output may not look grammatically correct (they love to do this on the AP Exam—remember, it's not a grammar test!), will compile without error. Choice (D) is fine because the numerical value is concatenated with the string literals, producing a string literal that can be displayed. Choice (E) uses string literal that is simply an empty space, which is valid. Therefore, (C) is the answer because "Java" is missing the left-hand quotation mark.

The Four Data Types—int, double, boolean, char

When the programmer wants to assign data to a variable, he or she must first decide what *type* of data will be stored. For the AP Exam, there are four data types that make up the **primitive data** forms—i.e., the basic types of data. More complex data forms will be discussed later.

integer *(int)* represents an integer number: positive numbers, negative numbers, and zero, with no decimals or fractions. Integers can store non-decimal values from –2,147,483,648 to 2,147,483,647, inclusive. That's a lot of values.

double represents a number that can be positive, negative, or zero, and can be a fraction or decimal…pretty much any number you can think of. It also has a much bigger breadth of upper and lower limits than an integer; it can express numbers with decades of significant digits. If you have to store an integer that is larger than the limits listed above, you must store the data as a double.

On the AP Exam, you do not have to memorize the upper and lower limits of these numerical data types; you do, however, need to know that a double must be declared for a number that is larger than an integer can store.

boolean represents a value that is either true or false. In machine code, true is represented by 1 (or any nonzero value) and false is represented by 0. This data type is excellent for storing or using yes/no data, such as the responses to: Are you hungry? Are you excited about the AP Exam? Is this chapter boring?

character *(char)* represents any single character that can be represented on a computer; this type includes any character you can type on the keyboard, including letters, numbers, spaces, and special characters like slashes, dashes, and the like. Char values are stored using a single quotation mark or apostrophe ('). The values of the capital letters A thru Z are 65–90 and lowercase letters are 97–122 (browse to unicode-table.com/en for a fancier, more complete listing of these values). Although the AP Exam does not require the memorization of these codes (thankfully), you should know their relative placement in the table. For example, you should know that character "A" comes before (has a lower numerical value) than character "B"; you should also note that every capital letter character comes before the lowercase letters. Therefore, "a" actually comes *after* "Z."

You've Got Character, The Test Doesn't
It's useful to know how char works, but it won't be on the AP Exam, so don't stress over it!

Arithmetic Operations

The most primitive uses for the first computers were to perform complex calculations. They were basically gigantic calculators. As a result, one of the most basic operations we use in Java involves arithmetic.

The symbols +, -, *, and / represent the operations of addition, subtraction, multiplication, and division, respectively. The operator % is also used in Java; called the "modulus" operator, this symbol will produce the numerical remainder of a division. For example, 3%2 would evaluate to 1, since 3 divided by 2 yields 1, with 1 as a remainder. These operations can be performed intuitively on numerical values; they can also be performed on variables that store numerical values.

Speaking of math, back to our triangle example...

Consider the following statement in a program:

```
int side2 = 2, side3 = 3;
```

(Note that you can write multiple assignment statements in a single line, as long as the data types are the same.)

If the programmer wanted to write a statement that found the sum of these data and assigned the result to another variable called sumOfSides, he or she could easily write

```
sumOfSides = 2 + 3; // method 1
```

But this statement is less useful than

```
sumOfSides = side2 + side3; // method 2
```

Since the data is assigned to variables, for which values can vary, method 2 will reflect those changes while method 1 will not.

This same technique can be applied to all of the mathematical operators. Remember that a mixture of mathematical operations follows a specific order of **precedence**. Java will perform the multiplication and division operations (including modulus), from left to right, followed by the addition and subtraction operations in the same order. If the programmer wants to change the order of precedence of the operators, he or she can use parentheses.

Consider these lines of code:

```
System.out.print(3 - 4/5); // statement 3
System.out.print(3 -(4/5)); // statement 4
System.out.print((3 - 4)/5); // statement 5
```

In statement 3, the division would occur first, followed by the subtraction of three minus the answer.

In statement 4, the same thing would happen, so it is mathematically equivalent to statement 3.

In statement 5, the parentheses override the order of operations, so the subtraction occurs followed by the answer being divided by 5.

Okay, here's where it gets crazy. Can you predict the output of these statements? Believe it or not, the output of statements 3 and 4 is 3; the output of statement 5 is 0. These results demonstrate the fact that data in Java is **strongly typed**.

When you perform a mathematical operation on two integers, Java will return the answer as an integer, as well. Therefore, although 4/5 is actually 0.8, Java will return a value of 0. Likewise, Java will evaluate 5/4 to be 1. The decimal part is cut off (not rounded), so the result will also be an integer. Negative numbers work the same way. Java will return –4/5 as 0 and –5/4 as –1. Strange, huh?

As is true with all computer science, there is a workaround for this called **casting**. Casting is a process through which data is forced to "look like" another type of data to the compiler. Think of someone who is cast in a show to play a part; although the actor has a personal identity, he or she assumes the new identity for the audience. The following modifications to statement 3 demonstrate different ways of casting:

```
System.out.print(3 -(double)(4)/5); // statement 3.1
System.out.print(3 - 4/(double)5); // statement 3.2
```

These statements will cast 4 and 5, respectively, to be double values of 4.0 and 5.0. As a result, the division will be "upgraded" to a division between double values, not integers, and the desired result will be returned. The following statements, although they will compile without error, will not display the desired result of 2.2.

```
System.out.print((double)3 - 4/5); // statement 3.3
System.out.print(3 - (double)(4/5)); // statement 3.4
```

Casting has a higher precedence than arithmetic operators, except parentheses, of course. Therefore, statement 3.3 will first convert 3 to 3.0, but will then perform integer division before completing the subtracting. The result is 3.0. In statement 3.4, the result of dividing the integers is casted to a double; since the integer division evaluates to 0, the cast will simply make the result 0.0, yielding an output of 3.0 once again. Very tricky!

The **increment operator** (++) is used to increase the value of a number by one. For example, if the value of a variable x is 3, then x++ will increment the value of x to 4. This has the exact same effect as writing $x = x + 1$, and is nothing more than convenient shorthand.

Conversely, the **decrement operator** (--) is used to quickly decrease the value of a number by one. For example, if the value of a variable named x is 3, then x-- decreases the value of x to 2. This has the exact same effect as writing $x = x - 1$.

Other shortcut operators include +=, -=, *=, /=, and %=. These shortcuts perform the indicated operation and assign the result to the original variable. For example,

```
a += b;
```

is an equivalent command to

```
a = a + b;
```

If `int a` has been assigned the value 6 and `int b` has been assigned the value 3, the following table indicates the results of the shortcut operations.

Shortcut Command	Equivalent Command	Resulting value of a
a += b	a = a + b	9
a -= b	a = a - b	3
a *= b	a = a * b	18
a /= b	a = a / b	2
a %= b	a = a % b	0

4. Consider the following code segment:

```
int a = 3;
int b = 6;
int c = 8;
int d = a/b;
c /= d;
System.out.print(c);
```

Which of the following will be output by the code segment?

(A) 4
(B) 8
(C) 12
(D) 16
(E) There will be no output because of a run-time error.

Here's How to Crack It

Go through the coding one step at a time. The first three lines initialize a as 3, b as 6, and c as 8. The fourth line initializes d as a/b, which is 3/6. However, note that this is integer division, so the result must be an integer. In normal arithmetic 3/6 = 0.5. In Java, integer division cuts off the decimal part, so the d = 0. The command c /= d is equivalent to c = c/d. However, this requires dividing by 0, which is not allowed in Java (or normal arithmetic for that matter). In Java, dividing by 0 will cause an `ArithmeticException`, which is a type of run-time error, so the answer is (E).

Give Me a Break

Humans are pretty smart when it comes to guessing intent For instance, you probably noticed that there's a missing period between this sentence and the one before it. (If not, slow down: AP Computer Science A Exam questions require close reading when looking for errors.) Computers, on the other hand, are literal—more annoyingly so, probably, than those teachers who ask if you're physically capable of going to the bathroom when you ask if you can go. To that end, then, it's crucial that you end each complete statement (i.e., sentence) with a semicolon, which is our way of telling the Java compiler that it's reached the end of a step. This doesn't mean that you need to place a semicolon after every line—remember that line breaks exist only to make code more readable to humans—but you must place one after any complete declaration or statement.

Study Break
Speaking of breaks, don't burn yourself out and overdo it with your AP Comp Sci preparation. Take it day by day and read a chapter, then work the end-of-chapter drills each day, then every so often, give yourself a break! Go for a walk, call a friend, listen to a favorite song.

CHAPTER 3 REVIEW DRILL

Answers to the review questions can be found in Chapter 13.

1. Consider the following code segment:

```
1    int a = 10;
2    double b = 10.7;
3    double c = a + b;
4    int d = a + c;
5    System.out.println(c + " " + d);
```

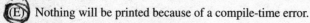

What will be output as a result of executing the code segment?

(A) 20   20
(B) 20.0   30
(C) 20.7   31
(D) 20.7   30.7
(E) Nothing will be printed because of a compile-time error.

2. Consider the following code segment:

```
1    int a = 10;
2    double b = 10.7;
3    int d = a + b;
```

Line 3 will not compile in the code segment above. With which of the following statements could we replace this line so that it compiles?

I.   int d = (int) a + b;
II. int d = (int) (a + b);
III. int d = a + (int) b;

(A) I
(B) II
(C) III
(D) I and III
(E) II and III

3. Consider the following code segment.

```
1    int a = 11;
2    int b = 4;
3    double x = 11;
4    double y = 4;
5    System.out.print(a/b);
6    System.out.print(", ");
7    System.out.print(x/y);
8    System.out.print(", ");
9    System.out.print(a/y);
```

What is printed as a result of executing the code segment?

(A) 3, 2.75, 3
(B) 3, 2.75, 2.75
(C) 2, 3, 2
(D) 2, 2.75, 2.75
(E) Nothing will be printed because of a compile-time error.

Summary

- Good use of commenting, identifiers, and white space does not affect the execution of the program but can help to make the program coding easier to interpret for both the programmer and other readers.

- Compilers turn the Java code into binary code. Invalid code will prevent this and cause a compile-time error.

- Logical errors do not prevent the program from compiling but cause undesired results.

- Runtime errors also do not prevent the program from compiling but instead call the program to halt unexpectedly during execution.

- The AP Computer Science A Exam uses `System.out.print()` and `System.out.println()` for output. Any input is assumed and does not need to be coded by the student.

- Variables must be initialized with a data type. They are assigned values using the "=" operator.

- The primitive data types that are tested are `int`, `double`, and `boolean`. `String` is a non-primative type that is also tested extensively.

- The `int` and `double` operators +, −, *, /, and % are tested on the AP Computer Science A Exam.

- Additional math operations can be performed using the Math class.

- The "+" is used to concatenate strings.

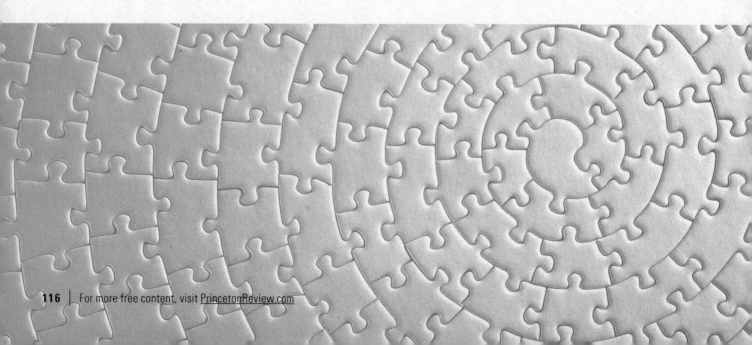

KEY TERMS

Computer Science
programming style
commenting
in-line or short comments
long comments
identifiers
white space
interpreter
binary
compiling
compile-time error
logical error
run-time error
string literal (string)
escape sequence
assign
assignment operator
variable
concatenation operator
primitive data
integer
double
boolean
character
precedence
strongly typed
casting
increment operator (++)
decrement operator (--)

Chapter 4
Using Objects

THE MATH CLASS

Part of the AP Computer Science Java subset is the `Math` class. The `Math` class allows for additional mathematical operations. The methods of the `Math` class are static. There will be more on static methods later, but, for now, understand that to call the methods of the `Math` class, the programmer must type `Math.` before the name of the method. The `Math` class contains many methods, but only a few are part of the AP Computer Science Java Subset.

Command	Return
`Math.abs(x) //x is an int`	An int equal to the absolute value of x
`Math.abs(x) //x is a double`	A double equal to the absolute value of x
`Math.pow(base, exponent)`	A double equal to the base raised to the exponent
`Math.sqrt(x)`	A double equal to the square root of x
`Math.random()`	A random double in the range [0, 1)

Understanding operator precedence is essential for multiple-choice questions on the AP Exam and, perhaps more importantly, for showing off on social media when those "solve this problem" memes pop up and everyone argues over the right answer.

---

5. A math teacher is writing a program that will correctly calculate the area of a circle. Recall that the area of a circle is pi times the radius squared (πr^2). Assuming Math.PI returns an accurate decimal approximation of pi, which of the following statements WILL NOT calculate an accurate area of a circle with radius 22 ?

   (A) `r*r*Math.PI;` // r is the int 22
   (B) `r*r*Math.PI;` // r is the double 22.0
   (C) `(double)r*r*Math.PI;` // r is the int 22
   (D) `(double)(r*r)*Math.PI;` // r is the int 22
   (E) All of the above choices will calculate an accurate area.

Here's How to Crack It

Choice (A) will use integer multiplication for `r*r` but will then convert everything to doubles when it multiplies by `Math.PI`, a double. Choice (B) is obviously correct. Choices (C) and (D) will cast some of the values to double, but as stated above, this will not impact the result in an undesired way. Therefore, the answer is (E).

It is important to note that the `Math.PI` is a static variable of the Math class. Therefore, it can be called only if the class has been imported by putting the following statement at the top of the class coding:

```
import java.lang.Math;
```

MORE STRINGS

While the Char data type is not directly tested, it can be useful to understand that the data in the String class is an array of characters. Therefore, strings have many analogous tools to arrays. Consider the coding below.

```
String sample = "Sample".

System.out.print(sample.length());
```

The coding will output the number 6. The `length()` method of the String class will output the number of characters in the string much as length is the number of elements in an array. Furthermore, the strings use indexes in much the same way. The index of the first character in a string is 0, and the index of the last character is `length()` − 1.

Indexes are useful when dealing with substrings, which are portions of strings. The `String` class has two substring methods. One has two integer parameters

```
String substring (int from, int to)
```

This method returns as a `String` object, the substring starting at index from and ending at index to−1. Note that the character at index to will NOT be included in the substring. Therefore, using the `String` sample from above, the command

```
System.out.print(sample.substring(1, 4))
```

will display

```
amp
```

Note that

```
System.out.println(sample.substring(1, 7));
```

will result in an `IndexOutOfBoundsException` since the index 7 − 1 = 6 is outside the bounds of the string.

The other substring method works similarly but uses only one parameter to indicate the starting index. The resulting substring will continue to the end of the string. Therefore, the command

```
System.out.print(sample.substring(1))
```

will display

```
ample
```

This process can be reversed using the `indexOf` method of the String class. This method takes a substring as a parameter and returns the first occurrence of that substring. For example,

```
sample.indexOf("amp")
```

will return 1, as the substring 1 first occurs at index 1. However,

```
sample.indexOf("amb")
```

will return −1 as this substring does not occur.

---

8. Consider the following code segment:

```
String s = "This is the beginning";
String t = s.substring(5);
int n = t.IndexOf("the");
```

Which of the following will be the value of n ?

(A) −1
(B) 3
(C) 7
(D) 9
(E) n will have no value because of a run-time error.

Here's How to Crack It

The question asks for the value of n, which is `IndexOf` "the" in `String t`, which is a substring of `s`. First determine t, which is the substring beginning at the index 5 of s. Remember to start with 0 and to count the spaces as characters. Index 0 is 'T', index 1 is 'h', index 2 is 'i', index 3 is 's', and index 4 is the space. Therefore, index 5 is the 'i' at the beginning of "is". There is only one parameter in the call of the `substring` method, so continue to the end of `String s` to get that `String t` is assigned "is the beginning". Now, find the index of "the". Since index 0 is 'i', index 1 is 's', and index 2 is the space, the substring "the" begins at index 3. Therefore, the value of n is 3, which is (B).

Chapter 5
Boolean Expressions
and If Statements

Now that we have some tools to make the computer accomplish a simple task, let's discuss how to make our programs a little more…interesting.

When you wake up in the morning, some tasks occur automatically, while others may depend on a decision. For example, if your alarm clock sounds at 6:00 A.M.…wait, what if it doesn't? If it sounds at 6:00 A.M., you proceed with your morning rituals; if it does not sound, you wake up late and have to speed up, or change, your routine. When you sit down to eat your favorite breakfast cereal… none is left! Now what?

Most, if not all, of the actions we perform depend on decisions. These decisions affect whether or not we perform the action, or even how we perform the action. Programs possess this exact ability to make decisions and react accordingly. In this way, the programmer can *control the flow* of the program.

THE IF STATEMENT

If you read the above examples closely, you will literally find the word *if* as a pivotal word in your decision of what action to perform next. The reserved word **if** is a **conditional statement** used in Java when the programmer wants to **control the flow** of the program—i.e., if he or she wants Line 2 to occur ONLY if a condition in Line 1 is true.

The syntax of a simple if statement is

> if (condition) statement;

Syntax statements in this book will be presented in *pseudocode* in order to illustrate the general form, and then further examples will be given. Pseudocode is not Java code that will compile, but it shows the format of the Java statements that we will write later.

Consider an instance when you are asking a parent whether you can go out to the mall with a friend on Friday night. The (classic) parent response usually looks something like this: *If you clean your room, you can go to the mall on Friday*.

In pseudocode, the parent's response could be written as

> if (you clean your room) go to the mall;

In this example, "you clean your room" is the **condition** of the if statement and "go to the mall" is the *statement*. The condition in an if statement must have a boolean result. Note that if you do clean your room (true), you will go to the mall; however, if you do not clean your room (false), you will not go to the mall. The if statement is written in this way; the programmer is now controlling the flow of the program. Thus, "go to the mall" will occur if the condition is true, but will be skipped if the condition is false. Another popular (pseudocode) way to write this statement is

> if (you clean your room)
>   go to the mall;

This construction simply uses white space to make the code more readable. The AP Exam may present an if statement in either of these formats.

Let's try a code example. Consider the following lines from a Java program:

```
int num1 = 4, num2 = 5;
if (num1 == num2)
    System.out.print("The numbers are the same.");
```

Since we have an if statement, one of two possibilities could occur, based on whether num1 has the same value of num2…(1) the program would display the string literal "The numbers are the same." if the condition is true, or (2) the program will not display any output if the condition is false.

Note the use, here, of the **boolean operator** == (also known as equality operator); do not confuse this boolean operator with the assignment operator =. A boolean operator asks a question, while an assignment operator executes a command. num1 = 4 *assigns* the value of 4 to the variable num1, while num1 == num2 *determines whether* the two values are equal. The assignment statement produces no other result, while the boolean statement returns a truth value based on the comparison.

Wouldn't it be nice if conditions in life depended on just one comparison, as our previous code example did? If we dig a bit deeper into our alarm clock example from before, there are probably a few more decisions that need to be made in order to begin your morning rituals; a few of these decisions might be, "is it a school day?"… "do I feel healthy?"… "is my blanket glued to my mattress, trapping me between them?" Note that each of these questions, regardless of its plausibility, has a true or false (boolean) answer.

If (see how many times we use this word?) the programmer wants to incorporate a more complicated condition into our code, he or she must create a **compound condition**. Compound conditions include at least one boolean operator; all of these and their meanings are as follows:

&&	logical *and*
||	logical *or*
!	logical *not*
==	is equal to
!=	is not equal to

Let's explore how each of these can be incorporated into a program.

Consider a situation in which you need a study break and decide to visit your local bakery for a snack. Your favorite dessert is typically Italian cannoli but you will also accept an apple turnover. But apple turnovers are somewhat dry, so you will buy one only if they are selling coffee that day.

Since this example is relatively complicated, let's break it into chunks.

> When attacking a complicated programming situation, break it into chunks and tackle each part, one by one.

We will use pseudocode for this example.

Let's outline the conditions presented in this example, in order:

- The bakery has cannoli.

- The bakery has apple turnovers.

- The bakery has coffee.

The complication here is that some of these decisions depend on others. For example, if the bakery DOES have cannoli, then it doesn't matter whether it has apple turnovers. Again, step by step…start with condition (1)

        if (bakery has cannoli) buy dessert;

Now, another decision must be made, based on this decision; if the bakery DOES have cannoli, we get our desired dessert. If it does NOT have cannoli, we must try the apple turnover.

if (bakery has cannoli)

        buy dessert; // occurs only if bakery has cannoli

else if (bakery has apple turnovers) // occurs only if bakery has no cannoli

        buy dessert; // occurs only if bakery has apple turnovers

Note the *else* keyword used here. else is used if the programmer wants a statement to execute if the condition is false. It's not that easy, though…we must consider the coffee. Since you will buy an apple turnover only if there is ALSO coffee for sale, the && operator is appropriate here:

1 if (bakery has cannoli)

2   buy dessert; // bakery has cannoli

3 else if (bakery has apple turnovers && bakery has coffee) // no cannoli

4   buy dessert; // bakery has apple turnovers AND coffee

This pseudocode seems to work, but we must check for logical errors.

> Remember that logical errors will not be caught by the compiler, and that we cannot test for logical errors on a pencil-and-paper test.

Using the numbered lines of pseudocode, let's trace the possibilities using a **trace table**.

has cannoli: line 1, condition is true -> line 2, buy dessert

no cannoli, no turnovers, no coffee: line 1, false -> line 3, false -> no dessert

no cannoli, yes turnovers, no coffee: line 1, false -> line 3, false -> no dessert

no cannoli, no turnovers, yes coffee: line 1, false -> line 3, false -> no dessert

no cannoli, yes turnovers, yes coffee: line 1, false -> line 3, true -> line 4, buy dessert

Moral of the story: This bakery had better get itself together.

There is a lot of Java here! Controlling the flow of a program can be difficult and confusing, which is why it is a popular topic on the AP Exam. But it is also important because most programs, like most things we do in life, rely on conditions and react accordingly.

To make things more complicated (or more life-like…), consider a further idea…. What if we want to execute SEVERAL commands when a condition is true (or false) instead of just one? For example, using the bakery case, let's say that buying cannoli is so exciting that we must devour it right away. In other words, if the conditions are met for the bakery having cannoli, we want to buy it AND eat it. The pseudocode would look something like:

1 if (bakery has cannoli)

2 {

3   buy dessert; // bakery has cannoli

4   eat dessert;

5 }

6 else if (bakery has apple turnovers && bakery has coffee) // no cannoli

7   buy dessert; // bakery has apple turnovers AND coffee

The { and } symbols in lines 2 and 5 indicate **blocking**, a technique used in flow control statements that allows the programmer to execute a series of commands (instead of just one) when a given condition is satisfied.

Use blocking to execute more than one statement based on a condition.

Consider an expression that has an AND operator, and two expressions X, Y.

To evaluate X && Y

First evaluate X. If X is FALSE then stop: the whole expression is FALSE. Since the operator is AND and the evaluated result of expression X is FALSE, in this situation X controls the final value of the output.

Otherwise, if X is TRUE, then evaluate Y and perform the AND operation of the two values. Here the expression Y controls the final value of the output. This idea is called short-circuit evaluation.

Since false && anything is false, there is no need to continue after the first false has been evaluated. In Java programmers, use this idea frequently.

AND Truth Table

Input A	Input B	Output
1	0	0
1	0	0
0	0	0
1	1	1

Consider an expression that has an OR operator, and two expressions X, Y.

To evaluate **X || Y**

First evaluate X. If X is TRUE then stop: the whole expression is true. Because of the operator value and the evaluated result of X, the expression X controls the final value of the output.

Otherwise, if X is TRUE, then evaluate Y and perform the OR operation of the two values. In this situation, the expression Y controls the final value of the output. This idea is called short-circuit evaluation.

Since true || anything is true, there is no need to continue after the first true has been evaluated.

OR Truth Table

Input A	Input B	Output
1	0	1
0	1	1
1	1	1
0	0	0

1. Consider the following code.

```
int x = 0;
if (x == 0)
    System.out.print("1");
else
    System.out.print("2");
    System.out.print("3");
```

Which of the following best describes the result of executing the code segment?

(A) Since the value of x is 0, the first print statement will be performed, producing 1 as the output.

(B) Since the value of x is 0, the first print statement will be performed, producing 13 as the output.

(C) Since the value of x is 0, the first print statement will be performed, producing 123 as the output.

(D) == is not the correct boolean operator, so a syntax error will be produced by the compiler prior to execution.

(E) == is not the correct boolean operator, so a logical error will be produced by the compiler prior to execution.

Here's How to Crack It

Since x is assigned to 0, the condition of the if statement will be true, performing the first print statement and outputting 1. The else statement will then be skipped, so 2 will not be outputted, eliminating (C). The trick here, however, is that the third print statement is NOT part of the else statement since it is not blocked with {}, even though it is (incorrectly) indented. This will output 3, eliminating (A), (D), and (E). Furthermore, == is a valid boolean operator so (D) and (E) are clearly incorrect (and a compiler will never produce a logical error). The correct answer is (B).

Before we move on, let's scrutinize the boolean operator situation a bit further.

Often, the truth values of a situation are simply abbreviated to a single letter. This action occurs because most real programs involve dozens, or more, of conditions and variables. As a result, it is important (and essential for the AP Exam) to evaluate the **truth value** of a bunch of random boolean variables, completely out of context.

If we look at the bakery example one more time (seriously, just once), the line

buy dessert;

occurs twice. Good programming style attempts to repeat the same lines of code as little as possible, if ever. Therefore, we can rearrange the boolean operators in the following way, creating the same result:

if (bakery has cannoli OR (bakery has apple turnovers AND bakery has coffee))

buy dessert;

That is a hefty boolean condition; however, it (1) eliminates the repetition of code and (2) provides a more "elegant" programming solution. "elegant" is a relative term, of course, but the AP Exam often uses this subjective term to write code and to confuse you. Either way, you should be familiar with both ways.

> The AP Exam Free-Response Questions (FRQs) do not require you to write code with "elegance"; in the FRQs; they will accept any code solution as long as it fulfills the specifications of the question.

To sum up, let's create a truth table of various combinations of boolean conditions, simply called A and B, and the truth possibilities based on those combinations. Since there are two variables, there are four possible combinations of their truth values: they are both true, only one of them is true (both ways), and neither is true. These possibilities are shown in the first two columns below. In subsequent columns, the truth values are shown for the boolean statements shown in the first row.

A	B	A&&B	A||B	!A	!B	!(A&&B)	!A||!B
T	T	T	T	F	F	F	F
T	F	F	T	F	T	T	T
F	T	F	T	T	F	T	T
F	F	F	F	T	T	T	T

An && (and) expression is true if BOTH A and B are true; a || (or) expression is true if EITHER A or B is true, or if they are both true. The ! (not) operator simply reverses the truth value of the variable. Note that the truth values of the last two expressions are identical; these results are an illustration of De Morgan's Law, which is similar to the "distributive property" of boolean expressions. Applying a ! (not) operator to an expression reverses the truth value of each variable and changes an && to an ||, or vice versa. If this law is applied to !(A&&B), the result is !A||!B, as shown in the last column.

> The intricacies of if statements that we just explored will apply to all flow control statements, so understand them here before you move on to the next section.

Augustus De Morgan was a British mathematician and logician in the 19th century. DeMorgan's Law can be used to simplify complicated Boolean expressions. The basic concept is to know that an expression can be rewritten so as to simplify and logically hold the same value. For example logically speaking

!TRUE = FALSE

!FALSE = TRUE

Then the 2 laws are stated as follows:

```
1. !(a && b) is equivalent to !a || !b
2. !(a || b) is equivalent to !a && !b
```

The first law is primarily to get rid of the negation, while the second law is to swap the && to an ||. Because of these two reasons, the two laws are very useful.

Consider the following example:
If (!(x >=0 AND y<=100), then first convert it into something that doesn't have NOTs.

 Applying De Morgan's First Law:
 if (!(x >= 0) OR !(y <= 100) then...
 This can now be rewritten as follows:
 !(x >= 0) = x < 0
 and
 !(y <= 100) = y > 100
Putting this all together, we have the following simplified expression:
 if (x < 0) OR (y > 100)

2. Consider the following code segment.

```
boolean a = true, b = false;
if (/ * missing code * /)
    System.out.print("Nice job.");
else
    System.out.print("Nicer job.");
```

Which of the following could be used to replace / * missing code * / so that the output of this block of code is "Nicer job."?

I. `a && !b`
II. `!a || b`
III. `!a && b`

(A) I only
(B) I and II only
(C) I and III only
(D) II and III only
(E) I, II, and III

Roman numeral problems are only as annoying as their hardest option; look at the options and do the easiest one first, which is often not I. Then use Process of Elimination.

Here's How to Crack It

Ahh, the dreaded "Roman numeral" problems that the College Board loves to torture us with. If "Nicer job." has to be displayed, then the condition must evaluate to *false*. The options show relationships between a and b, and boolean "and" is easier to evaluate since it's false whenever *any* variable is false, so start with Statements I and III. Statement I is `a && !b`. Since b is false, `!b` is true. Since both a and `!b` are true, `a && !b` is true. Therefore, Statement I would output `Nice job.` instead of `Nicer job`. Eliminate (A), (B), (C), and (E), which include Statement I. Only one choice remains, so there is no need to continue. However, to see why Statements II and III do work, note that, since a is true, `!a` is false. Therefore, `!a || b` is an "or" statement with two false statements and is therefore false. Also, `!a && b` is an "and" statement with at least one false statement (actually two in this instance) and, therefore, false. Thus, both Statements II and III will output `Nicer job`. The answer is (D).

3. Suppose p and q are declared as boolean variables and have been initialized to unknown truth values.

What does the following boolean expression evaluate to?

(!p && !q) || !(p || q)

(A) The expression always evaluates to true.

(B) The expression always evaluates to false.

(C) The expression evaluates to true whenever p is false.

(D) The expression evaluates to true whenever q is false.

(E) The expression evaluates to false whenever p and q have opposite truth values.

Here's How to Crack It

Using DeMorgan's Law, we can see that the truth value of the left expression (!p && !q) will be the same as the truth value of the right expression !(p || q). Anytime both parts of an "or" statement have the same truth value, the value of the "or" statement is also the same as the value of each part, so we can test our choices using the easier side, which is the right side. Through a quick trial-and-error and looking at the answer choices, let p and q be false; the right expression will evaluate to true, making the whole expression true and eliminating (B). Now let both p and q be true; the right expression will evaluate to false, making the whole expression false and eliminating (A), (C), and (D). Similar guess-and-check can be used to finish the job, but you've already eliminated four choices. Through Process of Elimination, (E) is correct. To see why (E) is correct, set p as true and q as false. Because p is true, the statement (p || q) is true, so !(p || q) is false. Similarly, set p as false and q as true. Because q is true, the statement (p || q) is true, so !(p || q) is false. Therefore, in both cases in which p and q have opposite truth values, the statement is false.

Trial-and-error and Process of Elimination are both useful techniques for boolean expression problems.

CHAPTER 5 REVIEW DRILL

Answers to the review questions can be found in Chapter 13.

1. Consider the following code segment:

```
for (int i = 200; i > 0; i /= 3)
{
    if (i % 2 == 0)
        System.out.print(i + "  ");
}
```

   What is the output as a result of executing the code segment?

   (A) 200 66 22 7 2
   (B) 66 22 7 2
   (C) 200 66 22 2
   (D) 200 66 22
   (E) 7

2. Consider the following statement:

```
int i = x % 50;
```

   If x is a positive integer, which of the following could NOT be the value of i after the statement above executes?

   (A) 0
   (B) 10
   (C) 25
   (D) 40
   (E) 50

Summary

o Values can be compared to form boolean statements using == (equals), != (not equal), < (less than), <= (less than or equal to), > (greater than), and >= (greater than or equal to).

o Boolean statements can be combined using && (and), || (or), and ! (not).

o If statements can be used to allow a command or series of commands to be executed once only if a certain boolean statement is true. Else statements can be used to execute a different statement if that condition is not met.

KEY TERMS

if
conditional statement
flow control
condition
boolean operator ==
compound condition
&& (logical and)
|| (logical or)
! (logical not)
== (is equal to)
!= (is not equal to)
trace table
blocking
truth value

Chapter 6
Iteration

THE WHILE STATEMENT

When the programmer wants a statement (or multiple statements) to occur repeatedly, he or she has two options: (1) copy and paste the statement as many times as necessary (inefficient and ugly), or (2) write a conditional statement called a **loop** (efficient and "elegant").

> On the AP Exam, you will be expected to know two types of loops:
> *while* and *for*.

The syntax of a **while loop** is as follows:

        while (condition) statement;

Note its similarity to the if statement. The *while* statement is a loop that does exactly what its name implies: the loop cycles again and again, *while* the condition is true. Consider a paint-soaked paintbrush that you just used to paint your bedroom. Hopefully, you will not store the paintbrush away until it is no longer dirty. A while loop that could represent this situation in pseudocode would look like:

1 while (paintbrush is dirty)

2   do not put away paintbrush;

3 put away paintbrush;

Note that if the condition is true (paintbrush is dirty), line 2 will continue to execute, over and over again, until the condition is false (paintbrush is not dirty). Once the condition is false, line 2 is skipped and line 3 is finally executed.

Unfortunately, this loop is fundamentally flawed. Although its logic SEEMS to be correct, it is not. Within the statement(s) of a loop, the variable(s) in the condition must be modified so that there is a chance that the truth value of the condition will be changed. How will the paintbrush become less dirty—is this a self-cleaning paintbrush? Probably not. Therefore, the paintbrush will actually remain dirty and Java will keep executing line 2, forever. When this happens, the programmer has written an **infinite loop**, which is a logical error and is therefore undesirable. Ever have your computer randomly "freeze" in the middle of your work, leaving it unresponsive and causing you to lose that perfectly sculpted digital picture that you just spent an hour perfecting? That is an infinite loop and is definitely not desirable.

On the AP Exam, you must trace code in MCQs and detect infinite loops. You must also write code in FRQs that is free of infinite loops.

While loops, like if statements, are therefore dependent on the condition. If the condition is more intricate, as it usually is (Do we put the paintbrush away if it is not dirty but it is wet? Not dirty but it is still not CLEAN?), we can use the techniques outlined in the previous section. Boolean operators are mandatory and compound conditions and/or blocking are appropriate, when necessary. A more realistic pseudocode representation of our paintbrush example could be

```
1    while (paintbrush is dirty && paintbrush is wet) // ! means NOT wet

2    {

3            clean paintbrush; // is it COMPLETELY clean?

4            dry paintbrush; // is it COMPLETELY dry?

5            do not put paintbrush away;

6    }

7    put paintbrush away;
```

In this example, the paintbrush will continue to be cleaned and dried (and not put away) until it is either NOT dirty or NOT wet, or both, at which point the condition will be false and the paintbrush will be put away. Remember that an && condition is true only if both conditions are true; therefore, if the paintbrush is not dirty but is still wet (or vice versa), it will be put away. Is this the desired result? Who cares?! Reading code is not about logical understanding of a situation; rather, it is about understanding the code and its result.

It is also worth noting here that an && statement may be **short-circuited**. Since both boolean statements on either side of the && must be true, a false result from the first statement will automatically render the condition false. As a result, Java will completely skip the second condition, bypassing the rest of the condition.

4. Consider the following code segment.

```
int val1 = 2, val2 = 22, val3 = 78;
while (val2 % val1 == 0 || val2 % 3 == 0)
{
    val3++;
    val2--;
}
```

What will val3 contain after the code segment is executed?

(A) 77

(B) 78

(C) 79

(D) 80

(E) None of the above

Here's How to Crack It

Tracing the loop is the best way to handle this type of problem. Remember that % returns the remainder of the division between the two numbers. In order for the condition to be true, there first must be no remainder when dividing val2 by val1. Since 22/2 = 11, there is no remainder, and the condition will be true (an "or" statement will be true if its first condition is true), and the loop statements will execute, incrementing val3 to 79 and decrementing val2 to 21. Since there are no visible statements that would decrement val3 below 79, we can eliminate (A) and (B). Execution then returns to the condition; this time, we have 21/2, which does yield a remainder so we check the rest of the division, and 21 % 3 does not yield a remainder, so the condition is true overall and the loop statements execute again. We now have val3 = 80 and val2 = 20, eliminating (C). Again we try to evaluate the condition, which will be true since 20/2 has no remainder, increasing val3 to 81 and decreasing val2 to 19. We can now eliminate (D). By Process of Elimination, (E) is the answer. (In case you are wondering, it will take several more loop iterations before the condition is finally false, but it will get there eventually. Try it for practice!)

When tracing loops, make a table of values for each variable to organize your work.

THE FOR STATEMENT

A *for* statement is another type of loop. **For loops** and while loops are equally effective in controlling the flow of a program when a statement (or set of statements) is to be executed repeatedly. The syntax is quite different, however:

> for (initializer; condition; incrementer) statement;

Since the for loop requires more components, it can potentially avoid an infinite loop situation, although there is no guarantee. Let's try a pseudocode example. Consider a younger brother or sister who is learning to count to 22. He or she will start with 1 and continue counting until he or she reaches 22, and then stop. The counting process repeats until the condition is met. Pseudocode may look like:

for (start with 1; not yet reached 22; go to the next number)

> count the number;

The execution of a for loop is more difficult to understand. Here are the steps:

1. The initializer will occur first, beginning the process.
2. The condition will be checked to make sure it is true.
3. The statement(s) will execute.
4. The incrementer will occur, changing the number.
5. See step (1) and keep repeating (1) to (4), until (2) is false.
6. The loop ends.

A code example of this situation, outputting the current number to the screen, could be:

```
for (int num = 1; num <= 22; num++)

    System.out.println(num);
```

This code will produce each counting number and output it to the screen, each on a separate line. Once again, remember that boolean operators are mandatory and compound conditions and/or blocking are appropriate, when necessary.

> **Take Note:** for loops and while loops are interchangeable, although one method may look more elegant than the other.

For and while statements are loops; if statements are not.

On the AP Exam, MCQs may show you several loop structures in both formats and ask you questions that compare the results, so you should practice working between them. FRQs that ask you to write a loop are equally as correct if you decide to write a for loop or a while loop.

The following two code examples involving loops have identical results:

```
int num = 1;
while (num <= 3)
{
    System.out.println(num);
    num++;
}
System.out.println("Done");

---

for (int num = 1; num <= 3; num++)
    System.out.println(num);
System.out.println("Done");
```

Each set of code is equally as effective and equally as respected in both the programming world and on the AP Exam. But MCQs could use either format, or both, so you should familiarize yourself with both.

> While loops perform the blocked statement(s) once, and then evaluate the condition to determine whether the loop continues; for loops evaluate the condition first and then perform the blocked statement(s) if the condition is initially true.

5. What will be the output when the following code is evaluated?

```
for (int k = 0; k < 3; k++)
{
    for (int j = 1; j < 4; j++)
    {
        System.out.print(j + " ");
    } System.out.println();
}
```

1 2 3

(A) 1 2 3 4
     1 2 3 4
     1 2 3 4

(B) 0 1 2
     0 1 2
     0 1 2
     0 1 2

(C) 1 2 3
     1 2 3
     1 2 3

(D) 1 2 3
     1 2 3
     1 2 3
     1 2 3

(E) 1 2 3 4
     1 2 3 4
     1 2 3 4
     1 2 3 4

Here's How to Crack It

One glance at the condition in the outer for loop reveals that it will iterate a total of 3 times (k = 0, 1, and 2). The same will occur for the inner loop (j = 1, 2, and 3). Answers that involve loops of 4 can be eliminated, ruling out every choice except (C). There is no need to continue. However, to see why (C) works, work through the two loops. The outer loop sets k = 0, then j = 1. It prints 1 and a space, then increments j to 2. It prints 2 and a space, then increments j to 3. It prints 3 and a space, then increments j to 4. Since 4 is not less than 4, it terminates the inner loop. System.out.println() prints a line break. Then k is incremented to 1. Since k does not effect the output or the value of j, the loop again prints 1 2 3, before printing a line break. The value of k increments to 2, printing a third line of 1 2 3. Finally, k is incremented to 3, which terminates the outer loop, leaving (C) as the result of the print. The answer is (C).

6. Consider the following code fragments. Assume someNum has been correctly defined and initialized as a positive integer.

```
I. for (int i = 0; i < someNum; i++)
   {
           someNum--;
   }
II. for (int i = 1; i < someNum - 1; i++)
   {
           someNum -=1;
   }
III.int i = 0;
   while (i < someNum)
   {
           i++;
           someNum--;
   }
```

All of the following statements are true about these code fragments EXCEPT

(A) The for loops in I and II can be rewritten as while loops with the same result.
(B) The value of someNum after execution of I and III is the same.
(C) The value of i after execution of II and III is the same.
(D) At least two out of I, II, and III have different numbers of iterations.
(E) I, II, and III all produce different results.

Here's How to Crack It

For an "except" question, cross out the original sentence and rewrite it without the negative so that it's easier to understand. In this case, rewrite the question to say, "Which is false?" Eliminate (A) since every for loop can be rewritten as a while loop, and vice versa. For the remaining choices, let someNum equal a positive non-zero value (not too big)...let's try 5.

I.	i	someNum
	0	5
	1	4
	2	3
	3	2

II.	i	someNum	someNum-1

	1	5	4
	2	4	3
	3	3	2

III.	i	someNum
	0	5
	1	4
	2	3
	3	2

From these trace tables of values, (C), (D), and (E) are all true. Choice (B) is the only false statement, so (B) is the answer.

———————○———————

———————○———————

7. Consider the following code segment:

```
for (int i = 1; i < 100; i = i * 2)
{
    if (i / 50 == 0)
        System.out.print(i + " ");
}
```

What is printed as a result of executing the code segment?

(A) 1 2 4 8 16 32 64
(B) 1 2 4 8 16 32
(C) 2 4 8 16 32 64
(D) 2 4 8 16 32
(E) 4 8 16 32 64

Here's How to Crack It

The initial condition for execution to enter the loop is i = 1. Since 1/50 = 0 in integer division, 1 will be displayed, so eliminate (C), (D), and (E). The difference between (A) and (B) is the 64 at the end, so let's skip the output in between and focus on the 64. If i = 64, the if statement will be false, and thus 64 will not be printed. Therefore, the answer is (B).

———————○———————

Synopsis

Here's a quick synopsis of which concepts from this chapter you can expect to find on the exam, and which you won't.

Don't Forget This!

Head over to your free online student tools to download a printable version of this chart and other important pages from within this book.

	Concepts Covered on the AP Computer Science A Exam	Concepts Not Covered on the AP Computer Science A Exam
Primitives	• int • double • boolean	• short • long • byte • char • float
Increment / Decrement Operators	• x++ • x--	• ++x • --x
Logical Operators	• == • != • < • <= • > • >= • && • || • !	• & • | • ^ • << • >> • >>>
Conditional Statements	• if/else • for • while	• do/while • switch • plain and labeled break • continue
Miscellaneous		• ?: (ternary operator) • User input • JavaDoc comments

CHAPTER 6 REVIEW DRILL

Answers to the review questions can be found in Chapter 13.

1. Consider the following output:

```
0   1
0   2   4
0   3   6   9
0   4   8   12   16
```

Which of the following code segments will produce this output?

(A)
```
for (int x = 1; x < 5; x++)
{
    for (int z = 0; z <= x; z++)
    {
        System.out.print(x * z + "   ");
    }
    System.out.println(" ");
}
```

(B)
```
for (int x = 1; x <= 5; x++)
{
    for (int z = 0; z < x; z++)
    {
        System.out.print(x * z + "   ");
    }
    System.out.println(" ");
}
```

(C)
```
for (int x = 1; x < 5; x++)
{
    for (int z = 0; z <= 4; z++)
    {
        System.out.print(x * z + "   ");
    }
    System.out.println(" ");
}
```

(D)
```
for (int x = 1; x < 5; x++)
{
    for (int z = 0; z <= 4; z += 2)
    {
        System.out.print(x * z + "   ");
    }
    System.out.println(" ");
}
```

(E)
```
for (int x = 1; x <= 5; x++
{
    for (int z = 0; z <= x; z++)
    {
        System.out.print(x * z + "   ");
    }
    System.out.println(" ");
}
```

2. The speed limit of a stretch of highway is 55 miles per hour (mph). The highway patrol issues speeding tickets to anyone caught going faster than 55 miles per hour. The fine for speeding is based on the following scale:

Speed	Fine
greater than 55 mph but less than 65 mph	$100
greater than or equal to 65 mph but less than 75 mph	$150
greater than or equal to 75 mph	$300

If the value of the int variable speed is the speed of a driver who was pulled over for going faster than 55 mph, which of the following code segments will assign the correct value to the int variable fine?

```
I.    if (speed >= 75)
         fine = 300;
      if (speed >= 65 && speed < 75)
         fine = 150;
      if (speed > 55 && speed < 65)
         fine = 100;
II.   if (speed >= 75)
         fine = 300;
      if (65 <= speed < 75)
         fine = 150;
      if (55 < speed < 65)
         fine = 100;
III.  if (speed >= 75)
         fine = 300;
      if (speed >= 65)
         fine = 150;
      if (speed > 55)
         fine = 100;
```

(A) I only
(B) II only
(C) III only
(D) I and II
(E) I and III

3. Consider the following code segment:

```
int x = 10;
int y = 3;
boolean b = true;
for (int i = 0, i < 15; i += 5)
{
    x = x + y;
    b = (x % y == 2);
    if (!b)
    {
        y++;
        i += 5;
    }
}
```

What is the value of x after the code segment executes?

(A) 10
(B) 15
(C) 17
(D) 22
(E) 25

4. In the following statement, a and b are boolean variables:

```
boolean c = (a && b) || !(a | | b);
```

Under what conditions will the value of c be true?

(A) Only when the value of a is different than the value of b
(B) Only when the value of a is the same as the value of b
(C) Only when a and b are both true
(D) Only when a and b are both false
(E) The value of c will be true for all values of a and b.

5. Consider the following code segment:

```
while ((x > y) || y >= z)
{
    System.out.print("*");
}
```

In the code segment above, x, y, and z are the variables of type int. Which of the following must be true after the code segment has executed?

(A) x > y || y >= z
(B) x <= y || y > z
(C) x > y && y >= z
(D) x < y && y <= z
(E) x <= y && y < z

6. Consider the following code segment:

```
int a = 0;
for (int i = 0; i < 10; i ++)
{
    for (int k = 0; k <= 5; k++)
    {
        for (int z = 1; z <= 16; z = z * 2)
        {
            a++;
        }
    }
}
```

What is the value of a after the code segment executes?

(A) 31
(B) 180
(C) 200
(D) 300
(E) 400

7. Consider the following code segment:

```
int x = 10;
int y = x / 3;
int z = x % 2;
x++;
System.out.println(x)
```

What is printed as a result of executing the code segment above?

(A) 2
(B) 4
(C) 10
(D) 11
(E) 15

8. Consider the following code segment:

```
int a = 10;
double b = 3.7;
int c = 4;
int x = (int) (a + b);
double y = (double) a / c;
double z = (double) (a / c);
double w = x + y + z;
System.out.println(w);
```

What is printed as a result of evaluating the code above?

(A) 10

(B) 15

(C) 15.5

(D) 17

(E) 17.5

9. Consider the following code segments:

```
I.    int x = 10;
      int y = 20;
      int z = 0;
      if (x < y && 10 < y/z)
      {
            System.out.println("Homer");
      }
      else
      {
            System.out.println("Bart");
      }
II.   int x = 10;
      int y = 20;
      int z = 0;
      if (x > y && 10 < y/z)
            System.out.println("Homer");
      else
        System.out.println("Bart");
III.  int x = 10;
      int y = 20;
      int z = 0;
      if (x < y || 10 < y/z)
            System.out.println("Homer");
      else
            System.out.println("Bart");
```

Which of the code segments above will run without error?

(A) I only

(B) II only

(C) III only

(D) II and III

(E) I, II, and III

Summary

o   While statements can be used to cause a command or series of commands to execute while a certain boolean statement is true.

o   For statements are similar to while statements but include the initialization of a variable before the looping and a modification of the variable after each execution of the loop.

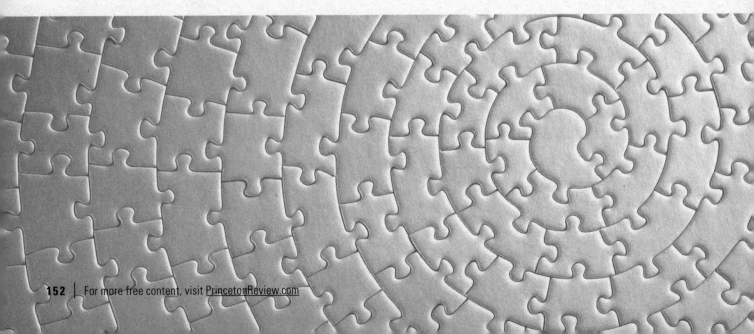

KEY TERMS

loop
while loop
infinite loop
short-circuited
for loop

Chapter 7
Writing Classes

When a group of statements, including control structures, is assembled into a single unit, the unit is called a **class**. Similar to a word processing document or a picture file stored on your computer, a class is stored on your computer in a file. Unlike a word processing document, however, a class must follow specific rules in order to conform to Java and, as a result, to be understood by the compiler. Remember that your brilliantly constructed program is useless unless the compiler can successfully translate it into machine code.

DESIGN & STRUCTURE

The structure of a class, at this level anyway, is straightforward. Take all of the statements you've written before this chapter, put curly brackets around them, kind of like a huge block, name it, and save it. The naming conventions for a class are similar to those of a variable, except that they should begin with a capital letter. The name of the class should reference the purpose or function of the class. For example, a class that calculates a GPA might be called GPA or GradePointAvg. The way we declare a class in Java is using the header:

```
public class GradePointAvg
{
    // statements not shown
}
```

Well, Actually...
This is a convention but not a rule. You can have all of the code on a single line if your heart so desires, but that would be very bad form.

Note that the statements in the class reside at least one tab stop across the page. If the programmer would like to use more white space within the structures of the class, they will be tabbed further into the page:

```
public class GradePointAvg
{
    // other code and variable declarations not shown

    while (/* condition not shown */)
    {
        // looped statements not shown
    }
}
```

Typically, variable declarations are placed into the code first, right after the class header, as a sort of "setup" for the rest of the class. Of course, this is not a rule, but it is a good guideline in order to keep your code readable.

On the AP Exam, your code must be readable (not just legible), quickly and easily.

This class would be saved to the computer as GradePointAvg.java; the .java extension helps the compiler to recognize the file as containing Java code. If the code compiles (there are no syntax errors), the compiler will create another file in the same folder called GradePointAvg.class; this file is unreadable to the programmer because it is encoded in machine language. The computer, however, uses this file to execute the program. The .java file is called the **source code** of the program, since it defines the program's actions and functions.

Remember that classes are executed top-down—i.e., line 1 followed by line 2, etc. If the programmer wants to alter top-down execution, he or she must use a flow control structure, as we studied before.

———————○———————

1. Which of the following class declarations would cause a compile-time error? Assume the rest of the code compiles as intended.

   (A) `public class Calculus`
   (B) `public class apCalculus`
   (C) `public class APCalculus`
   (D) `public class 4APCalculus`
   (E) `public class APCalculus extends Calculus`

Here's How to Crack It

Choice (A) and (C) follow the format as discussed above. The naming conventions of a class name are that we *should* begin with a capital letter; however, this is not required by the compiler, so (B) does not cause an error. Be careful when the College Board uses programming techniques in the answer choices that you may not know; in this case, the *extends* keyword comes in a later section of this book, so you may choose it here if you have never seen it. However, it is used properly, so (E) does not cause an error, but you would not be able to use POE if you didn't know this. The real problem with (D) is that it begins with a numerical character, which is not allowed in a class name. The answer is (D).

———————○———————

> POE is a great tool, but it isn't always enough on an AP Exam. Know your stuff!

METHODS

Picture a Java class as a closet, with essentially limitless possibilities. If you were to declare a single shelf to hold, say, board game boxes…that would be a great way to organize your collection of games, toys, and other sophisticated possessions.

A class is organized in this way using **methods**.

> A method is a group of code that performs a specific task.

Although a class can simply contain a list of commands, any program that accomplishes a task could easily balloon to 100 lines of code, or more. Instead of writing a class that contains a giant list of disorganized code, writing separate methods for each small task (within the overarching task) is an excellent way to make your code more readable. In addition, method-based classes enable easier flow control.

To understand this concept, let's break down a bright, sunny Saturday in the middle of the summer (don't worry—you will make it). Perhaps some of the activities you would do might include getting out of bed (obviously), eating breakfast, taking a shower, getting ready for the beach, driving to the beach, enjoying the beach, and eating lunch. Each of these activities has its own specific components; that is, part of eating breakfast includes drinking orange juice and taking a daily vitamin supplement. The pseudocode of a program that simulates these Saturday's activities might look like this:

```
public class Saturday1
{
    hear alarm;
    turn off alarm;
    get out of bed;
    make breakfast;
    eat breakfast; ...
```

You get the idea…. A long list of commands that occur top-down. Now, consider each of these general activities as a separate grouping of smaller activities, called a method. Each small activity will be defined later, but your Saturday class would look much cleaner:

```
public class Saturday2
{
    wake up method; // includes alarm
    eat breakfast method; // includes preparation, OJ,
                          // vitamin, etc.
    take a shower method; // includes preparing for the
                          // shower, etc.
    beach method; // includes prep for the beach, driving
                  // to the beach, etc.
    eat lunch method;
}
```

The result is a cleaner, more structured class that is easier to read. A class that is created to control a larger program, such as Saturday2, is called a **driver class** because it *drives* the program through its general structure which will, in turn, execute the smaller commands. Note also that if, for some reason, the programmer wanted the simulation to take a shower before eating breakfast, the two lines would be switched in Saturday2 and the job is done. Performing the same change in Saturday1 would involve switching multiple lines of code. Even more poignant would be a simulation that repeats method calls, such as one that represents your extra hungry older brother, who eats breakfast twice. The driver would simply call the breakfast method twice (or use a loop to call it more than twice) and the job is completed.

An **object class** is a different kind of class which houses the "guts" of the methods that the driver class calls. As you understand this setup, you will see that your driver classes begin to shorten, while your object classes expand. For example, the driver of a car truly performs a relatively small set of actions in order to drive the car: start the engine, buckle the seatbelt, check the mirrors, accelerate, brake. The driver does not actually understand (nor does he need to) exactly how these operations work, he just does them. How does the accelerator pedal ACTUALLY make the car move more quickly? Doesn't matter. The "driver" just operates the pedal and the rest happens under the hood. The object class is the "under the hood" class. It defines all of the aspects of an object; more specifically, it defines what the object *has* and what the object *does*.

The object class referred to in this section should not be confused with the Object class in the Java language which is the Parent class of all classes. The Object class is part of the Java.lang package. Every class in Java is a descendent of this class. Every class in Java Inherits the methods of the Object class.

> For the AP Exam, you must be able to write, troubleshoot, and understand object AND driver classes, as well as understand how they interact. These skills are HUGE in the FRQs!

Back to the breakfast example...

Pseudocode for the object class might look something like this:

```
public class Saturday3
{
    wake up(...)
    {
        hear alarm
        turn off alarm
        get out of bed
    }


    breakfast(...)
    {
        make breakfast;
        eat breakfast;
    }
```

Since our object class could be used for any day of the week, not just Saturday, *BeachDay* might be a more appropriate name for this class. The driver class from before, which executes a series of actions for this particular day, might be called *Saturday*.

2. Which of the following statements would best describe an efficient design to represent a pair of sunglasses?

   (A) Three classes: UnfoldGlasses, CleanGlasses, and WearGlasses
   (B) An UnfoldGlasses class with methods CleanGlasses and WearGlasses
   (C) A PairOfSunglasses class with boolean variables unfolded, cleaned, and worn
   (D) A PairOfSunglasses class with methods that unfold, clean, and wear the objects in the class
   (E) A UseSunglasses class with statements that unfold, clean, and wear the sunglasses

Here's How to Crack It

Design questions must account for efficiency and "beauty," since the former isn't formally tested on the FRQs and the latter is not tested in the FRQs. Since a pair of sunglasses is best represented as an object—it has attributes and can do tasks—eliminate (A), (B), and (E). Since the tasks of a `PairOfSunglasses` object would best be performed in a method, (C) is not appropriate. The answer is (D).

One more item that needs to be mentioned…do you see how each method in the object class has a "title," or **header**? The header is used to indicate the overall function of a method.

This is a Java book, right? So let's look at some Java. These two classes are designed to simulate a phone downloading and opening a new app.

```
1 import Phone;
2 public class UsePhoneApp
3 {
4   public UsePhoneApp()  // just do it, we'll explain later
5   {
6       Phone myPhone = new Phone();
7       myPhone.downloadApp();
8       myPhone.openApp();
9       myPhone.closeApp();
10 }
11 }
```

```
1 public class Phone
2 {
3   private boolean hasApp;
4   public Phone()
5   {
6       hasApp = false;
7   }
8   public void downloadApp()
9   {
10      hasApp = true;
11  }
12
13 public void closeApp()  // closes the app
14 {
15     if (hasApp)
16         System.out.println ("App is closed.");
17 }
18
19 public void openApp()  // opens the app
20 {
21     if (hasApp)
22         System.out.println ("App is running...");
23 }
24 }
```

OUTPUT:

```
App is running...
App is closed.
```

There are many components in this program; first, note that we now have two classes that make up a single program. In isolation, neither of these classes would produce a useful result. The UsePhoneApp class would not compile because the compiler does not understand the methods if they are not present (compiler: what does openApp mean?); the Phone class would compile but would not actually perform any actions without UsePhoneApp (compiler: when do I openApp, and on which phone?). In order to allow the UsePhoneApp class to access the Phone class, the line

```
import Phone;
```

must be used at the top of the file above the class declaration.

Lines 4–7 in Phone make up a special kind of method called a **constructor**. An object must be constructed before it can perform any actions, just as a car must be built before it can be driven. Line 6 in UsePhoneApp calls this constructor method, which "builds" the Phone object; this command must occur before the non-constructor methods are called; otherwise the compiler will return an error. Imagine someone pressing an imaginary accelerator pedal and trying to drive somewhere, without a car. Interesting, but not possible.

Line 3 of Phone defines whether the Phone has an app (true) or does not (false). This is the sole attribute of a Phone object in our program; more complex programs may have dozens or even hundreds of attributes (a phone, in reality, has many more attributes, such as a screen, volume buttons, etc.). The programmer should write these attributes, called **instance variables** or **fields**. Following the data fields is the constructor, as we stated before, and then a series of methods that control what the Phone *can do*.

> An object class defines what an object HAS and DOES.

A method has several components. The method header is built in a very specific way; its syntax is as follows:

```
visibility returnType methodName (param1, param2, ...)
```

The visibility of a method can be public or private, depending on the situation (more on this later). The **return type** identifies what type of data, if any, will be returned from the method after its commands are executed. The name of a method, similar to the name of a variable, should be an intuitive name that summarizes the function of the method; it should conform to the same specifications as a variable name (begin with a lowercase letter, etc.). The **parameters**, which are optional, are the data that the method needs in order to perform its job.

In our previous example, the method header for closeApp was:

```
public void closeApp()
```

This is functional, but it is also relatively simple for the example. Its visibility is public, its return type is void (there is no information returned), and it does not have parameters. A more realistic method to close an app on a phone might require information regarding when it should be closed, and might return data whether or not it was closed successfully. Thus, the revised method header might look like

```
public boolean closeApp (int minutes)
```

Note that the single parameter, minutes, is defined with its type. Since minutes will be a temporary variable that exists only during the execution of this method, it must be defined as new, right in the header. A method can have any number of parameters, depending on the programmer's design decisions for the program.

A method must begin with a header, containing a visibility modifier (private or public), a return type or void if no information will be returned, and a method name. Parameter(s) are optional, depending on the method's requirements to perform its task.

The ultimate purpose of a method is to perform some sort of task with respect to the object. Note that openApp() and closeApp() simply access the data field hasApp and react accordingly; i.e., the message is displayed only if the value hasApp is true. downloadApp() is more profound, in a way; rather than simply accessing data, it actually changes the value of a data field—in this case, updates hasApp to true once the "app" is "downloaded". As a result, it is common in Java to label methods like openApp() and closeApp() as **accessor methods** and to label methods like downloadApp() as **mutator methods**.

We have mentioned a car in several examples in this chapter, but it's a great way to understand these concepts. When you want to start a car, you have to go through a series of steps. Since all of those steps perform, ultimately, a single action—the car starting—a method would be a great way to keep the "car starting" commands in a single, convenient unit. As a programmer, you would have to decide what data the method would need in order to work (parameter(s)) and what data, if any, the method would return. Does the car need a key to start? A password code? Does the brake pedal have to be depressed? This information would all be accepted through parameters. Should the method return whether the car has started? How long it took to start? A code that represents whether it needs an oil change? These are all examples of possible return data.

In some cases, there may be a situation in which the car can be started multiple ways—for example, the owner has a push-button starter and a remote starter. The designer could write two startCar methods (or three, or four...), each one performing the same task but requiring different information (parameters) to do the task. This process is called **overloading** and can be accomplished by writing two or more methods with identical names but different types and/or numbers of parameters.

PreCondition:

A precondition is a comment that is intended to inform the user more about the condition of the method and can guarantee it to be true.

In the AP Exam, the precondition shows up as a comment immediately above the method. It is the responsibility of the program that calls the method not to pass parameters that violate the precondition.

```
/*** preconditon
```

.... a and b are positive integers

```
*/

public int sum(int a, int b)

{

}
```

PostCondition:

A postcondition is a comment that is intended to guarantee the user calling the method of a result that occurs as the result of calling the method.

In the AP Exam, the postcondition is written as a comment either before or within the method as shown in the example below. The method designer is responsible for making sure that these conditions are met.

```
public int sum100(int a, int b)

{

<code>

//// postcondition—returns a 100 if sum is greater than 100 or the value of sum

if (sum < 100)

        return sum;

else

        return 100;}
```

A method may accept any number of parameters, but may return only one data value or object.

As a final example for this section, consider a programmer who is trying to write an object class that represents a book (like this book, only arbitrarily more interesting). Some of the data the programmer may consider are:

- What does a book *have*? A cover, pages, words, …

- What can a book *do*? It can be read, be skimmed, be put away, …

From this information, the programmer can begin to write the object class. He or she must first determine which item(s) on his or her list are relevant to the situation, so as to keep the object class as efficient as possible. For example, if the programmer is designing a book to be used as a paperweight, it is probably not important to discuss how many words are in the book, so that data field would not be incorporated into the program. Likewise, if the programmer is not a student studying a ridiculous number of books in a short amount of time (sound familiar?), then it may not be relevant to have a method that skims the book, rather than reading it closely. The class will then be built based on these decisions.

As you can see, the **planning** of the program is equally as important, if not more important, than the actual writing of the program. In some classes, your teacher may remind you to "write an outline" or "write a first draft" before you compose the final product, and you might skip that step and go right to end unit, and still be successful. For programming at any profound level, which is required in this course to some extent, planning is essential in order for your program to work well and in order to increase your efficiency. Remember, the AP Exam is strictly timed.

> The AP Exam tests the planning of a class by presenting a LENGTHY description of the requirements, along with other interacting classes in the project.

COMPOSITION

Now that we have written classes to run a program, we must get these classes to interact correctly in order to create a functioning program. We have the driver, we have the car, now we need to put the driver into the car to eagerly drive to the AP Computer Science A Exam on exam day.

The driver and object classes must reside in the same folder on the computer. If you are using an interactive development environment (as opposed to command line programming), you often have to create a "Project" or some similar structure in the software that will hold all of the program's files in one place. Remember that the driver depends on the object class in order to compile, and the object class depends on the driver to make it actually do anything.

Consider a program that will take "flower" objects and "plant" them into a garden. The flower objects might be outlined in an object class called…Flower. One class would perform the planting, so we can call it MakeGarden.

Suppose the Flower constructor method has the following header:

```
public Flower(int xPosition, int yPosition)
```

where xPosition and yPosition are horizontal and vertical coordinates in the garden, respectively, where the flower object will be planted. Our driver would have to first "create" the flowers, and then plant them accordingly.

> In order to create an object, we must instantiate the object using its corresponding class.

Each time we instantiate a flower object, we must assign it an *object reference variable*; like the fancy name implies, this is just a variable name. Some lines in MakeGarden might look like this:

```
Flower f1 = new Flower(2, 1);
Flower f2 = new Flower(2, 2);
Flower f3 = new Flower(2, 3);
```

These lines will instantiate three different flower objects, each containing its own **instance data**. f1, f2, and f3 are used to distinguish between the objects. We can then use these objects to perform methods. Consider a plant method in the Flower class; this method would "plant" the flower and might have the following header:

```
public void plant()
```

In MakeGarden, we must invoke this method through the objects. Let's say we only want to plant f1 and f3, but not f2. We would add the following lines:

```
f1.plant();
f3.plant();
```

Now let's say the plant method, instead, returns whether or not the plant was successfully planted. This altered plant method might have the header:

```
public boolean plant()
```

Now we can use the returned data to output an appropriate message in the driver:

```
if (f1.plant())

  System.out.print("Planted successfully.");

else

  System.out.print("There was a problem.");
```

Because we are invoking f1.plant, f1 should be planted as requested. Since the plant method returns a boolean value, we can place f1.plant in the context of an if statement (it produces a truth value so it is considered a condition) and now it also functions as part of a control structure. Awesome!

Let's add to our garden situation. As you know, other items can appear in a garden, besides flowers. Plants, bushes, and weeds can appear in gardens. Each of these items would probably have its own object class, since their instance data and methods would be different from those of a flower. For example, a flower has flower petals, while a plant does not; weeds often grow on their own without water, whereas most flowers and plants do not. Regardless, separate object classes can be created for each of these object types, and the driver can hold them all together, as long as they are all stored in the same folder on the computer.

Assuming each of these object classes has been created and each corresponding object class has a plant method as outlined above, MakeGarden might include these lines:

```
Flower f1 = new Flower();
Flower f2 = new Flower();
Plant p1 = new Plant();
Plant p2 = new Plant();
Weed w1 = new Weed();
if (f1.plant())
System.out.println("Planted successfully");
if (f2.plant())
System.out.println("Planted successfully");
if (p1.plant())
System.out.println("Planted successfully");
if (w1.plant())
System.out.println("You have a weed.");
```

Note that `MakeGarden` does not instantiate any Bush objects, and does not attempt to plant the p2 object. Note also that we cannot see the entire class! The programmer has the task of deciding which objects to instantiate of which type, when and if to use them, and how to use them appropriately, based on their class specifications. Still think you can go directly to the final draft?

Let's add another layer. Programmers often recognize that an object is actually composed of many smaller, or more basic, objects. If you think about a flower, it actually has several parts, each of which *has* data and *does* particular actions. As a result, we could write an object class for, say, the stalk and the root system. The `Stalk` class and the `RootSystem` class, then, would reside as attributes of each flower. Their classes, again, must be placed in the same folder as the rest of the program's classes. The programmer can then set up the `Flower` class as follows:

```
public class Flower
{
    // other data not shown
    private Stalk st;
    private RootSystem rootSys;

    public Flower()
    {
        st = new Stalk();
        rootSys = new RootSystem();
        // other commands not shown
    }

    // other methods not shown
}
```

This means that every `Flower` object *has* a stalk and a root system. The Flower class, then, is called an **aggregate class** because it is made up of, among other data, instances of other classes. This setup is more realistic; think of any object in your room, and you can probably see pretty quickly that it is made of smaller objects, each with its own data and methods. A laptop computer has keys, ports, and a screen, which can all be considered as objects because they *have* stuff and *do* stuff. A dresser has drawers, but we can go even deeper…a drawer has walls and a floor and can be opened or closed…the floor of a drawer has a shape and is made of a certain material and can be broken if the drawer is overstuffed…you get the idea. Luckily, as the programmer, we get to decide the detail of the object classes, and the answer typically lies in the desired function of the program, as we stated before. Do you REALLY need to know what material the floor of the drawer is made of? Most people do not, although a furniture retailer might. Again, it all depends on the application.

> The FRQs on the AP Exam will present some sort of context and will often tell you exactly what class(es) and/or method(s) to write, so they don't get a wild variety of solutions from test-takers around the world.

Otherwise, they could literally be forced to read thousands of completely different approaches to a given task. This fact is not good for our creativity, but it's great for scoring a 5; save your creative juices for those extra college classes you can take when you AP out of CS!

Use class Chair and method sitOnChair to answer Questions 3 and 4.

```java
public class Chair
{
    private int numberOfLegs = 4;
    private boolean padded;

    public Chair(boolean soft)
    {
        if (soft) padded = true;
        else padded = false;
    }
}

public void sitOnChair( )
{
        <program statements>
}
```

3. The method sitOnChair belongs to another class and is supposed to allow the user to "sit" on a Chair if the chair is padded. Which of the following code segments could be used to replace <program statements> so that sitOnChair will work as intended?

I. `Chair c = new Chair(true);`
    `c.sit();`
II. `Chair c = new Chair(true);`
III. `Chair c = new Chair(true);`
    `if (c.padded) System.out.print("You are sitting.");`

(A) I only
(B) II only
(C) III only
(D) I, II, and III
(E) None

Here's How to Crack It

Since (A), (B), and (C) allow the selection of only one option, we must test check all of them. We've got this! Remember that an object must (1) be instantiated in the executing class, and (2) be associated only with methods that are defined in its class. Option I instantiates a `Chair` correctly, but then attempts to invoke a sit() method, which is not defined in `Chair` (or anywhere); eliminate (A) and (D). Option II correctly instantiates a `Chair` but does not attempt to "sit"; eliminate (B). Option III is incorrect because it also attempts to access padded, which is private data in `Chair` and therefore not accessible directly; eliminate (C). Since no option is valid, (E) is the answer.

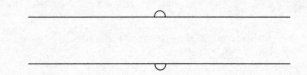

4. Which of the following modifications, if any, would help to make the Chair class MOST useful to the sitOnChair method, based on the task attempted in Question 3?

   (A) Adding an accessor method that returns the value of numberOfLegs
   (B) Adding an accessor method that returns the value of padded
   (C) Adding a mutator method that changes the value of numberOfLegs
   (D) Adding a mutator method that changes the value of padded
   (E) Adding an accessor method that returns the values of both numberOfLegs and padded

Here's How to Crack It

The situation presented in Question 4 requires the information regarding whether the chair is padded. `numberOfLegs` is irrelevant here, regardless of your personal bias; eliminate (A), (C), and (E). Since the padded attribute of the chair does not have to be changed, eliminate (D). The answer is (B).

Do not get "emotional" about a situation presented; follow the specifications carefully and don't assume the programmer's intentions.

5. Consider the following method:

```
public int halfRoot(int n)
{
        return Math.sqrt(n) / 2;
}
```

Which of the following method calls would cause a run-time error?

(A) halfRoot(-2)
(B) halfRoot(3)
(C) halfRoot((int)2.0)
(D) halfRoot(3.0)
(E) None will cause a run-time error.

Here's How to Crack It
The heading of the method definition requires an integer parameter. Choices (A) and (B) directly use integers. Even though (A) uses a negative, this doesn't result in an error. In math class, this doesn't result in a real number. However, in Java, this results in NaN. While this is not a preferred result, it is not strictly an error. Choice (C) casts a double as an integer and thus would compile and run correctly. Choice (D) gives a double parameter when an integer is required. This would cause an error. While this error would appear to cause an IllegalArgumentException, it will instead cause a compiler-time error rather than a run-time error. The IllegalArgumentException would arise only if the programmer deliberately throws it if an argument is legal in Java terms but inappropriate for the purposes of the program. (For example, a program intended to find the factorial of an integer might be designed to throw an IllegalArgumentException if it takes a negative parameter.) Since none of these results in a run-time error, the answer is (E).

REFERENCES
All of this data that is passed from driver classes to object classes and vice versa creates a complicated operation that's occurring behind the scenes. Consider this example: the programmer decides that he or she wants to write a class that represents a vinyl record player (for music), or "turntable". The driver class will then operate the turntable, turning it on and off, controlling it, and putting on/taking off the desired record. For this program, we will have three classes: Turntable and Record, which represent each of these objects, and PlayRecord will be the driver that relates them.

In theory, we would have to perform the following steps in the driver:

- create (instantiate) a turntable object
- create one or more record objects
- place the record onto the turntable
- switch on the turntable

Some code from these classes might look like this:

```
public class Record
{
    // data not shown

    public Record()
    // constructor code and other methods not shown
}
public class Turntable
{
    private Record r;
    // other data not shown

    public Turntable(Record r1)
    {
        r = r1;
        // other statements not shown
    }

    // other methods not shown
}
public class PlayRecord
{
    public static void play()
    {
        Record rec = new Record();
        Turntable tt = new Turntable(rec);
        // other statements not shown
    }
    // other methods not shown
}
```

In this example, note that Turntable is an aggregate class since part of its instance data involves another object. More importantly for this section, note the instantiation of the Record object in the driver, the "passing" of that object to the Turntable class, and the assignment r = r1. When an object is passed to another class and, as a result, received through a parameter, a **reference** is created to the object. Think of it this way: if you just picked up your favorite Taylor Swift record (you know you love her) and wanted to play it, you wouldn't need two copies of the album. In the same way, we don't have to create a copy of the Record object, we just need to create another reference to it in order for it to be used in the Turntable class. This is the only way the Turntable class can use this record, since it was instantiated in the driver. The record can then be used in context (in this case, assigned to the data field r) and then the reference will disappear once the constructor is over. Since the reference is not an actual copy of the object, its life is not affected.

Another way to think of references is to think of a superhero with his or her secret identity. Clark Kent was just another name for the person; he was still Superman the whole time. They were the same guy with the same superpowers, the same attributes, and the same ability to perform cool superhero actions. Therefore, "Clark Kent" was simply a reference created to *refer* to the same guy.

It is extremely important to know that primitive data is not copied by reference; it is copied by value itself.

> When received as a parameter, primitive data is actually copied, while object data will simply receive a new reference to the object itself. Primitives are copied by value; objects are copied by reference.

Here's the really confusing part or maybe, not really. If a copy of a primitive data value is made, then the two copies (the original and the new one) exist exclusively. Therefore, if you change the value of one copy, the other is not affected. On the other hand, if a new reference to an object is made, then a modification of the object through the reference will be reflected by all references. Again, the superhero example: if Superman dyed his hair blond because it was all the rage, then both Clark Kent and Superman will have blond hair. They are two names that reference the same guy, so any changes will be reflected in all the references. If we suddenly decided that Superman/Clark Kent should be called "Blue Guy" instead of either of these two names, we are *still* referring to the same guy; he now has three *aliases* instead of two.

This is important for understanding object equality. Two objects are considered equivalent only if they are, in fact, the same object. In the superhero example above, Clark Kent is equal to Superman, since they are the exact same person.

Now imagine that Superman has an identical twin brother named Duperman with alter ego Klarc Tenk. Since Duperman and Klarc Tenk are the same person, Duperman is equal to Klarc Tenk. Therefore, in Java `Duperman == Klarc Tenk` is true. However, even though they are identical twins, Superman and Duperman are different people. Therefore, Superman is not equal to Duperman. In Java, Superman and Duperman could be identified as identical twins using the `equals` method of the Object class. The `equals` method takes an Object parameter and returns true if and only if the two object have identical data, regardless of whether they are the same object. While the boolean statement `Superman == Duperman` is false, the statement `Superman.equals(Duperman)` is true.

this keyword:

Sometimes to call a method it may be necessary for the calling object to be able to refer to itself. When an object calls a method, an implicit reference is assigned to the calling object. The name of this implicit reference is *this*. The keyword *this* is a reference to the current calling object and may be used as an object variable.

Eg. this.mySize

Use the following incomplete class declarations to answer Questions 6 and 7.

```java
public class Number
{
    private int value;

    public Number(int someNum)
    {
        if (someNum >= 0)
            value = someNum;
    }

    public int changeVal(int newVal)
    {
        /* missing code */
    }

    public int getValue()
    {
        return value;
    }
}

public class NumChanger
{
    public void change()
    {
        Number n1 = new Number(5);
        Number n2 = new Number(5);
        int sum1 = n1.getValue() + n2.getValue();
        int oldn1Val = n1.changeValue(10);
        n2 = n1;
        int sum2 = n1.getValue() + n2.getValue();
        System.out.print(sum1 + " " + sum2);
    }

    //other methods not shown
}
```

6. The changeVal method in Number should reassign value to be the value taken as the parameter and return the original value. Which of the following code segments should be used to replace / * *missing code* * / so that changeVal will work as intended?

(A)
```
value = newVal;
return value;
```
(B)
```
value = newVal;
return 5;
```
(C)
```
int oldVal = value
value = newVal;
```
(D)
```
int oldVal = value;
value = newVal;
return value;
```
(E)
```
int oldVal = value;
value = newVal;
return oldVal;
```

Here's How to Crack It

To accomplish the task, two events must occur: value must be reset to the parameter value and the old value must be returned. Choice (C) does not attempt to return any value, so it cannot be correct. The remaining answer choices attempt to accomplish both events; however, if value is reset and its new value is returned, the second event is done incorrectly. The original value must be stored, so eliminate (A) and (B) as a result. Choice (D) stores the old value but returns the new value, since it has been reassigned to newVal, so it is not correct. Since (E) stores the old value, reassigns value, and returns the old value, (E) is the answer.

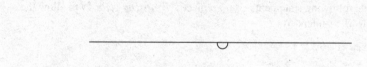

7. What will be printed as a result of executing the change method? Assume changeVal in the Number class works as intended.

(A) 5 5
(B) 5 10
(C) 10 5
(D) 10 10
(E) None of these

Here's How to Crack It

The College Board LOVES to write MCQs with confusing object references like this. Remember that setting an object "equal" to another object merely means that the two identifiers reference the same object (like Superman and Clark Kent). sum1 will be assigned to the sum of the values of n1 and n2, which is 10, so the first number printed will be 10. Eliminate (A) and (B) as a result. oldn1Val is irrelevant here but n1.changeValue(10) makes n1 have a value of 10. n2 = n1 will now have variable n2 reference the same object as n1, which has a value of 10 from the previous statement. Therefore, n1.getValue and n2.getValue will both return 10, so sum2 will be 10 + 10 = 20. As a result, the second number printed will be 20 and (C) and (D) can be eliminated. The answer is (E).

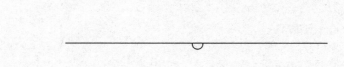

8. The following method is intended to output "Strings match." if the two strings contain identical data and otherwise print "Strings do not match."

```
public void match(String s, String t)
{
    if (/ * missing code * /)
        System.out.println("Strings match.");
    else
        System.out.println("Strings do not match.");
}
```

Which of the following statements could replace / * missing code * / to allow the method to work as intended?

I.   s.compareTo(t) == 0
II. compareTo(s, t) == 0
III. s == t

(A) I only
(B) III only
(C) I and III only
(D) II and III only
(E) I, II, and III

Here's How to Crack It

This question is testing the proper way to determine whether two strings contain identical data. Go through each statement one at a time. Statement I uses the `compareTo` method. The `compareTo` method of the `String` class takes on another string as a parameter and returns an int. If the two strings contain identical data, the return is 0. (Note that this can also be applied to other objects, as the `Object` class has a similar `compareTo` method.) Therefore, Statement I will cause the method to work as intended. Eliminate (B) and (D), which do not include Statement I. Statement II also uses `compareTo`. However, since `compareTo` is a non-static method of the `String` class, it must be invoked by a `String` object. Also, the `compareTo` method takes only one parameter. Therefore, Statement II would cause a compile-time error. Eliminate (E), which contains it. Now, look at Statement III. When the == operator is applied to objects, the result is true only if the references are the same. If two objects have different references but contain identical data, the return will be `false`. The above method needs for the return to be `true` in this case. Although this does not cause a compile-time or run-time error, the method will not work as intended. Therefore, eliminate (C), which contains Statement III. The answer is (A).

STATIC MODIFIER

The **static** keyword can appear in two contexts at this level. A **static variable** is an attribute that is shared among all instances of a class. When the value of this variable is changed, the alteration is reflected by all of the objects instantiated through that class. A classic example of a static variable is the high score list on a video game. Consider video game MKA, the latest in a series of popular games on portable devices. After you fire up the MKA app, you start a new game and play until you lose...then, since you are addicted to the game, you start over. If each game of MKA you play is considered an object of the same class, a static variable might be the high score. Every time you start (or instantiate) a new game, the high score remains the same from when it was initially set. Once a new high score is set, every new game will reflect the new high score, rendering the old high score non-existent (or 2nd best, etc.).

In an object class, a static variable is declared with the rest of the instance data at the top of the class, preceded by the keyword static. Static variables are often used for identification numbers or for counters. Consider this short program:

```
public class Box
{
    private static int boxNumber = 0;
    // other data fields not shown

    public Box()
    {
        boxNumber++;
        // other statements not shown
    }
}
public class BoxCreator
{
    public BoxCreator()
    {
        Box box1 = new Box();
        Box box2 = new Box();
    }
}
```

As each Box object is instantiated in BoxCreator, the static variable in the Box class will be updated. That way, the next time a box is created, the box number value is incremented for all box objects. The static variable is not an attribute of each individual box; rather, it is a shared value among all boxes. Contrast this set-up with a non-static declaration of boxNumber; every time a box is instantiated, its boxNumber would start as 0 and then be incremented, making every box have the same boxNumber value of 1.

In order to show this structure is actually working, let's create an accessor method to let the driver "see," or access, the value of boxNumber. This method is necessary for this result since boxNumber has been declared private. A non-constructor method that is designed to access and/or modify a static variable is a **static method** and must be declared as such. To add this functionality and test it, here are our new object and driver classes:

```
public class Box
{
    private static int boxNumber = 0;
    // other data fields not shown

    public Box()
    {
        boxNumber++;
        // other statements not shown
    }

    static public int getBoxNum()
    {
        return boxNumber;
    }
}
public class BoxCreator
{
    public BoxCreator()
    {
        Box box1 = new Box();
        Box box2 = new Box();
        System.out.print (Box.getBoxNum() + " boxes
        created so far.");
    }
}
```

Notice the method call from BoxCreator does not use an object reference variable; rather, the class is used directly. Since static variables are shared among all instances, the programmer needs to access static methods (and therefore, static variables) through the class itself.

---

9. A class called ComputerMouse has a static variable connector and a static method getConnector. Which of the following statements is true based on this information?

(A) In order to invoke getConnector, a new ComputerMouse object does not need to be instantiated; getConnector must be called directly through the object class.

(B) In order to invoke getConnector, a new ComputerMouse object must be instantiated and then getConnector must be called through that object.

(C) Since connector is declared static, getConnector is shared among all objects in the program.

(D) Since connector is declared static, ComputerMouse objects cannot be mutated during execution.

(E) Since connector is declared static, all of the methods in ComputerMouse must also be declared static.

Here's How to Crack It

The AP Exam tests rote knowledge as well as reasoning; this question can be answered correctly only if you know how static works. A static method must be called directly through the class, so (A) looks good so far, but eliminate (B). Choice (C) is incorrect because `getConnector` will be shared among all `ComputerMouse` objects, not all objects in general. Choice (D) is nonsensical since static is not related to mutations. Choice (E) would be correct if it said "all of the methods in ComputerMouse that access or mutate connector." The answer is (A).

Do not be afraid of answer choices (A) or (E).

CHAPTER 7 REVIEW DRILL

Answers to the review questions can be found in Chapter 13.

1. A development team is building an online bookstore that customers can use to order books. Information about inventory and customer orders is kept in a database. Code must be developed that will store and retrieve data from the database. The development team decides to put the database code in separate classes from the rest of the program. Which of the following would be an advantage of this plan?

   I.   The database access code could be reused in other applications that also need to access the database.
   II. The database access code can be tested independently. It will be possible to test the database access code before the interface is developed.
   III. A team of programmers can be assigned to work just on the code that is used to access the database. The programmers can work independently from other programmers, such as those who develop the user interface.

   (A) I only
   (B) II only
   (C) III only
   (D) I and II only
   (E) I, II, and III

2. In Java, instance fields (also known as instance variables) and methods can be designated public or private. Which of the following best characterizes the designation that should be used?

   (A) Instance fields and methods should always be public. This makes it easier for client programs to access data fields and use the methods of the class.
   (B) Instance fields should be either public or private, depending on whether or not it is beneficial for client programs to access them directly. All methods should be public. A private method is useless because a client program can't access it.
   (C) Keep all methods and instance fields private. This enforces encapsulation.
   (D) Instance fields should always be private so that clients can't directly access them. Methods can be either public or private.
   (E) All instance fields should be public so client programs can access them, and all methods should be private.

3. Which of the following are signs of a well-designed program?

   I.   Clients know how data is stored in the class.
   II. Classes and methods can be tested independently.
   III. The implementation of a method can be changed without changing the programs that use the method.

   (A) I only
   (B) II only
   (C) II and III
   (D) I and II
   (E) I, II, and III

4. Consider the following classes:

```
public class Sample
{
    public void writeMe(Object obj)
    {
        System.out.println("object");
    }
    public void writeMe(String s)
    {
        System.out.println("string");
    }
}
```

What will be the result of executing the following?

```
Sample s = new Sample( );
String tmp = new String("hi");
s.writeMe(tmp);
```

(A) Compile-time error
(B) "hi"
(C) "object"
(D) "string"
(E) Run-time error

5. Consider the following class:

```
public class Sample
{
    public void writeMe(Object obj)
    {
        System.out.println("object");
    }
    public void writeMe(String s)
    {
        System.out.println("string");
    }
}
```

What will be the result of executing the following?

```
Sample s = new Sample( );
Object tmp = new Object( );
s.writeMe(tmp);
```

(A) Compile-time error
(B) "string"
(C) "object"
(D) "tmp"
(E) Run-time error

6. Consider the following class:

```
public class Sample
{
    public void writeMe(Object obj)
    {
        System.out.println("object");
    }
    public void writeMe(String s)
    {
        System.out.println("string");
    }
}
```

What will be the result of executing the following?

```
Sample s = new Sample( );
Object tmp = new String("hi");
s.writeMe(tmp);
```

(A) Compile-time error
(B) "hi"
(C) "object"
(D) "string"
(E) Run-time error

7. Consider the following class:

```
public class Sample
{
    public void writeMe(Object obj)
    {
        System.out.println("object");
    }
    public void writeMe(String s)
    {
        System.out.println("string");
    }
}
```

What will be the result of executing the following?

```
Sample s = new Sample( );
String tmp = new Object( );
s.writeMe(tmp);
```

(A) Compile-time error
(B) "hi"
(C) "object"
(D) "string"
(E) Run-time error

8. Consider the following class:

```
public class Sample
{
    int val = 0;
}
```

Is val an attribute or a method?

(A) Neither: a compile-time error occurs when we try to execute this code.

(B) val is an attribute.

(C) val is a method.

(D) val is both an attribute and a method.

(E) Neither, val is a primitive.

9. Consider the following class:

```
public class Sample
{
    public String writeMe(String s)
    {
        System.out.println("object");
    }
    public void writeMe(String s)
    {
        System.out.println("string");
    }
}
```

What will be the result of executing the following?

```
Sample s = new Sample( );
Object tmp = new Object( );
s.writeMe(tmp);
```

(A) Compile-time error

(B) "hi"

(C) "object"

(D) "string"

(E) Run-time error

Summary

o A class is an assembly of control statements. A class can contain methods and variables. On the AP Computer Science A Exam, all class methods are public and can be accessed by other classes, and all class variables are private and cannot be accessed by other classes.

o A method is a group of code that performs a specific task.

o A method can take any number of variables of specified types as input parameters and return one value of a specified type as output. However, methods need not take any parameters or return any values.

o An object is a specific instance of a class. An object is identified by one or more references.

o For static class, all methods and variables must be called by the class name. For non-static variables, all methods and variables must be called by object references.

o On the AP Computer Science A Exam, all object variables are private and thus cannot be called by other classes, and all object methods are public and thus can be called by other classes.

KEY TERMS

class
source code
methods
driver class
object class
header
constructor
instance data/data fields
instance variables/fields
return type
parameters
accessor methods
mutator methods
overloading
precondition
postcondition
planning
aggregate class
reference
static
static variable
static method

Chapter 8
Array

Now that we understand how to store data and manipulate it, the next step is to understand how to organize it. Imagine creating a program that keeps track of hundreds of entries per day, such as a factory that produces bottles of aspirin. Using the skills we have learned thus far, you would have to write a class representing an aspirin bottle, instantiate each individual bottle separately, and use an object reference variable for each. Imagine invoking a method on every one of those objects? You're looking at some serious lines of code...not to mention, some serious *repetition* of code, which is bad style. Let's discuss an **array** structure, the fundamental object that organizes data in an intuitive way.

PRIMITIVES & OBJECTS

In order to instantiate an array, you must first decide what type of objects will be contained in the array. Suppose you are creating a program that will keep track of your test grades in your APCS class. Since grades are usually represented by an integer number, you will create an array of integers. The syntax for instantiating an array of integers is

```
int <identifier> [] = new int [<array size>];
```

This format is used if you do not yet know the values that will be stored in the array. Alternatively, if you already know the data values, you can instantiate the array using an **initializer list**:

```
int <identifier> [] = {<data1>, <data2>, …, <data n>};
```

Notice the square brackets—these are standard characters in Java that signify an array is present. The braces (curly brackets) indicate an initializer list. In the beginning of the semester, you do not yet know your grades. In order to create an array called `testGrades` that will eventually store your first 5 test grades, you could write a statement like this:

```
int testGrades[] = new int[5];
```

This array object will store your test grades and keep them organized using **index numbers**. Just like your tests might be organized as Chapter 1 Test, Chapter 2 Test, etc., your data will be accessed through particular index numbers in the array. The tricky part is that array indexes start with the number 0 instead of 1. Therefore, if your Chapter 1 Test is the first test score in the array, it will be stored at index 0. If the first test you have in APCS reviews a previous course, then it's Chapter 0 instead of Chapter 1. If you did not instantiate the array using an initializer list, then you will assign data values, using the index number; you will do the same process to access the data, regardless of how you created the array. For example, if you scored a 95 on the first test, you could write the line:

```
testGrades[0] = 95;
```

Let's say that, after looking over your test, you realize that your teacher made a grading error and you actually scored a 98. You can either increment the data value or reassign it:

```
testGrades[0] += 3;
```

or

```
testGrades[0] = 98;
```

You can also perform any integer operation and also display the value to the user, with that same format.

Let's step it up a notch. Suppose, after all 5 tests are complete, your teacher feels that the scores are too high and decides to deflate the grades. (You didn't think this book would discuss only *nice* teachers, did you?) The programmer can use a simple loop in order to **span** the array and change every value accordingly, rather than writing 5 separate lines. Since an array's length is well-defined, a for loop is usually appropriate for arrays. Provided that the array is **full**, meaning all 5 values are assigned, the following loop will span the array and subtract 2 points from every grade:

```
for (int index = 0; index < 5; index++)
    testGrades[index] -= 2;
```

Note the values of index will be 0, 1, 2, 3, and 4, even though it stores 5 elements. Since the index numbers start at 0, you must stop spanning the array before index 5, or your will receive an **ArrayIndexOutOfBoundsException** and the program execution will be interrupted, which is never desirable.

Much better than writing multiple lines, right? Whether you use an array or not, the loop systematically changes every value. We are just scratching the surface of the usefulness of arrays, and we have already improved our coding efficiency.

The AP Exam will require you to read, interpret, and write arrays; FRQs are loaded with arrays and will specifically state that an array must be created.

The programmer needs to ensure that every element of the array contains a value, or undesired results may occur. In an array of primitives, the value of an unassigned element will default to 0. Consider the following code segment that will calculate the average of your 5 test grades:

```
int total = 0, len = testGrades.length;
double average;
for (int index = 0; index < len; index++)
    total += testGrades[index];
average = (double)total / len;
```

If all 5 of your test grades are stored in the array, this code segment will calculate the average. If you did not input one of your scores, however, it will remain stored as 0 and incorrectly drag down your average, which is (definitely) an undesired result. Even worse, your teacher's grade deflation will make that grade negative!

There is an alternative way to execute the previous code segment. This involves using an **enhanced-for loop**. An enhanced-for loop can be used to automatically go through each element of an array.

```
int total = 0, len = testGrades.length;
double average;
for (int grade : testGrades)
    total += grade;
average = (double)total / len;
```

In the enhanced-for statement, a previously declared array or an `ArrayList` (more on `ArrayLists` later) must be referenced after the colon. The loop will iterate for each element on the list, beginning with index 0 to index `length-1`. However, no variable is used to refer to the current index. Instead, the element located at the current index is stored as the variable declared before the colon. (The variable must be of the same type stored in the array.) Therefore, the enhanced-for loop above stores each element, one at a time in increasing order by index, of the array testGrades as int grade. It then adds each grade to total. Thus, the enhanced-for loop has the same functionality as the for loop in the previous example.

---

1. Consider the following code segment:

```
final int[] a1 = {1, 2};
int[] b1 = {3, 4};
a1 = b1;
System.out.print(a1[1]);
```

What is printed as a result of executing the code segment?

(A) 2
(B) 3
(C) 4
(D) Nothing is printed due to a compile-time error.
(E) Nothing is printed due to a run-time error.

Here's How to Crack It

This is an easy one if you know your compiler. Since a1 is declared final, its reference cannot be changed. In the third line, the programmer attempts to change a1 to reference the second array, which is not allowed. The answer is (D).

---

2. Consider the following incomplete method:

```
public static int mod3(int[] a)
{
    int count = 0;
    for (int i = 0; i < a.length; i++)
    {
        // code not shown
    }
    return count;
}
```

Method Mod3 is intended to return the number of integers in the array numbers that are evenly divisible by 3. Which of the following code segments could be used to replace // code not shown so that Mod3 will work as intended?

I.
```
if (i % 3) == 0)
{
  count++;
}
```
II.
```
if (a[i] % 3 == 0)
{
  count++;
}
```
III.
```
while (a[i] % 3 == 0)
{
  count++;
}
```

(A) I only
(B) II only
(C) III only
(D) I and II
(E) II and III

Here's How to Crack It

Option I is checking whether i—the counter—is divisible by 3, rather than the element in the array itself, so I is incorrect, eliminating (A) and (D). The process needs to be looped in order to span the entire array, but the hidden code is already in a loop, so Option III is incorrect, eliminating (C) and (E). By Process of Elimination, (B) is the answer.

Since objects are typically used to represent real-world phenomena, arrays are also commonly used to organize and manipulate objects. Suppose you have an object class that represents a pair of sneakers. The following code segment would instantiate an array that would store 5 of these objects:

```
PairOfSneakers collection[] = new PairOfSneakers[5];
```

Since each element is an object, however, the default value for each object is **null**. Since null is not a valid object, operations performed on null will result in a **NullPointerException**, another error that will halt the execution of the program. Without getting into the specifics of the PairOfSneakers class, a statement that could assign an instantiated pair of sneakers called jordans is

```
collection[0] = jordans;
```

Now suppose PairOfSneakers has a tie() method that will tie the laces of the corresponding pair of sneakers; i.e., jordans.tie() will tie that pair. At this point, index 0 references the jordans object—remember objects are referenced, not copied—but indexes 1–4 are null. As a result, the following statement will cause a NullPointerException:

```
for (int i = 0; i < collection.length; i++)
    collection[i].tie();
```

> When using a loop to span an array of objects, be sure the array is full to avoid undesired results.

```
public int[] someMethod (int[] array, int value)
{
    for (int i = 1, i < array.length-1; i++)
        array[i-1] += value;
    return array;
}
```

3. Which of the following statements is true about the method someMethod?

(A) The method will not return any value.
(B) The method will not return the correct value.
(C) The method will cause a run-time error.
(D) The method will not increment the first element of the array by value.
(E) The method will not increment the last element of the array by value.

Here's How to Crack It

The return value must be an array of integers, so eliminate (A) and (B) because `array[i]` is an integer. At no point will the code segment call for an index of less than 0 or greater than or equal to `array.length`, so there will be no run-time error. The remaining answer choices prove that this question is messing around with the spanning of the array (and with your brain). The loop purposely offsets the way it (supposedly) spans the array because…well, you don't expect a straightforward MCQ on this exam, do you? Index 0 is incremented because the method increments element `i-1`, and `i` is initialized with a value of 1. By the same reasoning, index 4 is not addressed because the last value of `i` will be less than `array.length-1`. The answer is (E).

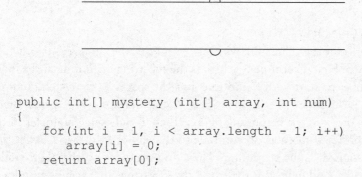

```
public int[] mystery (int[] array, int num)
{
    for(int i = 1, i < array.length - 1; i++)
        array[i] = 0;
    return array[0];
}
```

4. Which of the following modifications will make the method compile, based on the information given?

   (A) Change int[] array in the method header parameter to int[] numbers.
   (B) Change array.length-1 to array.length in the loop statement.
   (C) Change array[i-1] = 0; to array[i] = 0;.
   (D) Change the return statement to return array;.
   (E) None of these choices will make the method compile.

Here's How to Crack It

The problem with this method is the discrepancy between the return type `int[]` and the type of value that the method attempts to return `int`; (D) addresses this issue. Choice (A) will have no effect on the outcome of the method because array is simply the name of the variable that references the array. Choices (B) and (C), although valid, will not correct the return type issue. Choice (C) will cause a problem. Choice (E) is incorrect, again, because the return type issue is keeping the method from compiling. The answer is (D).

One last item before we start manipulating the data contained in the array…the constant value returned by `arrayName.length` is very useful when spanning the area and/or attempting to identify the size of the array. This constant is always available for the programmer's use.

5. Consider the following code segment:

```
String s = "This is the beginning";
String t = s.substring(5);
int n = t.IndexOf("the");
```

Which of the following will be the value of n?

(A) −1
(B) 3
(C) 7
(D) 9
(E) n will have no value because of a run-time error.

Here's How to Crack It

The question asks for the value of n, which is IndexOf "the" in String t, which is a substring of s. First determine t, which is the substring beginning at the index 5 of s. Remember to start with 0 and to count the spaces as characters. Index 0 is 'T', index 1 is 'h', index 2 is 'i', index 3 is 's', and index 4 is the space. Therefore, index 5 is the 'i' at the beginning of "is". There is only one parameter in the call of the substring method, so continue to the end of String s to get that String t is assigned "is the beginning". Now, find the index of "the". Since index 0 is 'i', index 1 is 's', and index 2 is the space, the substring "the" begins at index 3. Therefore, the value of n is 3, which is (B).

Arrays	ArrayList
After an array is created, it cannot be resized.	ArrayLists will automatically resize as new elements are added.
No import statement is needed to use an array, unless the array holds elements that require an import statement.	You must import java.util.ArrayList, or use the full package name whenever you use an ArrayList.
Elements are accessed using index notation (e.g., myArray[2]).	Elements are accessed using methods of the ArrayList class (e.g., myList.get(2), myList.add("George")).
Arrays can be constructed to hold either primitives or object references.	ArrayList instances can hold only object references, not primitives. The Integer and Double wrapper classes must be used to store integer and double primitives in an ArrayList.

Each array can be declared for only one type of element. For example, if an array is declared to hold Strings, you cannot store an Integer in it.	An ArrayList can hold a heterogeneous collection of objects. For example, the following is perfectly legal (though not recommended):
	`ArrayList list = new ArrayList( );`
	`list.add(new String("A String"));`
	`list.add(new Integer(4));`

CHAPTER 8 REVIEW DRILL

Answers to review questions can be found in Chapter 13.

1. Consider the following code segment:

```
String[] s = new String[2];
String[] t = {"Michael", "Megan", "Chelsea"};
s = t;
System.out.print(s.length);
```

What is printed as a result of executing the code segment?

(A) 1

(B) 2

(C) 3

(D) Nothing will be printed due to a compile-time error.

(E) Nothing will be printed due to a run-time error.

2. Consider the following code segment:

```
final int[] a1 = {1, 2};
int[] b1 = {3, 4};
a1 = b1;
System.out.print(a1[1]);
```

What is printed as a result of executing the code segment?

(A) 2

(B) 3

(C) 4

(D) Nothing will be printed due to a compile-time error.

(E) Nothing will be printed due to a run-time error.

3. Consider the following code segment:

```
final int[] myArray = {1, 2};
myArray[1] = 3;
System.out.print(myArray[1]);
```

What is printed as a result of executing the code segment?

(A) 1

(B) 2

(C) 3

(D) Nothing will be printed due to a run-time error.

(E) Nothing will be printed due to a compile-time error.

4. Consider the following incomplete method:

```
public static int Mod3(int[] numbers)
{
    int count = 0;
    for (int i = 0; i < numbers.length; i++)
    {
        / * mystery code * /
    }
    return count;
}
```

Method Mod3 is intended to return the number of integers in the array numbers that are evenly divisible by 3. Which of the following code segments could be used to replace / * mystery code * / so that Mod3 will work as intended?

I. ```
    if (i % 3 = = 0)
    {
        count++;
    }
    ```

II. ```
    if (numbers[i] % 3 = = 0)
    {
        count++;
    }
    ```

III. ```
     while (numbers[i] % 3 = = 0)
     {
         count++;
     }
     ```

(A) I only
(B) II only
(C) III only
(D) I and II
(E) II and III

5. Consider the following code segment:

```
ArrayList list = new ArrayList( );
list.add("A");
list.add("B");
list.add(0, "C");
list.add("D");
list.set(2, "E");
list.remove(1);
System.out.println(list);
```

What is printed as a result of executing the code segment?

(A) [A, B, C, D, E]
(B) [A, B, D, E]
(C) [C, E, D]
(D) [A, D, E]
(E) [A, C, D, E]
```

6. Consider the following data fields and method:

```
private ArrayList letters;
// precondition: letters.size( ) > 0
// letters contains String objects
public void letterRemover( )
{
    int i = 0;
    while (i < letters.size( ))
    {
        if (letters.get(i).equals("A"))
            letters.remove(i);
        i++;
    }
}
```

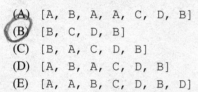

Assume that ArrayList letters originally contains the following String values:

[A, B, A, A, C, D, B]

What will letters contain as a result of executing letterRemover( )?

(A) [A, B, A, A, C, D, B]
(B) [B, C, D, B]
(C) [B, A, C, D, B]
(D) [A, B, A, C, D, B]
(E) [A, A, B, C, D, B, D]

7. Consider the following method:

```
private ArrayList myList;
// precondition: myList.size( ) > 0
// myListcontains String objects
public void myMethod( )
{
    for (int i = 0; i < myList.size( ) - 1; i++)
    {
        myList.remove(i);
        System.out.print(myList.get(i) + " ");
    }
}
```

Assume that myList originally contains the following String values:

[A, B, C, D, E]

What will be printed when the method above executes?

(A) A B C D E
(B) A C E
(C) B D E
(D) B D
(E) Nothing will be printed due to an IndexOutOfBoundsException.

8. Consider the following code segment:

```
int[][] numbers = new int [4][4];
initializeIt(numbers);
int total = 0;
for (int z = 0; z < numbers.length; z++)
{
    total += numbers[z][numbers [0].length - 1 - z];
}
```

The call to initializeIt() on the second line initializes the array numbers so that it looks like the following:

```
1 2 5 3
7 9 4 0
3 3 2 5
4 5 8 1
```

What will be the value of total after the code has executed?

(A) 11
(B) 12
(C) 13
(D) 14
(E) 15

9. Consider the following code segment:

```
int[][] numbers = new int[3][6];
initializeIt(numbers);
int total = 0;
for (int j = 0; j < numbers.length; j++)
{
    for (int k = 0; k < numbers[0].length; k += 2)
    {
        total+= numbers[j][k];
    }
}
```

The call to initializeIt() on the second line initializes the array numbers so that it looks like the following:

```
2 4 6 3 2 1
5 6 7 4 2 9
4 0 5 6 4 2
```

What will be the value of total after the code has executed?

(A) 18
(B) 35
(C) 37
(D) 72
(E) 101

10. Consider the following code segment:

```
ArrayList list = new ArrayList( );
for (int i = 1; i <= 8; i++)
{
    list.add(new Integer(i));
}
for (int j = 1; j < list.size( ); j++)
{
    list.set(j / 2, list.get(j));
}
System.out.println(list);
```

What is printed as a result of executing the code segment?

(A) [2, 4, 6, 8, 5, 6, 7, 8]
(B) [1, 2, 3, 4, 5, 6, 7, 8]
(C) [1, 2, 3, 4]
(D) [1, 2, 3, 4, 1, 2, 3, 4]
(E) [2, 2, 4, 4, 6, 6, 8, 8]

11. Consider the following code segment:

```
int[][] num = new int[4][4];
for (int i = 0; i < num.length; i++)
{
    for (int k = 0; k < num[0].length; k++)
    {
        num[i][k] = i * k;
    }
}
```

What are the contents of num after the code segment has executed?

(A) 0 0 0 0
    0 1 2 3
    0 2 4 6
    0 3 6 9
(B) 0 1 2 3
    1 2 3 4
    2 3 4 5
    3 4 5 6
(C) 0 3 6 9
    0 2 4 6
    0 1 2 3
    0 0 0 0
(D) 1 1 1 1
    2 2 2 2
    3 3 3 3
    4 4 4 4
(E) 0 0 0 0
    1 2 3 4
    2 4 6 8
    3 6 9 12

Summary

- An array is a grouping of fixed length of variables of the same data type or objects of the same class.

- Arrays are indexed beginning at 0 and ending at length –1.

- A two-dimensional array is an array of arrays. On the AP Computer Science A Exam, these arrays will always be the same length. Also, arrays of dimension greater than 2 are not tested.

- `ArrayLists` are lists of objects of variable length.

- An enhanced-for loop automatically performs the loop for each element of an array or `ArrayList`.

- A sequential search looks for an element of an array or `ArrayList` beginning at index 0 until the desired element is found and returns the index. If the element is not found, it returns –1.

- A binary search begins searching in the middle of an array of `ArrayList` and moves to higher or lower indexes to find the desired element. A binary search is more efficient but can be used only on an ordered list.

- A select sort orders an array or `ArrayList` by swapping lower elements to lower indexes.

- An insertion sort orders an array or `ArrayList` by finding the appropriate location for an element, shifting other elements to take its place, and then placing the element into the appropriate location.

- A merge sort orders an array or `ArrayList` by recursively dividing the array or `ArrayList` into smaller pieces. The smaller pieces are sorted and merged with other pieces.

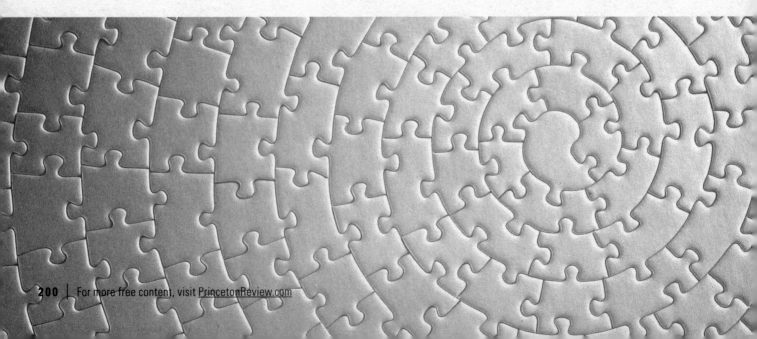

KEY TERMS

array
initializer list
index numbers
span
full
ArrayIndexOutOfBoundsException
enhanced-for loop
null
NullPointerException

Chapter 9
Array List

SEARCHES

Once data is stored in an array, a common task is to methodically search the array for given data. Consider a line of parked cars in the "Curbside To Go" section of your local chain restaurant. When the server is bringing the food to a particular car, he or she must use a given attribute—say, a license plate number—to find the correct car. Once the correct car is found, the server can deliver the food and then go back inside for the next order, beginning the process all over again…and again…and again. Poor kid.

This same technique is used for searching an array. In APCS, we have two methods of searching arrays, the **sequential search** and the **binary search**. Since each of these search methods uses a distinct formula to search through the arrays, they are commonly referred to as **search algorithms**.

The chain restaurant example given above is an example of a sequential search. All of the cars are "lined up" and the server begins with the first car, checking its license plate number against the one he or she is looking for. If it's correct, the server delivers the food and returns. If not, he or she moves on to the next car and repeats the process; this all ends when either (1) the correct car is found or (2) the correct car is not in the line at all. This sequential process works just fine, although it can be very tedious. The server would have to do much more work if the desired car were at the end of the line, as opposed to the beginning. Remember, we are programming a computer: the server cannot simply "look" at all of the plates at once, like we would in real life. The computer does not know how to "look," unless we know how to write the program that enables it!

A code segment that performs a linear search for a number target in array of integers nums might look like this:

```
for (int i = 0; i < nums.length; i++)
    if (nums[i] == target)
        System.out.print("Found at " + i);
```

This segment will correctly traverse the array, searching for target, starting with index 0 and continuing to index length-1, as desired. Remember that nums. length is the size of the array and therefore nums[length] would be out of bounds. When target is found, the print statement displays its index number. This process will continue until the end of the array is reached. Note that, if target is never found, there will be no output.

When writing search algorithms and other structures that span entire arrays, programmers often implement the enhanced-for loop, which is designed specifically for spanning entire arrays. In cases in which spanning the ENTIRE array is not the intent or would cause a run-time error, the enhanced-for loop should not be used. Assuming nums from the previous example would not cause such a problem, the same code segment can be written as an enhanced-for loop structure like this:

```
for (int i: nums)
    if (nums[i] == target)
        System.out.print("Found at " + i);
```

Each time the loop iterates, i will be assigned the value of the next element in the array. This structure automatically ensures that i does not go out of bounds. Nice! Just remember that an enhanced for-loop (also known as for-each loop) is appropriate only for full arrays.

A binary search is much more efficient; think of it as a "divide-and-conquer" mechanism. Instead of our restaurant server starting with the beginning of the line of cars, he or she will start with the middle car. Depending on whether the license plate is "greater" than that car's or less, the server will move in the appropriate direction. (It is the programmer's decision to decide what "greater" or "lesser" means with respect to license plates.)

There is a huge obstacle with binary searches, however, or at least, for us with our current level of Java knowledge. Suppose the top 21 students in the senior class are lined up in a row. You are looking for a top 21 student named Kathy, whom you have never met, but you are not sure where she is in the line. If the students are not lined up in a particular order, a sequential search is your only option, and you might need all 21 tries to get to her if she is the last person. If they were sorted in alphabetical order by first name, though, you could divide and conquer. Go to the middle person and find out his or her name…if her name is Sara, you would move toward the front of the line and ignore the back. You then perform the same process, asking the name of the person halfway between the front of the line and Sara, and then ignore the appropriate side. Within a few tries, you will have Kathy.

Here is a code example of how a binary search might look for array nums when searching for target, assuming nums is sorted:

```java
int front = 0, back = nums.length - 1, middle = 0;
boolean isFound = false;
while((front <= back) && (!isFound))
{
    middle = (front + back) / 2;
    if (nums[middle] < target)
    {
        front = middle + 1;
    }
    else if(nums[middle] > target)
    {
        back = middle - 1;
    }
    else
    {
        isFound = true;
    }
}

if (isFound)
{
    System.out.println("Found at" + middle);
}
else
{
    System.out.println("Target Not Found");
}
```

On the AP Exam, you will not be required to WRITE a search algorithm; however, you will be required to RECOGNIZE a search algorithm and trace it, which can be done the easy way if you understand the algorithm, or the hard way by actually tracing the code, step by step. Try to identify the key characteristics of each search; for example, the "sum divided by 2" line is a good indicator of a binary search. The for-each loop will span the entire array, which may indicate a sequential search.

---

5. Which of the following statements is true, regarding search algorithms?

(A) Searching for a Twix in a row of unsorted candy is most efficient using a sequential search.

(B) Searching for a Twix in a row of unsorted candy is most efficient using a binary search.

(C) Searching for a Twix in a row of sorted candy is most efficient using a sequential search.

(D) Searching for a Twix in a row of sorted candy is most efficient using a binary search.

(E) None of these

Here's How to Crack It

Searching is usually more efficient using a binary search, provided the array is sorted. However, a binary search will require more than one comparison if the target is not in the middle, whereas a linear search will need only one comparison if the target is first in line. Therefore, each of the four situations presented in (A) through (D) could be the most efficient, depending on the position of the Twix. The answer is (E).

---

6. Assuming target is in array a, which of the following methods will correctly return the index of target in sorted array a ?

I.
```
public int findTarget(int[] a, int target)
{
for (int x = 0; x < a.length; x++)
  if (a[x] == target)
     return x;
}
```

II.
```
public int findTarget(int[] a, int target)
{
  for (int x: a)
  if (a[x] == target)
     return x;
  return -1;
}
```

III.
```
public int findTarget(int[] a, int target)
{
  int f = 0, h = a.length, g = 0;
  for (int i = 0; i < h; i++)
  {
     g = (f + h)/2;
     if (a[g] < target)
          f = g + 1;
     else if (a[g] > target)
          h = g - 1;
  }
  if (a[g] == target)
     return g;
  return -1;
  }
```

(A) I only
(B) II only
(C) I and II only
(D) II and III only
(E) I, II, and III

Here's How to Crack It

Notice that Options I and II look like linear searches, while III looks like a binary search. Option I will not compile because a non-void method must return data. An if statement without an else implies data may not be returned—even though the assumption states that will not occur—so the compiler will stop here. Eliminate (A), (C), and (E). Both (B) and (D) include Option II

Read Carefully!
This question is about a sorted array! Be sure you read the entire question carefully before you dive in.

so it must be correct; skip to Option III. Note that the variables are a bit confusing—but front/middle/back correspond to f/g/h, so they are in alphabetical order. Option III is a nice binary search and it avoids the return problem in Option I by returning −1 if target is not found, a common practice when writing search algorithms. Therefore, Options II and III are correct and (D) is the answer.

SORTS

Probably the most useful algorithms you will learn in this course are **sorting algorithms**—but they are also probably the most annoying to understand. If you've been keeping up, then you have a good start.

As the name implies, sort algorithms will take data in an array and rearrange it into a particular order. We already know that this technique is useful if we want to search for data using the binary search algorithm. But imagine this automated process in real life: a process that automatically sorts the cups in your cabinet in height order, a process that automatically takes your homework assignments and arranges them in time order, and a process that sorts your to-do list in priority order. Needless to say: sorting algorithms are extremely powerful.

The **selection sort** is the first sort algorithm we will discuss, and one of the three sorting algorithms you need to know for the AP Exam. This is a search-and-swap algorithm, and remember that the selection sort searches and swaps. Similar to a sequential search, the sort will first span the array for the lowest value. Once it finds the lowest value, it will swap its position in the array with the data at index 0. Now the first element is sorted. The process then repeats for index 1. The rest of the array will be searched for the lowest value and swapped with the data at index 1. Note that if the lowest value is already in position, it will stay there.

Consider the array below. We would like to sort this array from least to greatest.

8	6	10	2	4

Our strategy will be to first find the smallest element in the array, and put it in the first position. We will then find the smallest of the remaining elements and put that in the second position. We will continue to do this until the array is ordered.

We can start by looking at every element in the array (starting with the first element) and find the smallest element. It's easy for a person to quickly glance through the array and see which element is smallest, but the sorting algorithm that we will implement can compare only two elements at once. So here's how we can find the smallest element: take the number in the first cell in the array and assign it to a variable called smallestSoFar. We'll also assign the position of that value to a variable called position. In this case, smallestSoFar will equal 8 and position will be 0. Note that even though we are assigning 8 to smallestSoFar, the first cell of the array will contain 8; we didn't actually remove it.

Next we'll walk through the array and compare the next value to smallestSoFar. The next value is 6, which is less than 8, so smallestSoFar becomes 6 and position becomes 1.

```
smallestSoFar = 6;
position = 1;
```

8	6	10	2	4

Now let's look at the next value in the array. 10 is larger than 6, so smallestSoFar remains 6.

```
smallestSoFar = 6;
position = 1;
```

8	6	10	2	4

The next value in the array is 2. 2 is smaller than 6.

```
smallestSoFar = 2;
position = 3;
```

8	6	10	2	4

And finally we look at the last element, 4. Because 4 is greater than 2, and we are at the end of the array, we know that 2 is the smallest element.

```
smallestSoFar = 2;
position = 3;
```

8	6	10	2	4

Now we know that 2 is the smallest element in the array. Because we want to order the array from least to greatest, we need to put 2 in the first cell in the array. We don't simply want to overwrite the 8 that is in the first cell, though. What we'll do is swap the 2 with the 8 to get

2	6	10	8	4

We now have the smallest element in place. Next we'll need to find the second smallest element in the array. We can do this using the same approach we employed to find the smallest element. Because we know that 2 is the smallest element, we have to look at the elements only in positions 1 to 4 for the second smallest element.

Start by assigning 6 to smallestSoFar and 1 to position and then compare 6 to 10. Six is the smaller. Next, compare 6 to 8; 6 is still the smaller. Finally, compare 6 with 4. Four is smaller and because we have no more elements in the array, 4 must be the second smallest element in the array.

Swap 4 with the second element in the array to get

2	**4**	10	8	**6**

Make another pass through the array to find the third smallest element, and swap it into the third cell. The third smallest element is 6.

2	4	**6**	8	**10**

Finally, we look at the last two elements. Eight is smaller than 10, so we don't need to do anything. Our array is now sorted from least to greatest.

Implementation of a Selection Sort

Here is how a selection sort can be implemented in Java. The following implementation will sort the elements from least to greatest and will begin by sorting the smallest elements first.

```
//precondition: numbers is an array of ints
//postcondition: numbers is sorted in ascending order
1        public static void selectionSort1(int[] numbers)
2        {
3          for (int i = 0; i < numbers.length - 1; i++)
4          {
5            int position = i;
6            for (int k = i + 1; k < numbers.length; k++)
7            {
8               if (numbers[k] < numbers[position])
9               {
10                    position = k;
11              }
12           }
13           int temp = numbers[i];
14           numbers[i] = numbers[position];
15           numbers[position] = temp;
16         }
17       }
```

How could this be useful? Consider a case in which you have an unsorted array of 1,000 Student objects, and each Student object has a method that returns a grade-point average for that Student. What if you would like to find the five students with highest grade-point average? In this case, it would be a waste of time to sort the entire array. Instead, we can just run through five cycles of the second implementation of the selection sort shown above, and the top five students will be sorted.

The **insertion sort** is a little less intuitive. Rather than traversing the entire array, it compares the first two elements and depending on the comparison, inserts the second value "in front" of the first value into index 0, moving the first value to index 1. The first two elements are now sorted. Then the third element is checked, and the inserting continues. Note that here, also, an already-sorted element will remain in its position.

Below is an array with 9 elements. This array is sorted from least to greatest except for the last element.

2	3	5	8	11	14	17	22	15

We would like to move 15 so that the entire array is in order. First, we'll temporarily assign 15 to a variable. This will give us room to shift the other elements to the right if needed.

```
temp = 15
```

2	3	5	8	11	14	17	22	

We then compare 15 to the first element to its left: 22. Because 22 is larger than 15, we shift 22 to the right.

```
temp = 15
```

2	3	5	8	11	14	17	->	22

We then compare 15 to the next element: 17. Because 17 is larger, we shift that to the right also.

```
temp = 15
```

2	3	5	8	11	14	->	17	22

Next we compare 15 to 14. Because 15 is larger, we don't want to shift 14 to the right. Instead, we insert 15 into the empty cell in the array. Now the array is correctly sorted.

Insert 15

2	3	5	8	11	14	15	17	22

Now we'll look at how we can use the idea illustrated above to sort an entire array. This example will start at the beginning of the sorting process.

Here is the array that we are going to sort.

8	6	7	10

First, we'll look at just the first two elements of the array and make sure that they are sorted relative to each other.

8	6	7	10

To do this, we'll pull 6 (the number that is farthest to the right in our subarray) out of the array and temporarily assign it to a variable. We'll then compare 6 to 8. Because 8 is larger, shift 8 to the right and then put 6 in the cell where 8 was.

`temp = 6`

8 ->		7	10

Here's what the array looks like.

6	8	7	10

Now we need to put 7 in the proper place relative to 6 and 8. We start by assigning 7 temporarily to a variable.

`temp = 7`

6	8		10

We then compare 7 to the first number to its left: 8. Because 7 is less than 8, we shift 8 one place to the right.

`temp = 7`

6	->	8	10

Next, we'll compare 7 to the next number in the array: 6. Because 6 is less than 7, we don't want to shift 6 to the right. Instead, we will put 7 in the second cell. Our array now looks like the following:

6	7	8	10

Now we need to put 10 in its place relative to the first 3 elements in the array.

6	7	8	10

`temp = 10`

6	7	8	

First we compare 10 to 8; because 8 is smaller than 10, we don't need to shift 8 to the right. In fact, we can put 10 right back into the cell from which it came.

6	7	8	10

Implementation of an Insertion Sort

Here is how an insertion sort can be implemented in Java.

```
//precondition: x is an array of integers; x.length >= 0
//postcondition: x is sorted from least to greatest.
1   public static void insertionSort(int[] x)
2   {
3       for (int i = 1; i < x.length; i++)
4       {
5           int temp = x[i];
6           int j = i - 1;
7           while (j >= 0 && x[j] > temp)
8           {
9               x[j + 1] = x[j];
10              j--;
11          }
12          x[j + 1] = temp;
13      }
14  }
```

Note that like the selection sort, the insertion sort contains nested loops. In this case, we have a while loop nested within a for loop.

The for loop, beginning on line 3, proceeds from index 1 to the end of the array. The while loop goes through the array from i to 0 and shifts elements that are larger than temp to the right on line 9. On line 12, we put the value in temp into its proper place in the array.

Another type of sort used on the AP Exam is the **merge sort.** This is a more complex type that uses **recursion,** which is the technique of using a method to call itself. (Recursion will be further discussed in a later chapter.) A merge sort is like a divide-and-conquer. An array is split into two pieces. Each piece is sorted. The two sorted pieces are then merged together into one sorted list. In order to sort each of the two pieces, the same divide and conquer method is used.

Below is an array with 8 elements:

14	8	9	3	5	4	21	12

The merge sort will divide this array into two pieces:

14	8	9	3

5	4	21	12

Let's look at just the left half of the array. This array is divided in two pieces:

14	8

9	3

Each of these pieces is similarly divided into two pieces:

14

8

9

3

Since each remaining piece contains only one element, simply order the two from left to right:

8	14

3	9

Now merge the two sorted segments. Compare the first element in each piece. The smaller is 3, so this is the first element of the merged array. Now compare the first element in each piece that hasn't already been copied. These are 8 and 9. The smaller is 8, so this is the second element of the merged array. Again, compare the first element in each piece that hasn't already been copied. These are 14 and 9. The smaller is 9, so this is the third element of the merged array. Since the second array has no remaining elements that haven't already been copied, add the remaining element(s) on the first array into the merged array. The only remaining element is 14, so this is the fourth element:

3	8	9	14

Follow a similar process for the first array. Divide in two pieces:

5	4

21	12

Each of these pieces is similarly divided into two pieces:

5		4		21		12

Since each remaining piece contains only one element, simply order the two from left to right:

4	5

12	21

Now merge the two sorted segments. Compare the first element in each piece. The smaller is 4, so this is the first element of the merged array. Now compare the first element in each piece that hasn't already been copied. These are 5 and 12. The smaller is 5, so this is the second element of the merged array. Since the first array has no remaining elements that haven't already been copied, add the remaining elements from the second array into the merged array. The remaining elements, 12 and 21, become the third and fourth element of the merge array:

4	5	12	21

Thus, the two sorted pieces of the original array look like this:

3	8	9	14

4	5	12	21

Merge the two sorted arrays. Compare 3 and 4 to get that the first element is 3. Compare 8 and 4 to get that the second element is 4. Compare 8 and 5 to get that the third element is 5. Compare 8 and 12 to get that the fourth element is 8.

Compare 9 and 12 to get that the fifth element is 9. Compare 14 and 12 to get that the sixth element is 12. Compare 14 and 21 to get that the seventh element is 14. Since the first array has no uncopied elements, 21, which is the only remaining uncopied element on the second array, becomes the eighth element of the merged array. Below is the final array:

3	4	5	8	9	12	14	21

Implementation of a Merge Sort

Here's how a merge sort can be implemented in Java.

```
//precondition: x is an array in integers; x.length >= 0
//postcondition: x is sorted from least to greatest
1   public static void mergeSort (int[] x)
2   {
3       int[] temp = new int[x.length];
4       mergeSortHelper(x, 0, x.length - 1, temp);
5   }
6   public static void mergeSortHelper (int[] x, int low-
    Index, int highIndex, int temp)
7   {
8       if (lowIndex < highIndex)
9       {
10          int mid = (lowIndex + highIndex) / 2;
11          mergeSortHelper(x, lowIndex, mid, temp);
12          mergeSortHelper(x, mid + 1, highIndex, temp);
13          merge(x, lowIndex, mid, highIndex, temp);
14      }
15  }
16  public static void merge(int[] x, int lowIndex, int
    mid, int highIndex, temp)
17  {
18      int l = lowIndex;
19      int m = mid + 1;
20      int n = highIndex;
21      while (l <= mid && m <= highIndex)
22      {
23          if (x[l] < x[m])
24          {
25              temp[n] = x[l]
26              l++;
27          }
28          else
29          {
30              temp[n] = x[m];
31              m++;
32          }
33      n++;
34      }
35      while (l <= mid)
36      {
37          temp[n] = x[l];
38          l++;
39          n++;
40      }
```

```
41      while (m <= highIndex)
42      {
43          temp[n] = x[m];
44          m++;
45          n++;
46      }
47      for (n = lowIndex; n <= highIndex; n++)
48      {
49          x[n] = temp[k];
50      }
51  }
```

This is clearly a more complex sort than the other two and involves the use of multiple methods. The first method splits the array into two pieces, the second sorts the individual pieces, and the third merges the two pieces into one sorted array.

LISTS & ARRAYLISTS

There are two big limitations of the powerful array structure in Java: an array has a fixed length and it can store only one type of data. If you wanted to represent, say, a friend's collection of action figures, an array would require all of the action figures to be the same type. Generally speaking, they must *all* be flying superheroes, or they must *all* have protective body armor, etc.

Likewise, a collection of action figures represented as an array could store only a fixed number of action figures, no more and no less. If there are extra, unused slots, they stay there, which could be problematic if you have an array of helmeted heroes and you try to remove the helmet from every element in every index of the array. Once you reach the first empty spot, there is no hero and therefore no helmet, so the directions do not make sense; in Java, the compiler will return a `NullPointerException` for this situation.

> There are advantages and disadvantages to every structure that we study in Java.

An ArrayList addresses both of these issues. An ***ArrayList* object** is **dynamically sized**, expanding and compressing as elements are added and removed. An ArrayList can also store multiple types of data, without limit.

Let's use an example to understand the advantages and disadvantages of arrays versus ArrayLists. Consider your lunch bag that you take to school. If you wanted to represent your lunch bag using an array or ArrayList structure, which would be more accurate?

Naturally, the answer to this question depends on (1) the details of the objects in the bag—in this case, the types of lunch items—and (2) the programmer's choice of which is more appropriate. If your lunch contains a sandwich object, a fruit object, and a drink object, the ArrayList structure might be a better choice. Furthermore, as the components of the lunch are removed, the lunch bag theoretically shrinks (or can shrink). An ArrayList seems appropriate.

Let's consider the same lunch example, but this time, suppose the items are stored in a plastic container with compartments. Regardless of whether you have not yet eaten your lunch or you are done with your lunch, or anytime in between, the number and setup of the compartments do not change. We will discuss a workaround for "tricking" the array to think the lunch objects are all the same type. These facts and abilities render an array structure more appropriate, versus an ArrayList.

To further demonstrate the usefulness of an ArrayList structure, it is also possible to create a **typed ArrayList** which allows only objects of the same type to be stored in the list. This structure combines useful aspects of both arrays and ArrayLists.

In order to instantiate an ArrayList called lunchBag that will store the various components of our lunch, we use the following line of code:

```
ArrayList lunchBag = new ArrayList();
```

Note that, unlike the syntax we use for instantiating an array, neither the type of object nor the length of the list is defined initially.

In order to access data from within the list, particular methods must be invoked; unlike array structures in Java, there is not a convenient bracket notation available with lists. To return the second object, an Apple object, in the ArrayList and store it using the variable food, the line of code would be

```
Apple red = lunchBag.get (1);
```

There are several other useful methods available in the List class, and they are all mentioned in the AP Exam Quick Reference, although their functionality is (obviously) not given. These methods include add, set, remove, and size.

Bracket notation can be used only with array objects; lists must use the appropriate methods.

If the programmer decides it is more appropriate to keep the dynamic sizing ability of the ArrayList while fixing the type of data it can hold (just like an array), it would be instantiated as follows:

```
ArrayList<Apple> lunchBag = new ArrayList<Apple>();
```

One of the drawbacks of using ArrayList is that only objects can be stored in an ArrayList. The primitive data types int and double cannot be stored in ArrayLists. If a programmer wants to store integer and double data types, he or she must use the Integer or Double wrapper classes. Integer and Double objects can be created using integers and doubles, respectively, as parameters. For example,

```
Integer n = new Integer(5);
Double x = new Double(6.1);
```

To call the values, use the intValue() and doubleValue() methods. The following commands

```
int a = n.intValue();
int y = x.doubleValue();
```

assign a = 5 and y = 6.1.

Additionally, the AP Computer Science Java Subset includes the static variables MIN_VALUE and MAX_VALUE of the Integer class. These store the minimum and maximum possible values of the integer data type.

KEY TERMS

sequential search
binary search
search algorithms
sorting algorithms
selection sort
insertion sort
merge sort
recursion
ArrayList object
dynamically sized
typed ArrayList

Chapter 10
2D Arrays

2D ARRAYS

Two-dimensional, or 2D, arrays are structures that have entered, exited, and re-entered the required topics for the AP Exam. They are quite powerful and, at the same time, not too difficult to understand once you have mastered 1D array structures, which we studied in previous sections.

A great example of a 2D array is a stand-up soda machine, like you see in the mall or in front of the supermarket. You know the type, the one in which you drop money and hope desperately that the soda actually drops out.

Think of the soda machine as a set of **rows** across the machine, each having a different type of soda (let's say that the first row has cola, second has orange, etc.). Each of those rows can be considered as an array. Now consider the vertical **columns** down the machine; each column will have one of each type of soda, since it travels down the rows (first item is cola, second item is orange, etc.). *That* vertical column can also be considered as an array. The result is an "array of arrays," which Java quantifies as a 2D array, with index numbers assigned independently to each row and column location.

In the soda machine example, the very first cola in the upper left location of the 2D "array" would be located at index 0 of the first horizontal array, as well as index 0 of the first vertical array. The code to access this element (soda) in a 2D array (soda machine) already instantiated as `sodaMachine` would be `sodaMachine[0][0]`, with the first 0 being the row and the second 0 being the column. The second cola would be located at [0, 1], and the first orange would be located at [1, 0], and so on. For an m by n 2D array, with m being the number of rows and n being the number of columns, the last element in the lower right corner would be located at [m-1, n-1]. But you didn't forget that index numbers begin at 0 and end at (`array.length-1`), did you?

The methods and constants available for use with array structures are available for 2D array structures as well, because a 2D array is an array—just a fancy one. It's a little tricky, however; in order to, say, return the number of cola slots across the soda machine, you would use `sodaMachine.length`, as expected. In order to access the number of slots down the left side of the machine, however, you would use `sodaMachine[0].length`, meaning you want the length of the first column of the 2D array.

7. Consider the following code segment:

```
int[][] num = new int [4][4];
for (int i = 0; i < num.length; i++)
{
    for (int k = 0; k < num.length; k++)
    {
        num[i][k] = i * k;
    }
}
```

What are the contents of num after the code segment has executed?

(A) 0 0 0 0
     0 1 2 3
     0 2 4 6
     0 3 6 9

(B) 0 1 2 3
     1 2 3 4
     2 3 4 5
     3 4 5 6

(C) 0 3 6 9
     0 2 4 6
     0 1 2 3
     0 0 0 0

(D) 1 1 1 1
     2 2 2 2
     3 3 3 3
     4 4 4 4

(E) 0 0 0 0
     1 2 3 4
     2 4 6 8
     3 6 9 12

Here's How To Crack It

2D array questions are always intimidating. The first iteration of the outer loop will occur with `i = 0`. Looking at the inner loop, the `k` values will range from 0 to 3 before it terminates. Since `i = 0` and each iteration of the inner loop will multiply `i` by `k`, the first row of the array will be all zeroes. Eliminate (B), (C), and (D). Wow! Once that finishes, the outer loop will have its second iteration with `i = 1`. The inner loop will then start over with `k = 0`, and `i` times `k` will equal zero, as a result. The first number in the second row, then, will be 0. Eliminate (E) because its first number in the second row is 1, and the answer is (A).

Remember that an array, regardless of its dimensions, can store any one type of data, but not multiple types. Also remember that, as is true for most computer programming language rules, there is always a workaround! More on this later.

Chapter 11
Inheritance

Inheritance is the quintessential way—and the only way, for our purposes—to create direct relationships between classes. An **inheritance hierarchy** is designed in order to quantify this relationship, much like a family tree, and it defines the "parent" class and all of its "child" classes. A carefully designed hierarchy implemented as an inheritance relationship between classes is arguably the most powerful programming technique that you will learn in this course.

HIERARCHIES & DESIGN

The designing of the hierarchy is critical in implementing inheritance. As the programmer, you have limitless ways to design a hierarchy, so the importance of the planning process cannot be understated.

The first decision for the programmer/designer—yes, there are programmers who focus solely on *design*—is to define the parent class of the situation. Typically the parent class (**superclass**) is the most general form of the objects that will be instantiated in the overall program. Every other class in the program will lie lower in the hierarchy (**subclasses** of the superclass), but their objects will be more specific versions of the overall parent. This setup creates an *IS-A* relationship between the parent and the child classes.

Let's use potato chips as our example for this discussion (everyone loves food, right? If you don't, you should have realized that you won't like this book by now). If we are designing a hierarchy of classes to properly represent potato chips, there are a ridiculous number of possibilities—would the parent class be `PotatoChip`? `Potato`? `Snack`? `SaltySnack`? `JunkFood`? So we have to make a decision, based on the situation that we are given; if the programmer receives no context whatsoever, the design is very difficult and will produce unpredictable—yet all viable—results.

In this case, let's use `Snack` as the superclass. A `Snack` object is very general; there may be many subclasses in our situation. Let's define two subclasses for Snack, one for our purposes and an extra for practice: `PotatoChip` and `Cookie`. Since a potato chip (and a cookie) is a snack, the setup makes intuitive sense. Note how we define the relationship from the bottom (lowest subclasses) of the hierarchy to the top (highest superclass). Let us then define another, lower set of classes that will be subclasses of `PotatoChip`: `BBQChip` and `OnionChip`.

A visual representation of a hierarchy makes the design much easier to understand:

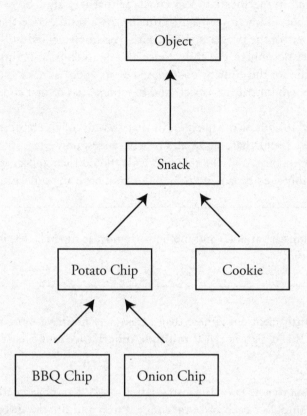

As you can see, there are several IS-A relationships here. A `BBQChip` IS-A `PotatoChip`, which IS-A `Snack`. A `BBQChip` also IS-A `Snack`, by inheritance. All of these relationships as designed in the hierarchy should make intuitive sense and/or conform to the given specifications.

> On the AP Exam, at least one FRQ and at least several MCQs typically focus on the design and/or implementation of inheritance relationships. Detailed specifications will be given in order to suppress the variety of exam responses to score.

Let's discuss the benefits of the setup we have created. When the programmer is ready to implement code, he or she should decide which variables and methods should be implemented, as well as their locations within the hierarchy. These variables and methods have a HAS-A relationship with the class to which they belong. This task is more formidable than it might seem; very general variables and methods should be closer to the top of the hierarchy, while more specifics should reside in lower subclasses. For example, virtually every snack food has some kind of flavor. Therefore, code to address the flavor of the snack food should be implemented in `Snack`, and it will be subsequently inherited by all of the subclasses …Since a `Snack` object HAS-A flavor, and a `PotatoChip` object IS-A `Snack`, a `PotatoChip` object also HAS-A flavor. What about an `OnionChip` object? It also HAS-A flavor, as described above.

Now consider code that addresses the crunch of an object in the hierarchy. Without any detail in specification, let's conclude that it is arguable whether a cookie is crunchy, but all potato chips are crunchy. As a result, code that addresses the crunchy aspect of the program should NOT be implemented in `Snack`; that way `Cookie` does not inherit the code. Since all potato chips are crunchy, the appropriate location for the crunchy code would be in `PotatoChip`, and `BBQChip` and `OnionChip` will inherit the aspects and functionalities of that code.

If we wanted to address the spiciness (is that a word?) of an object in our hierarchy, we might determine that, out of all of these classes, only the `BBQChip` has a spice factor worth quantifying. The spiciness code should then appear in `BBQChip` and will not be inherited because `BBQChip` does not have any subclasses.

> Classes inherit variables and methods from their superclasses, not the other way around.

It is also worth mentioning here that a class may not have more than one direct superclass. This design is called **multiple inheritance** and it is NOT allowed in Java.

It is important to note here that instantiating a `BBQChip` object with automatically instantiate an object each of both `PotatoChip` and Snack. In order for this to occur correctly, however, Java requires us to address their instantiation explicitly (this of this requirement as respecting the *PotatoChip*). Therefore, the constructor the `BBQChip` must first make a call to super(), which invokes the constructor of `PotatoChip`, its superclass. If the super constructor requires (a) parameter(s), then the super() call must include those parameters as well. Java will otherwise invoke super() on its own, often resulting in undesired results (broken chips?) and an easily-avoided missed point on an FRQ. As a rule, all classes in Java will instantiate the Object class, which is the ultimate generalization—think, if I look around the room right now, what isn't an object??

Consider the following class:

```java
public class College extends School
{
      // private data fields not shown

      // the only constructor in this class
      public College (String town, double tuition)
      {
          // code not shown
      }

      // other methods not shown
}
```

In order to write LawAcademy, a subclass of College, which of the following constructors is valid?

I.
```
public LawAcademy (String twn, double tuit)
{
    super.College(twn, tuit);
}
```

II.
```
public LawAcademy (String twn, double tuit)
{
    super(twn, tuit);
}
```

III.
```
public LawAcademy (String twn, double tuit, String st)
{
    super(st, tuit);
}
```

(A) II only

(B) I and II only

(C) I and III only

(D) II and III only

(E) I, II, and III

Here's How to Crack It:

The final answer is (D) but let's start with eliminations. This one has an easy eliminator—I—and a tempting eliminator—III. Super.College is not a valid reference, since the super-dot operator is different from the super() method. II is a typical way to handle the situation and so is fine. III brings in the extra parameter, which ends up being used as the first parameter (the String one) in the super call, rendering twn not used, but that doesn't matter. As long as the super constructor is called correctly, we are good. So (D) is the correct answer.

Let's tackle another.

Consider a class Recliner that extends a Chair class. Assuming both classes each have a no-parameter constructor, which of the following statements is not valid?

(A) Object a = new Recliner();

(B) Recliner b = new Chair();

(C) Chair c = new Chair();

(D) Chair d = new Recliner();

(E) All of the above choices are valid.

Here's How to Crack It

This question enforces the idea of creating references using hierarchies. According to the question, a Recliner is a Chair, not the other way around. Likewise any Java object is an Object. It is valid to declare a variable's type to be more generic than its referenced object, but not the other way around. Therefore, (B) is the only choice that breaks this rule; a Recliner is a Chair, not the other way around, as would be the only valid way to relate these two classes when declaring a variable. The correct answer is (B).

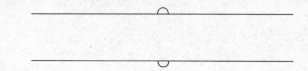

1. Consider the following two classes:

```
public class A
{
    public int method1(int x)
    {
        return 2;
    }
}
public class B extends A
{ /* code not shown */ }
```

Which of the following could be the signature of a method in class B that correctly overloads method1 in class A ?

(A) `public int method1(String x)`
(B) `public int method1(int y)`
(C) `private int method1(int x)`
(D) `public int method2(String x)`
(E) `public int method2(int y)`

Here's How to Crack It

Overloading a method means to create a new method with the same name, visibility, and return type, regardless of whether the method lies in the parent class or the child class. The parameter must be different, however, or the new method overrides the original method. Choice (B) will override `method1`, (C), (D), and (E) will create all new methods that are independent of `method1`, and (C) does not have the same visibility as `method1`. The answer is (A).

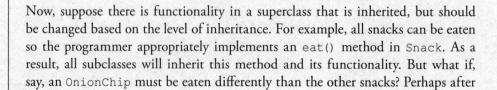

Now, suppose there is functionality in a superclass that is inherited, but should be changed based on the level of inheritance. For example, all snacks can be eaten so the programmer appropriately implements an `eat()` method in `Snack`. As a result, all subclasses will inherit this method and its functionality. But what if, say, an `OnionChip` must be eaten differently than the other snacks? Perhaps after a few chips, the "eater" would have to wipe his or her hands before he or she keeps eating. The desired `eat()` method—possessing the identical name, parameters, and return type—would be implemented in `OnionChip` and all objects of that class (and only that class, in this example) would use this new `eat()` method. The superclass's eat method has been **overridden** by this new version. The workaround for this situation would be to use the **super keyword**: `super.eat()`.

Though no longer part of the official Course Description as of fall 2019, it's pretty cool to know that another level of overriding involves method **abstraction**. Suppose that the programmer wants to force all subclasses to have the `eat()` method, but he or she decides that an `eat()` method's code in `Snack` is inappropriate; for example, all `Snack` objects can be eaten but the WAY they are eaten depends so much on the type of snack that superclass code for the method seems inappropriate. You would not eat a chip the same way you would eat a cookie, would you? Go with it. The `eat()` method can be declared abstract; in this design, the `Snack` class has now mandated every subclass to either (1) override the abstract method with code or (2) declare the method abstract once again, forcing its subclasses to override the abstract method.

2. Consider the following two classes:

```
public class Parent
{
    public void writeMe(String s)
    {
        System.out.println("Object");
    }
}
public class Child extends Parent
{
    public void writeMe(String s)
    {
        System.out.println("Object");
    }
}
```

Which of the following best describes the `writeMe` method of the `Child` class?

(A) An inherited method
(B) An overridden method
(C) An overloaded method
(D) An interface method
(E) An abstract method

Here's How to Crack It

Since the `writeMe` method in `Child` has the same name, return type, and parameter types, it is overriding `writeMe` in `Parent`. The answer is (B).

POLYMORPHISM

Polymorphism is a technique that, in a way, breaks all of the rules we think would happen in inheritance—and yet, it conforms to them at the same time.

Using our `Snack` example from above, including the overridden method in `OnionChip`, suppose several objects from various levels in the hierarchy reside in an untyped `ArrayList`. The programmer would like to, using a simple loop, simulate the user "eating" the chips in the list, regardless of their type. The loop will iterate through the list and automatically invoke the appropriate `eat()` method, including the overriden method for `OnionChip` objects, as desired. This is an example of polymorphism.

The word *polymorphism,* which means "many forms," can also apply to programs in a more profound manner. This process directly or indirectly involves virtually every technique we have learned in this book.

Suppose an interface called `Eatable` is implemented by all of the classes in the `Snack` hierarchy. Every class has either overriden the abstract methods from the interface, as normally required, or passed on the abstraction to a subclass.

Have you ever seen those snack bags that have multiple forms of snacks (for example, potato chips AND pretzels AND nacho chips…) in them? This example is similar; if you instantiated the "bag" as either a typed ArrayList or an array, you could fill the structure with instances of all of these classes by declaring the type as `Eatable`. Once the `eat()` method is invoked on all of the components of the list structure using a loop, each object will automatically invoke its corresponding eat method! Pretty awesome.

Use the information below to answer Questions 3 and 4.

————————◯————————

Consider the following declaration for a class that will be used to represent a rectangle:

```
public class Rectangle
{
    private double width;
    private double height;
    public Rectangle()
    {
        width = 0;
        height = 0;
    }
    public Rectangle(double w, double h)
    {
        width = w;
        height = h;
    }

    // postcondition: returns the height
    public double getHeight()
    {
        return height;
    }

    // postcondition: returns the width
    public double getWidth()
    {
        return width;
    }
}
```

The following incomplete class declaration is intended to extend the above class so the rectangles can be filled with a color when displayed:

```
public class FilledRectangle extends Rectangle
{
    private String color;
    // constructors go here

    public String getColor()
    {
       return color;
    }
}
```

Consider the following proposed constructors for this class:

```
I.   public FilledRectangle()
     {
         color = "red";
     }
```

```
II.  public FilledRectangle(double w, double h, String c)
     {
         super (w, h);
         color = c;
     }
```

```
III. public FilledRectangle(double w, double h, String c)
     {
         width = w;
         height = h;
         color = c;
     }
```

3. Which of these constructors would be legal for the FilledRectangle class?

(A) I only
(B) II only
(C) III only
(D) I and II
(E) I and III

Here's How to Crack It

This is an interesting one. Constructor II follows all of the rules nicely, invoking the super constructor and initializing the data field in its class, so Constructor II is good; eliminate (A), (C), and (E). Note that we do not have to check Constructor III now. For Constructor I, remember that the superclass's default constructor (the one with no parameters) will be invoked automatically if it is not called. Therefore, Constructor I is fine. Only one answer choice remains, so there is no need to continue. However, to see why Constructor III does not work, note that the variables width and height are private variables in Rectangle and, therefore, not inherited by FilledRectangle. Therefore, this will not compile. The answer is (D).

4. Based on the class declarations for Rectangle and FilledRectangle given above, which of the following code segments would be legal in a client class? Assume that the constructor that takes no arguments has been implemented for FilledRectangle.

I. ```
    FilledRectangle r1 = new Rectangle();
    double height = r1.getHeight();
    ```
II. ```
    Rectangle r2 = new FilledRectangle();
    double height = r2.getHeight();
    ```
III. ```
    Rectangle r3 = new FilledRectangle()
    r3.getColor();
    ```

Which of the code segments above are legal?

(A) None
(B) II only
(C) III only
(D) I and II
(E) II and III

## Here's How to Crack It

Since Segment II appears in the most answer choices, let's check that option first. A `FilledRectangle` may be declared as a `Rectangle` because it is a subclass of Rectangle, and a `FilledRectangle` inherits `getHeight` from `Rectangle` as well, so Segment II is legal; eliminate (A) and (C). A `Rectangle` cannot be declared as a `FilledRectangle` for the same reason, so Segment I is illegal and (D) can be eliminated. As for Segment III, a `Rectangle` object can invoke methods only from `Rectangle` (regardless of r3's identity as a `FilledRectangle`), so the second line is illegal. The answer is (B).
    ```

5. Consider the following class:

```
public class Cat
{
    private String name;
    private int age;

    public Cat(String name, int age){
        this.name = name;
        this.age = age;
    }
    public String toString()
    {
        return (name + ": " + age);
    }
}
```

Suppose another class were to include the following code segment:

```
Cat c = new Cat("Billi", 5);
System.out.println(c);
```

Which of the following will be the output of the code segment?

(A) c
(B) 5
(C) Billi
(D) Billi: 5
(E) There would be no output.

Here's How to Crack It

The first line of the code segment creates a `Cat` object with name initialized as `Billi` and age initialized as 5. The second line prints the `Cat` object c. When an object is used as the parameter to a print, the `toString` method of the `Object` class is called. In this case, however, that method is overridden by the `toString` method of the `Cat` class. This method returns the name of the `Cat`, concatenated with ":", concatenated with the `age` of the cat. Therefore, it prints `Billi: 5`, which is (D).

CHAPTER 11 REVIEW DRILL

Answers to the review questions can be found in Chapter 13.

1. Consider the following two classes:

```
public class Parent
{
    public void writeMe(String s)
    {
        System.out.println("object");
    }
}

public class Child extends Parent
{
    public void writeMe(String s)
    {
        System.out.println("object");
    }
}
```

Which of the following best describes the writeMe method of the Child class?

(A) An inherited method
(B) An overridden method
(C) An overloaded method
(D) An interface method
(E) An abstract method

2. How many classes can a given class extend?

(A) None
(B) 1
(C) 2
(D) As many as it needs to

3. Consider the following class:

```
public class Sample
{
    int var = 0;

    public static void writeMe(String string)
    {
        System.out.println("string");
    }
}
```

What is the result of executing the following?

```
Sample.writeMe("hello");
```

(A) This is not a legal call because there is no instance variable.
(B) "hello"
(C) "null"
(D) "string"
(E) Run-time error

4. Consider the following class:

```
public class Sample
{
    int static final var = 0;
}
```

What is the result of executing the following?

```
System.out.println(Sample.var);
```

(A) This is not a legal call because there is no instance variable.
(B) −1
(C) 0
(D) The value is unknowable.
(E) This is not a legal call because var is final.

For questions 5–6, consider the following class:

```
public class Sample
{
    String name;

    public Sample (String in)
    {
        name = in;
    }

    public void writeMe(String s)
    {
        String val = null;

        if (val.equals(s))
        {
            System.out.println("me");
        }
        else
        {
            System.out.println("you");
        }
    }
}
```

5. What will be the result of executing the following?

```
Sample s = new Sample( );
String tmp = new String("hi");
s.writeMe(tmp);
```

(A) Compile-time error
(B) Run-time error
(C) "hi"
(D) "string"
(E) "Sample"

6. What will be the result of executing the following?

```
Sample s = new Sample("sample");
String tmp = new String("hi");
s.writeMe(tmp);
```

(A) "hi"
(B) Run-time error
(C) "me"
(D) "sample"
(E) "you"

7. An apartment rental company has asked you to write a program to store information about the apartments that it has available for rent. For each apartment, they want to keep track of the following information: number of rooms, whether or not the apartment has a dishwasher, and whether or not pets are allowed. Which of the following is the best design?

(A) Use four unrelated classes: `Apartment`, `Rooms`, `Dishwasher`, and `Pets`.

(B) Use one class, `Apartment`, which has three subclasses: `Room`, `Dishwasher`, and `Pet`.

(C) Use one class, `Apartment`, which has three data fields: `int rooms`, `boolean hasDishwasher`, `boolean allowsPets`.

(D) Use three classes—`Pets`, `Rooms`, and `Dishwasher`—each with a subclass `Apartment`.

(E) Use four classes: `Apartment`, `Pets`, `Dishwasher`, and `Rooms`. The class `Apartment` contains instances of the other classes as attributes.

8. Consider the following class declarations:

```
public class Vehicle
{
    private int maxPassengers;
    public Vehicle( )
    {
        maxPassengers = 1;
    }
    public Vehicle(int x)
    {
        maxPassengers = x;
    }
    public int maxPassengers( )
    {
        return maxPassengers;
    }
}
public class Motorcycle extends Vehicle
{
    public Motorcycle( )
    {
        super(2);
    }
}
```

Which of the following code segments will NOT cause a compilation error?

(A) `Motorcycle m1 = new Motorcycle(3);`

(B) `Vehicle v1 = new Motorcycle(4);`

(C) `Motorcycle m2 = new Vehicle( );`

(D) `Vehicle v2 = new Motorcycle( );`

(E) `Vehicle v3 = new Vehicle( );`
`    int max = v3.maxPassengers;`

Summary

o   A subclass inherits from a superclass. A superclass is the most general form of an object. Subclasses are more specific types of the superclass.

o   A superclass can have more than one subclass, but a subclass can have only one superclass.

o   Subclasses inherit methods and variables from superclasses but can override these methods and variables.

o   The reserved word `super` can be used to call an overridden method or variable.

o   An object of a subclass is also an object of its superclass.

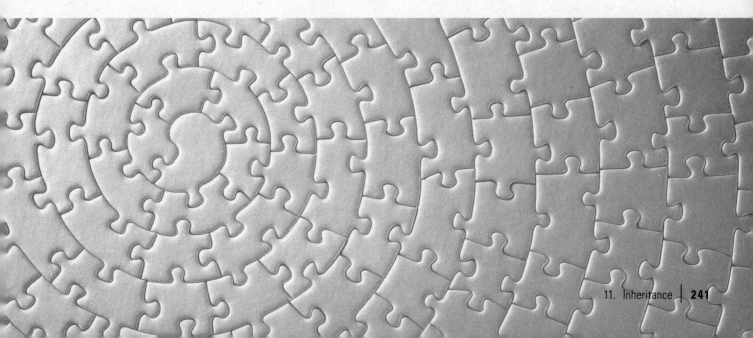

KEY TERMS

inheritance
inheritance hierarchy
superclass
subclass
multiple inheritance
override (overridden)
super keyword
abstraction
polymorphism

Chapter 12
Recursion

RECURSION

The final flow control structure that appears on the AP Exam is called **recursion**. It is not represented in the FRQs and appears at least once in the MCQs, but typically just a few times. This structure has a result similar to a loop, but approaches the task in a different manner.

Remember those little wind-up toys you played with when you were little? You know, the plastic teeth or bunny (or whatever) with the little white knob on the side? You would wind the knob over and over, and when you let go, the little teeth would walk across the table. The more you wound the knob, the longer the teeth would walk. Since the winding is the same action repeated, it can be considered a loop. The UNWINDING action, however, differentiates this situation from a while or for loop. When an unwinding or "winding down" occurs as a result of a "winding up," recursion is lurking in the shadows.

The distinguishing characteristic of a recursive method is a call to the very method itself; this statement is called a **recursive call**. In order to prevent an infinite loop, the recursive method includes a **base case**, which signals execution to stop recursing and return to each prior recursive call, finishing the job for each. Let's use an easy example to illustrate this somewhat confusing topic, and then we'll spice up the example a bit afterward.

Suppose you have a giant bag of small, multicolored, candy-coated chocolates. As a programmer, you naturally do not want to eat these candies in a haphazard manner; instead, you want to use some sort of algorithm. You decide that you will eat random candies, one at a time, until you reach your favorite color; when your favorite color is reached, you will systematically eat the same colors you ate previously, in backward order.

For example, if you eat red -> blue -> orange -> blue -> green, and green is your base case, you will then eat blue -> orange -> blue -> red and the recursion is complete. Pretty tough to remember, right? Well, a recursive method renders this task a cinch. In pseudocode,

```
eatCandy (color of current candy)
{
    if (current candy color is green)
        done eating;
    else
        eat more candy;
}
```

Although there is no for or while loop in the code, the recursive call to the method will exhibit a looping quality; unlike our previous loops, however, there is a forward/backward progression, as described above.

Let's add to this task: tell the user that you're done eating once you finish. Would adding the following line after the if-else statement accomplish this task?:

```
display I'm done;
```

The way recursion works, the task will be accomplished, although perhaps not according to plan. When the base case is reached, execution of the current method is completed, and then the process continues all the way back to the initial recursive call. Since the "I'm done" message is displayed after, and regardless of, the if/else, it will be displayed each time a recursive iteration completes. The result is the displaying of "I'm done" once for every candy that you ate. Ten candies, ten "I'm done" outputs. It works, but probably not as planned.

———————○———————

1. Consider the following method:

```
// precondition: x >= 0
public int mystery (int x)
{
    if (x == 0)
    {
        return 0;
    }
    else
    {
        return ((x % 10) + mystery (x / 10));
    }
}
```

Which of the following is returned as a result of the call mystery(3543)?

(A) 10
(B) 15
(C) 22
(D) 180
(E) Nothing is returned due to infinite recursion.

Here's How to Crack It

We hate these questions! But here we go, anyway. Eliminate (E) right away because there is a base case. Go through the recursion a few times and you will see that 3543 quickly loses digits because the method returns the sum of the units digit and the other digits. The units digit will be less than 10 and the recursion will occur 4 times, chopping off a digit each time and adding it to the overall sum. Therefore, the result will be 3 + 5 + 4 + 3 = 15. The answer is (B).

———————○———————

RECURSIVELY TRAVERSING ARRAYS

Although it is more common to use a for loop to step through an array, it is also possible to use a recursion. For example, say you have a lineup of football players, each of whom has a numbered helmet. You want to step through the lineup, and find the position of the person who has "9" written on his helmet:

A recursive solution for this problem is very easy to implement. You need to look through an array of int values and find the position of a specific value, if it's there.

First, we'll need to describe the problem in recursive terms.

- If we've looked through every item, then return −1.
- If the current item in the array is a match, return its position.
- Or else, restart the process with the next item in the array.

```java
public int findPosition
    (int nums[], int key, int currentIndex)
{
    //if we've already looked through
    //the entire array
    if (nums.length <= currentIndex)
        return -1;
    //if the next item in the array is match,
    //then return it
    if (nums[currentIndex] == key)
        return currentIndex;
    //else, step past the current item in the array,
    //and repeat the search on the next item
    return findPosition(nums, key, currentIndex + 1);
}
```

This example is slightly more subtle than the others because we're carrying information from one recursive call to the next. Specifically, we're using the currentIndex field to pass state information from one recursive call to another. Thus, the first recursive call starts looking at position 0, the next one at position 1, and so on.

Let's go back to our football-player example. You want to step through a lineup of football players and return the position of the player who has the helmet with "9" written on it. Your code would be of the following form:

```
int [] players = //represents the football players
int pos = findPosition(players, 9, 0);
```

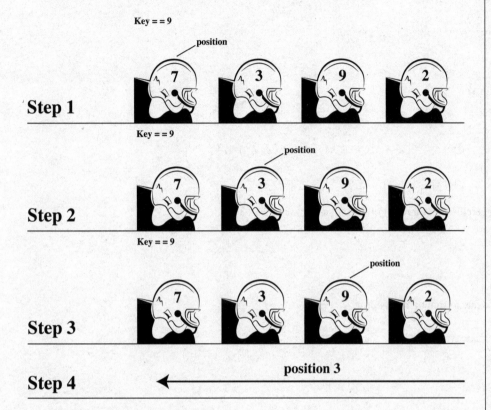

Study Break
Congratulations! You just tackled all of your AP Computer Science A content review! Take a study break, go for a walk, crank up some music, or eat your favorite snack.

CHAPTER 12 REVIEW DRILL

Answers to the review questions can be found in Chapter 13.

1. Consider the following method:

```
// precondition: x >= 0
public int mystery(int x)
{
        if (x == 0)
        {
            return 0;
        }
        else
        {
                return ((x % 10) + mystery(x / 10));
        }
}
```

Which of the following is returned as a result of the call `mystery(3543)`?

(A) 10

(B) 15

(C) 22

(D) 180

(E) Nothing is returned due to infinite recursion.

2. Consider the following recursive method:

```
public int mystery(int x)
{
    if (x == 1)
        return 2;
    else
        return 2 * mystery(x - 1);
}
```

What value is returned as a result of the call `mystery(6)`?

(A) 2

(B) 12

(C) 32

(D) 64

(E) 128

3. Consider the following recursive method:

```
public static int mystery(int x)
{
    if (x == 0)
    {
        return 0;
    }
    else
    {
        return (x + mystery(x / 2) + mystery(x / 4));
    }
}
```

What value is returned as a result of a call to mystery(10)?

(A) 10
(B) 12
(C) 20
(D) 22
(E) 35

4. Consider the following nonrecursive method:

```
//precondition: x >= 0
public static int mystery(int x)
{
    int sum = 0;
    while(x >= 0)
    {
        sum += x;
        x--;
    }
    return sum;
}
```

Which of the following recursive methods are equivalent to the method above?

```
I.   public static int mystery2(int x)
         {
             if (x == 0)
             {
                 return 0;
             }
             return (x + mystery2(x - 1));
         }
II.  public static int mystery3 (int x)
         {
             if (x == 0)
                 return 0;
             else
                 return mystery3(x - 1);
         }
III. public static int mystery4 (int x)
         {
             if (x == 1)
             {
                 return 1:
             }
             return (x + mystery 4(x - 1));
         }
```

(A) I only
(B) II only
(C) III only
(D) I and II
(E) II and III

5. Consider the following method:

```java
public int mystery(int x, int y)
{
    if (x >= 100 || y <= 0)
    {
        return 1;
    }
    else
    {
        return mystery(x + 10, y - 3);
    }
}
```

What value is returned by the call `mystery (30, 18)`?

(A) 0

(B) 1

(C) 6

(D) 7

(E) Nothing will be returned due to infinite recursion.

6. Consider the following incomplete method:

```java
public int mystery(int x)
{
    if (x <= 1)
    {
        return 1;
    }
    else
    {
        return (/* missing code */);
    }
}
```

Which of the following could be used to replace /* *missing code* */ so that the value of `mystery(10)` is 32 ?

(A) `mystery(x - 1) + mystery(x - 2)`

(B) `2 * mystery(x - 2)`

(C) `2 * mystery(x - 1)`

(D) `4 * mystery(x - 4)`

(E) `4 + mystery(x - 1)`

Summary

- Recursion is the use of a method to call itself. In order to avoid an infinite loop, any recursive method must have a base case that will cease recursion.

- Recursion can be used for searches, certain mathematical algorithms, or to repeat actions until a desired result is obtained.

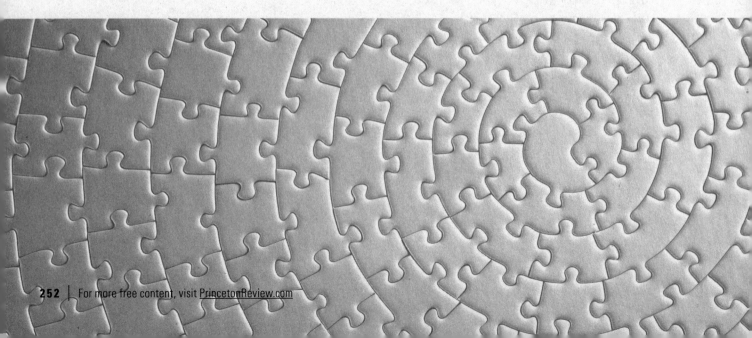

KEY TERMS

recursion
recursive call
base case

Chapter 13
Chapter Review
Drill Answers and
Explanations

CHAPTER 3

1. **E**   Start by examining line 3 in the code segment: `double c = a + b`. `a` is an integer variable and `b` is a double variable. When a double variable is added to an integer variable, the integer is automatically cast to a double before the addition takes place. Therefore, `a + b` will be 20.7; this value will be assigned to `c`.

    Now look at line 4: `int d = a + c`. Because `c` is a double, `a` will once again be cast to a double and `a + c` will be 30.7. This value, which is double, is then assigned to an integer variable. Because there is a loss of precision when a double value is assigned to an integer variable, the compiler will alert you. The correct answer is (E).

2. **E**   The key to this question is remembering that the cast operator `(int)` has precedence over the addition operator. First take a look at Statement I. In that case, `a` will first be cast to an int (which has no effect because it is already an int) and then it will be added to `b`, which is still a double: the result of the addition will be a double, so you haven't fixed the problem. You can therefore eliminate (A) and (D).

    In Statement II, `a + b` is enclosed in parentheses, so the addition will take place first. The result of adding `a` and `b` results in a double (20.7). This double is then cast to an int (20) and assigned to `d`. This is a legal assignment, so keep (B) and (E) and eliminate (C).

    Now, look at Statement III. Here, the double `b` (10.7) is first cast to an int (10). This int is added to `a`, which is also an int. When two ints are added, the result is also an int, so this expression is also valid. The correct answer is (E).

3. **D**   In line 5 of the code segment, divide `a` by `b`. Because both of the operands are integers, the result will be truncated to an int. 11 divided by 4 is 2.75, which is then truncated to 2. Now you know that the first number printed will be 2 (assuming you don't run into a compilation error later in the code), so get rid of (A) and (B).

    In line 7, once again divide 11 by 4. This time, however, the variables that hold these values are doubles. Therefore, the result of dividing 11 by 4 will also be a double: 2.75. Get rid of (C).

    In line 9, yet again divide 11 by 4. The variable that holds 11 is an integer, while the variable that holds 4 is a double. With arithmetic operators, if one of the operands is a double and the other an integer, the integer is automatically cast to a double and the result of the operation is a double. Therefore, you get 2.75 again. The correct answer is (D).

CHAPTER 5

1. **C** You may have seen a problem like this one before. Be careful not to make assumptions; instead, note that i starts at 200 and is divided by 3 after each pass through the for loop. Note that `i /= 3` is equivalent to `i = i / 3`, and integer division truncates the results. As you iterate through the loop, the values of i will be: 200, 66, 22, 7, 2.

    In the body of the loop, i is printed if `i % 2` equals 0. `i % 2` gives the remainder when i is divided by 2; i will give a remainder of 0 when divided by 2 whenever i is even. Therefore, 200, 66, 22, and 2 will be printed; 7 will not be printed. The correct answer is (C).

2. **E** In this question, you need to find the answer choice that doesn't work. If the answer to this question is not obvious to you, the best approach is to try each answer choice and see if it could be the value of i. If it can, then get rid of it.

    Start with (A). Could i be equal to 0? Because `x % 50` gives the remainder when x is divided by 50, for i to equal 0, x would have to be evenly divisible by 50. There are plenty of integers that would work for x (50, 100, 150…). In fact, any multiple of 50 would work.

    How about (B)? Is there a positive integer we can pick for x that leaves a remainder of 10 when divided by 50? Well, because 50 is evenly divisible by 50, 50 + 10, or 60, would leave a remainder of 10 when divided by 50. Other numbers that would work include 110 and 160. In fact, if you add 10 to any positive multiple of 50, you will get a number that leaves a remainder of 10 when divided by 50.

    Following the same logic, find numbers that leave a remainder of 25 and 40 when divided by 50. For example, 75 and 90 would work. Therefore, get rid of (C) and (D).

    The only choice left is (E). So why is it that you can't get a remainder of 50 if you divide a positive integer by 50? Consider what happens if you divide 98 by 50. You get a remainder of 48. What if you divide 99 by 50? Now the remainder is 49. It seems if you increase 99 to 100, the remainder will increase to 50! But wait—100 divided by 50 actually leaves a remainder of 0.

    The upshot of this example is that the value returned by the modulus operator will always be less than the operand to the right of the modulus operator. The correct answer is (E).

CHAPTER 6

1. **A** This question tests your ability to reason through a nested loop. The first thing you should note is that the output is triangular. The first row has two elements, the second has three elements, and so on. Generally, the output of a nested loop will be triangular if the conditional statement of the inner loop is dependent upon the value of the outer loop. If the two loops are independent, the output is usually rectangular.

Trace through each answer choice and see which one will give you the first row: 0 1.

The first time you go through the inner loop in (A), x will be 1, because z starts at 0 and the loop continues while z is less than or equal to 1, the inner loop will print out 0 1. So keep this choice. For (B), the condition of the inner loop is that z is strictly less than x, so this will only print out 0. Get rid of (B). Choice (C) will print out 0 1 2 3 4, so get rid of that too. Choice (D) will print 0 2 4 for the first line. Get rid of it. Choice (E) prints 0 1 for the first line, so keep it for now.

You are now down to (A) and (E). Rather than tracing through each segment in its entirety, see what the differences are between each segment.

The only difference is the outer for loop. In (A), it is

```
for (int x = 1; x < 5; x++)
```

And in (E), it is

```
for (int x = 1; x <= 5; x++) (note the extra equals sign)
```

In (E), because the body of the outer loop is evaluated 5 times, it will print out 5 rows of numbers. Because the answer we are looking for prints only 4 rows, the correct answer must be (A).

2.   **A**   Segment I works correctly, so get rid of (B) and (C).

Segment II is incorrect, because the conditional 65 <= speed < 75 is illegal. A variable can't be compared to two numbers at once. This code will therefore cause a compile-time error. Get rid of (D).

Segment III will compile and run, but it contains a logical error. Assume, for example, that a driver's speed is 85 mph. The driver should receive a fine of $300. If you trace through the code, you see that the value of the variable fine is, in fact, set to $300 in the body of the first if loop because the driver's speed is greater than or equal to 75. The problem is that the condition in the second if loop is also true: the driver's speed is greater than 65. The body of the second loop is executed and the fine is set to $150. Finally, the condition in the third loop is also true, so the fine is then set to $100. Because Segment III is incorrect, get rid of the final possible answer. Note that Segment III would have been correct if you had put else in front of the second and third loops. The correct answer is (A).

3.   **C**   This question tests your ability to trace through a convoluted piece of code. A few things to note:

The body of the if loop is executed only if b is false.

The variable i is incremented by 5, not by 1, in the for loop.

The variable i is also incremented by 5 in the body of the if loop. This is something you would not normally do in your own code, but it is something you may see on the exam. Don't assume the variable in the conditional of the for loop is only modified in the for loop.

4. **B** Keep in mind that `&&` returns true if both operands are true, `||` returns `true` if one or more of its operands are true, and `!` reverses a boolean value.

The best way to crack questions involving booleans is often to just assign true or false to the variables and evaluate the expression.

Break `(a && b) || !(a || b)` into two pieces: `(a && b)` and `!(a || b)`. The variable `c` will be assigned true if either of these pieces is true. `(a && b)` is true when both `a` and `b` are true. Therefore, get rid of (A) and (D).

See what happens if both `a` and `b` are false. Clearly `(a && b)` evaluates to false in this case, but what about `!(a || b)`? `(a || b)` is false if both `a` and `b` are false, but the `!` operator inverts the value to true. So because `!(a || b)` is true, `(a && b) || !(a || b)` evaluates to true. Therefore, `c` will be assigned true when both `a` and `b` are false, so get rid of (C).

You are left with (B) and (E). See what happens when `a` is false and `b` is true. `(a && b)` evaluates to false. `(a || b)` is true, so `!(a || b)` is false. Therefore, `(a && b) || !(a || b)` is false and you can get rid of (E). The correct answer is (B).

5. **E** The code will finish executing when the conditional in the while loop is false. In other words, when `!(x > y || y >= z)` is true. So figure out which of the answer choices is equivalent to `!(x > y || y >= z)`.

Here's how to solve it step by step:

Recall that `!(a || b)` is equivalent to `!a && !b`. So `!(x > y || y >= z)` becomes `!(x > y) && !(y >= z)`.

`!(x > y)` is equivalent to `x <= y`, so you now have `x <= y && !(y >= z)`.

`!(y >= z)` is equivalent to `y < z`, so you have `x <= y && y < z`. The correct answer is (E).

6. **D** Each time the incremental statement `a++` is evaluated, the value of `a` is increased by one. So to answer this question, you need to figure out how many times `a` is incremented.

The outer loop will be evaluated 10 times. The inner loop will be evaluated 6 times for each time that the outer loop is evaluated. The code in the body of the second loop will therefore execute `6 * 10` or 60 times. Note that the condition `k <= 5` evaluates to true when `k` equals 5. In the third loop, the value of `z` starts at 1 and is doubled after each pass through the loop. So the body of the innermost loop will execute when i equals 1, 2, 4, 8, and 16—or 5 times for each time the middle loop executes. Because `60 * 5` is 300, `a` will be incremented 300 times. The correct answer is (D).

7. **D** The trick to this question is that arithmetic operators don't modify their operands. So if `x` is 10 when we divide `x` by 3, the result is 3 but `x` remains the same. Likewise, taking the modulus of a number does not change the number itself. On the other hand, the post-increment operator `(++)` does change the value of the variable it operates on, so `x++` will increase the value of x by 1. The correct answer is (D).

8. **E** On the fourth line, a + b will be 13.7, but this result is cast to an int, so x will be 13. On the next line, a is first cast to a double and then divided by c. Because a is a double, c is automatically promoted to a double and the result of dividing the two is also a double. Therefore, y is 2.5.

On the next line, the parentheses cause the division to take place before the cast. Because a and c are ints, the result of dividing the two is truncated to an int, 2 in this case. The fact that we then cast the result to a double does not bring back the truncated decimal. Then z is equal to 2, so w = 13 + 2.5 + 2. The correct answer is (E).

9. **D** This question tests your understanding of short-circuit evaluation. In each code segment, pay attention to the conditional in the if statement.

In Segment I, the conditional statement is x < y && 10 < y/z. First, x < y is evaluated. Because x is 10 and y is 20, x < y evaluates to true. Then check 10 < y / z. Because you divide by zero here, a run-time exception occurs. You can eliminate (A) and (E).

Now look at Segment II. The conditional statement is x > y && 10 < y / z. Once again, first evaluate the operand to the left of the && operator. Because x is not greater than y, x > y evaluates to false. There's no need to evaluate the right-hand operand. With the && operator, if the left operand is false, the whole condition is false. Because the right-hand operand is not evaluated, y is never divided by z and a run-time exception does not occur. This means (B) and (D) are still possible.

In Segment III, the conditional statement is x < y || 10 < y / z. The left-hand side, x < y, evaluates to true. Notice that this time you have the or operator || in the middle of the conditional. With an or statement, if the left-hand side is true, the condition is true regardless of the value of the right side. Because the left side is true, there is no need to evaluate the right-hand side, and the division by 0 error never occurs. The correct answer is (D).

CHAPTER 7

1. **E** Because the database code can, in fact, be developed separately, tested separately, and possibly reused, all of the answers are correct. With questions like these, the easiest approach is to consider each candidate statement suspect, and look for ways in which they could be incorrect. If you find an incorrect one, cross it off, and cross any other answer that might "and" with that answer, because a combination of a true statement and a false statement is a false statement. Alternatively, when a candidate answer is true, put a star next to it. When you finish reading the questions, the one with the most stars wins.

In the above, because all three answers are true statements, we can cross off (A), (B), and (C), because they each say that only one statement is correct. Similarly, cross off (D), because it dismisses the third statement. The correct answer is (E).

2. **D**   While the Java language makes it possible to make data fields public, one of the golden rules on the AP Computer Science A Exam is that data fields should always be designated private. Note that constants that are declared as static and final can be public; however, static constants apply to the class as a whole (because of the keyword static) and thus, aren't data fields.

Because data fields must be private, get rid of any answer choice that states it can be public. So get rid of (A), (B), and (E).

Now look at (C). What would happen if all methods in a class were private? Instances of the class would be useless, because clients couldn't ask the class to do anything for them. Classes need public methods to be useful.

What about (D)? The first part is good, because data fields should be private. What about the second sentence? Above you saw that methods can be public. They can also be private. A private method is used internally by a class to help out a public method, but is not directly accessible by client programs. The correct answer is (D).

3. **C**   Statement I is incorrect, because it violates encapsulation. Thus, any answer that includes Statement I can be dismissed out of hand. Thus, dismiss (A), (D), and (E). The implementation of a method can be changed without changing its client programs, so Statement III is correct. Therefore, eliminate (B), which dismisses Statement III. Thus, the answer must be (C).

4. **D**   Both `writeMe` methods completely ignore the input that's passed into them, so there's no opportunity for `hi` to be printed. So (B) cannot be the answer. The code is syntactically correct, so (A) cannot be the answer. Along the same lines, you're not doing anything that requires casting, or dealing with null, or dividing by a number that could potentially be 0, so (E) is not the answer. That leaves (C) and (D). Because you're creating a String object and passing to a method that takes a String as a parameter, the existence of the `writeMe(Object obj)` method is inconsequential. Thus, the only valid answer is (D).

5. **C**   Both `writeMe` methods completely ignore the input that's passed into them, so there's no opportunity for `tmp` to be printed. So (D) cannot be the answer. The code is syntactically correct, so (A) cannot be the answer. Along the same lines, you're not doing anything that requires casting, or dealing with null, or dividing by a number that could potentially be 0, so (E) is not the answer. That leaves (B) and (C). Because you're creating an Object and passing to a method that takes an Object as a parameter, the existence of the `writeMe(String s)` method is inconsequential. Thus, the only valid answer is (C).

6. **C**   Both `writeMe` methods completely ignore the input that's passed into them, so there's no opportunity for `hi` to be printed. So (B) cannot be the answer. Use an Object reference to refer to a String instance, because a String IS-A Object. Thus, the code is not syntactically incorrect, so (A) is not the answer. That leaves (C), (D), and (E). Because you're not doing any sort of casting, (E) is also an unlikely candidate. That leaves (C) and (D). Now the question becomes, when making overloaded calls, does Java pay attention to the type of the reference (which in this case is Object)

or the type of the variable (which in this case is String)? It turns out that Java always pays attention to the type of the object, so (C) is correct.

7. **A** `tmp` is an `Object`, not a `String`; thus the code snipped `String tmp = new Object` is illegal. This code will generate a compile-time error. The correct answer is (A).

8. **B** This class is not declaring any methods at all, so (C) cannot possibly be correct. The code does not have any syntactical errors, so (A) cannot be correct. Choice (D) is nonsense, because nothing can be both an attribute and a method, and (E), while true, is irrelevant. Being a primitive does not imply that val cannot be an attribute, so the "neither" part of the question is a red herring. The correct answer is (B).

9. **A** Both `writeMe` methods have the same name and same parameter list, but they return different types. This is illegal. Thus, (A) is the right answer.

CHAPTER 8

1. **C** On line 1, an array of String is created and assigned to reference s. Note that the array to which s refers can hold only two Strings. This does not prevent you, however, from pointing s to another array that is not of length 2. This is exactly what happens on line 3; s is reassigned to the same array that t references. This array has a length of 3. The correct answer is (C).

Here is what this looks like:

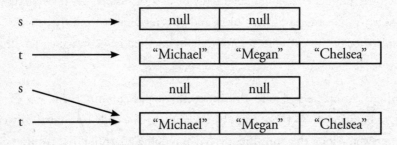

2. **D** In the code segment, the variable a1 is declared as final. This means that once you assign an array to it, a1 must always point to that array. A compile-time error will occur when you try to assign the array referenced by b1 to a1. The correct answer is (D).

3. **C** In the code segment, an array containing two integers is constructed and assigned to a variable named `myArray`. Because this reference is final, it cannot be assigned to another array. This does not prevent you, however, from changing the contents of the array that the variable `myArray` points to, as you do in the second line. The key here is that even though you change the contents of the array, it is still the same array. The correct answer is (C).

4. **B** In the for loop in the method `Mod3`, the variable `i` keeps track of the position in the array that you are inspecting for each iteration of the loop. `numbers[i]`, on the other hand, is the value that is located at position `i` in the array. Segment I will check to see if position `i` is divisible by 3; that is not what you are looking for, so (A) and (D) are incorrect. Segment II will check if the number that is stored in the array at position `i` is divisible by 3, which is what you are looking for. Segment III will go into an infinite loop the first time it encounters an element in the array that is divisible by 3, so (C) and (E) can be eliminated. Only Segment II will get the program to work as intended. The correct answer is (B).

5. **C** Walk through this step by step. Remember that the `add()` method that takes just one argument adds the argument to the end of the list. The following two lines of code add "A" and "B" to the ArrayList one after another:

    ```
    list.add("A")
    ```

    ```
    list.add("B")
    ```

    After the code above executes, the list looks like

    ```
    [A, B]
    ```

    The next statement, `list.add(0,  "C")`, adds "C" to the beginning of the list. Now the list looks like

    ```
    [C, A, B]
    ```

    After `list.add("D")` executes, the list looks like

    ```
    [C, A, B, D]
    ```

    The `set()` method replaces the value at the position indicated by the first argument. After `list.set(2,  "E")` executes, the list looks like

    ```
    [C, A, E, D]
    ```

    After `list.remove(1)` executes, the list looks like

    ```
    [C, E, D]
    ```

    The correct answer is therefore (C).

6. **C** The key to this question is that as elements are removed from an ArrayList, the elements to the right of the removed element are shifted to the left and their indexes are reduced by 1.

    On the first pass through the while loop, `i` will be 0. Because the String in position 0 of letters equals `A`, it will be removed and letters will look like

    ```
    [B, A, A, C, D, B]
    ```

The next time through the while loop, i will be 1. The letter in position 1 is equal to A, so it is removed. Now letters look like

```
[B, A, C, D, B]
```

On the next pass through the ArrayList, i is 2. The letter in position 2 is a C, so it is not removed. The while loop will continue to iterate through the ArrayList, but because none of the Strings in indexes higher than 2 are equal to A, nothing else will be removed.

The correct answer is therefore (C).

7. **D**   The first time through the for loop, the letter in position 0 is removed and myList looks like

```
[B, C, D, E]
```

The letter that is in position 0, which is now B, is printed.

The next time through the for loop, i is 1, so C, the letter in position 1, is removed. Now myList looks like

```
[B, D, E]
```

The letter that is in position 1, which is now D, is printed.

At this point, i is incremented to 2. The size of myList is also 2, so i is no longer less than myList.size(). The for loop does not execute again.

The correct answer is therefore (D).

8. **D**   The variable numbers.length is the number of rows in the two-dimensional array numbers. The variable numbers[0].length is the number of columns. Both the number of rows and the number of columns are 4.

On the first pass through the for loop, z is 0, and numbers[0].length - 1 - z is 3. So the value of numbers[0][3] is added to the total. So, numbers[0][3] is 3.

On the next pass, z is 1, numbers[0].length - 1 - z is 2, so the value of numbers[1][2] (which is 4) is added to the total.

On the next pass, add the value at numbers[2][1], which is 3, and on the final pass we add the value at numbers[4][0], which is 4.

As you can see, the for loop simply finds the sum of one of the diagonals of the array. The correct answer is (D).

9. **C**   Note that k is incremented by 2 in the inner for loop. The code segment will find the sum of all the integers in columns with an even index.

```
numbers[0][0] + numbers[0][2] + numbers[0][4] + numbers[1][0] + numbers[1][2] +
numbers[1][4] + numbers[2][0] + numbers[2][2] + numbers [2][4] = 37.
```

10.　**A**　The first for loop initializes the ArrayList list so that it looks like

```
[1, 2, 3, 4, 5, 6, 7, 8]
```

Now take a look at the second for loop. Note that the highest value that j will reach is 7, one less than the size of the list. In the body of the for loop, the index of the position that you are setting is j divided by 2; the index can therefore never be greater than 3, In other words, you won't be modifying any values other than those in the first 4 positions of the ArrayList. Knowing this, eliminate (D) and (E).

On the first pass through the loop, j is 1 and we call list.set(1 / 2, list.get(1)). Because the result of integer division is truncated, this call is equivalent to list.set(0, list.get(1)), so the value of the element at position 0 is the same as that of position 1 and the ArrayList is

```
[2, 2, 3, 4, 5, 6, 7, 8]
```

On the next pass through the for loop, i is 2 and call list.set(1, list.get(2)). The ArrayList looks like this:

```
[2, 3, 4, 5, 6, 7, 8]
```

On the next pass we call, list.get(1, list.get(3)). The ArrayList now looks like this:

```
[2, 4, 3, 4, 5, 6, 7, 8]
```

If you continue to iterate through the second for loop, the ArrayList will end up looking like this:

```
[2, 4, 6, 8, 5, 6, 7, 8]
```

The correct answer is (A).

11.　**A**　For each cell in the two-dimensional array, the code sets the value to the product of the indexes for that cell. For example, num[2][3] is set to 2 * 3 or 6. The correct answer is (A).

CHAPTER 11

1.　**B**　In this question, the Child class extends the Parent class. In both classes, the writeMe method has the same signature. Therefore, the writeMe method of the Child class overrides the writeMe method of the Parent class. Choice (A) is incorrect because an inherited method is one that would not be implemented in the Child class. Choice (C) is incorrect because an overloaded method is one in which the method name is the same but the signatures are different. Choices (D) and (E) are incorrect because the Child class is neither an interface nor an abstract method. Choice (B) is the correct answer.

2.　**B**　A class can, at most, directly extend one other class.

3. **D** Choice (A) is not relevant, because `writeMe` is a static method, and thus doesn't need an instance variable. The only print statement in the code explicitly writes out the hard-coded string `"hellostring"`, so (B) can't possibly be correct. And because we are not casting, dealing with elements that could be null, or dividing anything, (E) is very unlikely. Choice (C) is a possibility, but we're not using a null, nor are we doing anything that could result in a null value. Thus, the answer must be (D).

4. **C** Choice (A) is not relevant, because `writeMe` is a static method, and thus doesn't need an instance variable. The variable var is never initialized to –1, so (B) can't possibly be correct. Choice (D) can't be correct because Java doesn't allow values to be unknowable. They are always equal to their initialization value, or 0, if left uninitialized. And (E) is partially true, but irrelevant. Variables that are final can be displayed, but not changed. Thus, the answer must be (C).

5. **A** Because you've provided your own constructor for the `Sample` class, you must therefore provide all constructors that the code might use. This code will not compile, because you are attempting to create a Sample object by using the default constructor when you write `Sample s = new Sample();`. The correct answer is (A).

6. **B** This is a trick question. The only messages that are ever written are the hard-coded strings `"me"` and `"you"`, so neither (A) nor (D) can be the answer. That leaves (B), (C), and (E). If you trace through the logic of the code into the `writeMe` method, you can see that `"me"` is not equal to null, so (B) and (E) are left. Now comes the tricky part. The variable `"var"` is initialized to null, yet the code attempts to call methods on it. This will cause a runtime exception to be thrown because you cannot call methods on a null object. Therefore, (B) is the correct answer.

7. **C** This is a good question on which to use Process of Elimination. Don't try to find the best design right away. Instead, first get rid of the answer choices that you know are flawed.

    The use of the word *unrelated* is a tip-off that (A) is incorrect. In general, classes and data fields in a program will be related to each other; otherwise there would really be no point in writing the program in the first place.

    Now look at (B). Whenever you are trying to decide if one class is a subclass of the other, ask yourself if an instance of the proposed subclass IS-A instance of the proposed super class. For example, in this case you could ask if a `Pet` IS-A `Apartment`. Obviously not, so get rid of (B).

    Choice (C) looks good. Using primitive data fields allows us to store information about the `Apartment` within an instance of the class. Check the rest of the answer choices though.

    Like (B), (D) refers to subclasses. The difference this time is that `Apartment` is a subclass of the other classes. There are two problems here. First of all, the IS-A relationship doesn't hold. It would be incorrect to say that an `Apartment` IS-A `Pet`, `Room`, or `Dishwasher`. Here's the other problem: if `Apartment` is a subclass of all three of the other classes, then that means that `Apartment` has three immediate superclasses; in other words, `Apartment` extends three of the classes. However, in Java, a class can extend only one other class.

Finally, (E) uses a HAS-A relationship (this is also called composition). This design is similar to that of (C), except use objects instead of primitives, as you did in (C). In this case, using objects will be overkill. For example, the specification from the rental company states only that they want to know if the apartment has a dishwasher. A boolean can be used to store this information, so there's really no point in building a `Dishwasher` class. On the other hand, if the rental company had specified that they needed to store a lot of information about the type of dishwasher in each apartment, such as its color, manufacturer, and year of installation, then a `Dishwasher` class would be appropriate.

The correct answer is therefore (C).

8. **D** Choice (A) is incorrect because the `Motorcycle` class does not define a constructor that takes one argument. Note that unlike other methods, constructors are not inherited, so even though `Motorcycle` extends `Vehicle`, and `Vehicle` defines a constructor that takes one argument, `Motorcycles` will not inherit this constructor.

Choice (B) is incorrect for the same reason that (A) is incorrect. Even though the reference type is `Vehicle`, you are still constructing a `Motorcycle`, and the `Motorcycle` class does not define a constructor that takes one argument.

In (C), you are creating a `Vehicle` and assigning it to a reference of type `Motorcycle`. This is incorrect because a `Vehicle` is not necessarily a `Motorcycle`. The reference type of a variable must be the same class or a super class of the object that you are trying to assign to it. It cannot be a subclass.

Choice (D) is correct. Because the `Motorcycle` class extends the `Vehicle` class, a `Motorcycle` IS-A `Vehicle` and we can assign a `Motorcycle` instance to a `Vehicle` reference.

The first line in (E) is correct. However, in the second line, you are trying to access a private date member. To fix this, you would need to call the public method `maxPassengers()` instead. This would look like the following:

```
int max = v3.maxPassengers();
```

Always bear in mind that all data members on the exam will be private; only methods are public. Therefore, when you use dot notation on an instance of a class, the part that follows the dot should end in parentheses. The only exception to this that you will see on the exam is the length attribute of an array.

CHAPTER 12

1. **B**   In the method listed in the question, the base case occurs when x is equal to 0. Because the value that is initially passed to the method is 3543, the base case does not yet apply. See what happens on the line `return ((x % 10) + mystery(x / 10))`.

Make sure that you understand what `(x % 10)` and `(x / 10)` do. If x is a base 10 integer, `x % 10` will return the units digit. For example, `348 % 10` returns 8. If x is an int variable, then `x / 10` will remove the units digit. For example, `348 / 10` returns 34.

The expression within the return statement has two parts `(x % 10)` and `mystery(x / 10)`.

Take a look at `(x % 10)`. This returns the remainder when x is divided by 10. In this case, x is 3543, so 3543 % 10 is 3.

Now what about `(x / 10)`? 3543 / 10 is 354; integer division truncates the result.

So you now have

```
mystery(3543) - 3 + mystery(354).
```

Following the same logic as above, `mystery(354)` will be `(354 % 10) + mystery(354 / 10)` or `mystery(354) = 4 + mystery(35)`.

So what is `mystery(35)`?

```
mystery(35) = (35 % 10) + mystery(35 / 10)
```

Or simplified

```
mystery(35) = 5 + mystery(3);
```

And `mystery(3)`?

```
mystery(3) = (3 % 10) + mystery(3 / 10)
```

Or simplified

```
mystery(3) = 3 + mystery(0);
```

But `mystery(0)` equals 0 (this is the base case), so

```
mystery(3) = 3 + 0 = 3
```

```
mystery(35) = 5 + 3 = 8
```

```
mystery(354) = 4 + 8 = 12
```

```
mystery(3543) = 3 + 12 = 15.
```

The correct answer is (B).

2. **D**

```
mystery(6) = 2 * mystery(5)

    mystery(5) = 2 * mystery(4)

        mystery(4) = 2 * mystery(3)

            mystery(3) = 2 * mystery(2)

                mystery(2) = 2 * mystery(1)

                    mystery(1) = 2;
```

So `mystery(6)` = 2 * 2 * 2 * 2 * 2 * 2 = 64.

The correct answer is (D).

3. **D** On the first pass through the method, you get

```
10 + mystery(10 / 2) + mystery(10 / 4)
```

Which can be simplified to

```
10 + mystery(5) + mystery(2)
```

Now figure out what `mystery(5)` and `mystery(2)` are and add the results to 10.

First, solve `mystery(5)`

```
mystery(5) = 5 + mystery(5 / 2) + mystery(5 / 4) = 5 + mystery(2) + mystery(1)
```

```
mystery(2) = 2 + mystery(2 / 2) + mystery(2 / 4) = 2 + mystery(1) + mystery(0)
```

```
mystery(1) = 1 + mystery(1 / 2) + mystery(1 / 4) = 1 + mystery(0) + mystery(0)
```

Note that `mystery(0)` is our base case and returns 0. Working your way back up the recursive calls, you find that `mystery(1)` = 1, `mystery(2)` = 3, and `mystery(5)` = 9. Note that in solving `mystery(5)`, you ended up needing to solve `mystery(2)`.

So in the original equation, 10 + `mystery(5)` + `mystery(2)`, you can replace `mystery(5)` with 9 and `mystery(2)` with 3 to get 10 + 9 + 3, which equals 22. The correct answer is (D).

4. **A** For any non-negative number n that is passed as an argument to the non-recursive method `mystery()`, the method will return 0 + 1 + 2 + 3 + ... + n. For example, a call to `mystery(5)` will return 15(1 + 2 + 3 + 4 + 5). Note that the border case for `mystery()` occurs when 0 is passed to the method. In this case, the method returns 0.

Method I (method `mystery2()`) is equivalent to `mystery()`.

Method II (`mystery3()`) is not equivalent. Notice that `mystery2()` does not modify what is returned by the recursive call, whereas `mystery2()` adds x to the results of each recursive call. The method `mystery2()` will return 0 regardless of the value that is passed to the method.

Method III (`mystery4()`) is equivalent to `mystery()` except when x equals 0. If 0 is passed to the method, the loop will infinitely recurse. Because `mystery4()` doesn't handle the border case correctly, III is incorrect.

Only Method I is equivalent to the `mystery()` method, so (A) is correct.

5. **B**   You originally pass 30 and 18 to the method as x and y, respectively. Each time the method is recursively called, 10 is added to x and 3 is subtracted from y. Therefore, x will eventually become larger than 100 and y will become smaller than 0, so you know that the condition of the base case will eventually be met and infinite recursion won't occur.

Note that the base case returns 1. What about the non-base case? The method return `mystery` (`x + 10, y - 3`) simply returns whatever was returned by the call to `mystery()`; it doesn't modify it in any way. Because there's no modification of the return value, 1 is the only thing that is ever returned, no matter how many recursive calls occur. The correct answer is (B).

6. **B**   The best way to solve this problem is to trace through each answer choice. But don't necessarily start with (A). Start with the answer choice that you think you can solve most quickly. In this case, (A) will probably take longer to check because it has two recursive calls. Instead, start with (D). Why (D)? Because each recursive call reduces the integer that you pass as an argument by 4, there won't be as many recursive calls as there will be with the other choices.

With (D), the first time through the method, you have `mystery(10) = 4 * mystery(6)`. Find that `mystery(6) = 4 * mystery(2)` and `mystery(2) = 4 * mystery(-2)`. Finally, `mystery(-2)` equals 1 (the base case). Working your way back up the call stack, you get `mystery(2) = 4`, `mystery(6) = 16` and `mystery(10) = 64`. So (D) is incorrect.

The choice with the next fewest recursive calls is (B). For this choice, `mystery(10) = 2 * mystery(8)`; `mystery(8) = 2 * mystery(6)`; `mystery(6) = 2 * mystery(4)`; `mystery(4) = 2 * mystery(2)`; `mystery(2) = 2 * mystery(0)`; and `mystery(0) = 1`. Therefore, `mystery(2) = 2`; `mystery(4) = 4`; `mystery(6) = 8`; `mystery(8) = 16`; and `mystery(10) = 32`. The correct answer is (B).

Chapter 14
Required Lab Time and Suggested Labs

This book is intended to help you prepare for the AP Computer Science A Exam, but we would be remiss if we didn't discuss the lab requirements for the course, as outlined by the College Board. The AP Computer Science A course must include a minimum of 20 hours of hands-on, structured lab experiences to engage the student in individual and group problem solving. The College Board puts it this way: Each AP Computer Science A course must include a substantial laboratory component in which you design solutions to problems, express your solutions precisely (i.e., in the Java programming language), test your solutions, identify and correct errors (when mistakes occur), and compare possible solutions. Collectively, these laboratory experiences and activities should contain the following characteristics:

- Explore computing in context at a significant level, building upon existing code that provides examples of good style and appropriate use of programming language constructs.
- Contain a significant problem-solving component in which you study alternative approaches for solving a problem, solve new problems, or modify existing code to solve altered problems.
- Provide you with experience working with programs involving multiple interactive classes and may involve decomposing a program into classes and using inheritance, and other object-oriented concepts as identified in the AP Computer Science A topic outline.

The three labs that aligned with previous College Board AP Computer Science A course descriptions were: Picture, Elevens, and Magpie. The latest exemplar labs that the College Board lists on their website and the topics they involve are listed here:

- Consumer Review—manipulate strings in the context of a consumer review; you will parse string and call methods in the String class; work with conditional and iterative statements to complete methods
- Celebrity—a charades-like game; you will add and modify functionality in a GUI based application
- Data—this one gives you the freedom to explore a topic of interest to you; you will pose a question, determine a data source, write code, and process data in order to answer your question; you will combine content learned throughout the course, from conditional statements and iteration to class design and data structures
- Steganography—this lab uses the code from the College Board's previous Picture Lab (available online) and in this lab, you explore steganographic techniques of concealing messages or information within a picture; involves manipulation and traversal of data in a two-dimensional array

At the time that this book went to press, the College Board had not yet released the Student Guides for these 4 Labs, so be sure to visit the College Board's website for updates. The location of these Labs is: https://apcentral.collegeboard.org/courses/ap-computer-science-a/classroom-resources/lab-resource-page

Part VI
Practice Tests

Practice Test 2

AP® Computer Science A Exam

SECTION I: Multiple-Choice Questions

DO NOT OPEN THIS BOOKLET UNTIL YOU ARE TOLD TO DO SO.

At a Glance

Total Time
1 hour 30 minutes
Number of Questions
40
Percent of Total Score
50%
Writing Instrument
Pencil required

Instructions

Section I of this examination contains 40 multiple-choice questions. Fill in only the ovals for numbers 1 through 40 on your answer sheet.

Indicate all of your answers to the multiple-choice questions on the answer sheet. No credit will be given for anything written in this exam booklet, but you may use the booklet for notes or scratch work. After you have decided which of the suggested answers is best, completely fill in the corresponding oval on the answer sheet. Give only one answer to each question. If you change an answer, be sure that the previous mark is erased completely. Here is a sample question and answer.

Sample Question   Sample Answer

Chicago is a   (A) ● (C) (D) (E)
(A) state
(B) city
(C) country
(D) continent
(E) county

Use your time effectively, working as quickly as you can without losing accuracy. Do not spend too much time on any one question. Go on to other questions and come back to the ones you have not answered if you have time. It is not expected that everyone will know the answers to all the multiple-choice questions.

About Guessing

Many candidates wonder whether or not to guess the answers to questions about which they are not certain. Multiple-choice scores are based on the number of questions answered correctly. Points are not deducted for incorrect answers, and no points are awarded for unanswered questions. Because points are not deducted for incorrect answers, you are encouraged to answer all multiple-choice questions. On any questions you do not know the answer to, you should eliminate as many choices as you can, and then select the best answer among the remaining choices.

GO ON TO THE NEXT PAGE.

Java Quick Reference

Class Constructors and Methods	Explanation
String Class	
`String(String str)`	Constructs a new `String` object that represents the same sequence of characters as `str`
`int length()`	Returns the number of characters in a `String` object
`String substring(int from, int to)`	Returns the substring beginning at index `from` and ending at index `to - 1`
`String substring(int from)`	Returns `substring(from, length())`
`int indexOf(String str)`	Returns the index of the first occurrence of `str`; returns −1 if not found
`boolean equals(String other)`	Returns `true` if `this` is equal to `other`; returns `false` otherwise
`int compareTo(String other)`	Returns a value <0 if `this` is less than `other`; returns zero if `this` is equal to `other`; returns a value of >0 if `this` is greater than `other`
Integer Class	
`Integer(int value)`	Constructs a new `Integer` object that represents the specified `int` value
`Integer.MIN_VALUE`	The minimum value represented by an `int` or `Integer`
`Integer.MAX_VALUE`	The maximum value represented by an `int` or `Integer`
`int intValue()`	Returns the value of this `Integer` as an `int`
Double Class	
`Double(double value)`	Constructs a new `Double` object that represents the specified `double` value
`double doubleValue()`	Returns the value of this `Double` as a `double`
Math Class	
`static int abs(int x)`	Returns the absolute value of an `int` value
`static double abs(double x)`	Returns the absolute value of a `double` value
`static double pow(double base, double exponent)`	Returns the value of the first parameter raised to the power of the second parameter
`static double sqrt(double x)`	Returns the positive square root of a `double` value
`static double random()`	Returns a `double` value greater than or equal to `0.0` and less than `1.0`
ArrayList Class	
`int size()`	Returns the number of elements in the list
`boolean add(E obj)`	Appends `obj` to end of list; returns `true`
`void add(int index, E obj)`	Inserts `obj` at position index (`0 <= index <= size`), moving elements at position `index` and higher to the right (adds 1 to their indices) and adds 1 to size
`E get(int index)`	Returns the element at position `index` in the list
`E set(int index, E obj)`	Replaces the element at position `index` with `obj`; returns the element formerly at position `index`
`E remove(int index)`	Removes the element at position `index`, moving elements at position `index + 1` and higher to the left (subtracts 1 from their indices) and subtracts 1 from size; returns the element formerly at position `index`
Object Class	
`boolean equals(Object other)`	
`String toString()`	

GO ON TO THE NEXT PAGE.

COMPUTER SCIENCE A

SECTION I

Time—1 hour and 30 minutes

Number of Questions—40

Percent of total exam grade—50%

Directions: Determine the answer to each of the following questions or incomplete statements, using the available space for any necessary scratchwork. Then decide which is the best of the choices given and fill in the corresponding oval on the answer sheet. No credit will be given for anything written in the examination booklet. Do not spend too much time on any one problem.

Notes:
- Assume that the classes listed in the Quick Reference have been imported where appropriate.
- Assume that declarations of variables and methods appear within the context of an enclosing class.
- Assume that method calls that are not prefixed with an object or class name and are not shown within a complete class definition appear within the context of an enclosing class.
- Unless otherwise noted in the question, assume that parameters in the method calls are not `null` and that methods are called only when their preconditions are satisfied.

1. Consider the following methods.

```
public void trial()
{
        int a = 10;
        int b = 5;
        doubleValues(a, b);
        System.out.print(b);
        System.out.print(a);
}

public void doubleValues(int c, int d)
{
        c = c * 2;
        d = d * 2;
        System.out.print(c);
        System.out.print(d);
}
```

What is printed as the result of the call `trial()`?

(A) 2010

(B) 2010105

(C) 2010510

(D) 20102010

(E) 20101020

GO ON TO THE NEXT PAGE.

2. Consider the following method.

```
/**
 * Precondition: a > b > 0
 */
public static int mystery(int a, int b)
{
    int d = 0;
    for (int c = a; c > b; c--)
    {
        d = d + c;
    }
    return d;
}
```

What is returned by the call mystery(x, y)?

(A) The sum of all integers greater than y but less than or equal to x

(B) The sum of all integers greater than or equal to y but less than or equal to x

(C) The sum of all integers greater than y but less than x

(D) The sum of all integers greater than or equal to y but less than x

(E) The sum of all integers less than y but greater than or equal to x

3. Consider the following method.

```
public void mystery (int  n)
{
    int k;
    for (k = 0 ; k < n ; k++)
    {
        mystery(k);
        System.out.print (k);
    }
}
```

What is printed by the call mystery(3) ?

(A) 0123

(B) 00123

(C) 0010012

(D) 00100123

(E) 001001200100123

4. Consider an array of integers.

| 4 | 10 | 1 | 2 | 6 | 7 | 3 | 5 |

If selection sort is used to order the array from smallest to largest values, which of the following represents a possible state of the array at some point during the selection sort process?

(A) 1	4	10	2	3	6	7	5
(B) 1	2	4	6	10	7	3	5
(C) 1	2	3	10	6	7	4	5
(D) 4	3	1	2	6	7	10	5
(E) 5	3	7	6	2	1	10	4

GO ON TO THE NEXT PAGE.

5. Consider the following code segment:

```
int  k;
int  a[];
a = new int [7];
for (k = 0; k < a.length; k++)
{
    a[k] = a.length - k;
}
for (k = 0; k < a.length - 1; k++)
{
    a[k+1] = a[k];
}
```

What values will A contain after the code segment is executed?

(A)	1	1	2	3	4	5	6
(B)	1	2	3	4	5	6	7
(C)	6	6	5	4	3	2	1
(D)	7	7	6	5	4	3	2
(E)	7	7	7	7	7	7	7

GO ON TO THE NEXT PAGE.

Questions 6–7 refer to the following two classes.

```
public class PostOffice
{
    // constructor initializes boxes
    // to length 100
    public PostOffice()
    {   /* implementation not shown   */}

    // returns the P.O. Box based on the given P.O. Box number
    // 0 <= theBox < getNumBoxes()
    public Box getBox(int theBox)
    {    /* implementation not shown    */}
    // returns the number of p.o. boxes
    public int getNumBoxes()
    {    /* implementation not shown    */}


    // private data members and
    // other methods not shown
}


public class Box
{
    // constructor
    public Box()
    {   /* implementation not shown  */}

    // returns the number of this box
    public int getBoxNumber()
    {   /* implementation not shown    */}

    // returns the number of pieces
    // of mail in this box
    public int getMailCount()
    {   /* implementation not shown  */}
    // returns the given piece of mail
    // 0 <= thePiece < getMailCount()
    public Mail getMail(int thePiece)
    {   /* implementation not shown  */}
    // true if the box has been assigned
    // to a customer
    public boolean isAssigned()
    {   /* implementation not shown  */}
    // true if the box contains mail
    public boolean hasMail()
    {    /* implementation not shown  */}
    // private data members and
    // other methods not shown
}
public class Mail
{
    // private members, constructors, and
    // other methods not shown
}
```

GO ON TO THE NEXT PAGE.

6. Consider the following code segment:

```
PostOffice p[ ];
p = new PostOffice[10];
```

Assuming that the box has been assigned and that it has at least four pieces of mail waiting in it, what is the correct way of getting the fourth piece of mail from the 57th box of the 10th post office of p?

(A) `Mail m = p[10].getBox(57).getmail(4);`

(B) `Mail m = p[9].getBox(56).getMail(3);`

(C) `Mail m = p.getMail(57).getMail(4) [10];`

(D) `Mail m = getMail(getBox(p[9], 560, 3);`

(E) `Mail m = new Mail(10, 57, 4);`

GO ON TO THE NEXT PAGE.

7. Consider the incomplete function printEmptyBoxes given below. printEmptyBoxes should print the box numbers of all of the boxes that have been assigned to a customer but do not contain mail.

```
public void printEmptyBoxes (PostOffice[] p)
{
    for (int k = 0; k < p.length - 1 ; k++)
    {
        for (int x = 0; x < p[k].getNumBoxes() - 1 ; x++)
        {
            /* missing code */
        }
    }
}
```

Which of the following could be used to replace /* missing code */ so that printBoxesWithoutMail works as intended?

(A)
```
if (p[k].getBox(x).isAssigned() &&
!p[k].getBox(x).hasMail())
{
    System.out.println(p[k].getBox(x).getBoxNumber()) ;
}
```

(B)
```
if (p[x].getBox(k).isAssigned() &&
!p[x].getBox(k).hasMail())
{
  System.out.println(p[x].getBox(k).getBoxNumber());
}
```

(C)
```
if (p[k].getBox(x).isAssigned() &&
!p[k].getBox(x).hasMail())
{
    System.out.println (p[k].getBoxNumber (x));
}
```

(D)
```
if (p[x].getBox(k).isAssigned() &&
!p[x].getBox (k).hasMail())
{
    System.out.println(p[x].getBoxNumber(k));
 }
```

(E)
```
if (p[x].getBox(k).isAssigned() &&
p[x].getBox(k).getMail() == 0)
{
    System.out.println(k);
}
```

GO ON TO THE NEXT PAGE.

8. Assume that a and b are boolean variables that have been initialized. Consider the following code segment.

```
a = a && b;
b = a || b;
```

Which of the following statements is always true?

I. The final value of a is the same as the initial value of a.
II. The final value of b is the same as the initial value of b.
III. The final value of a is the same as the initial value of b.

(A) I only
(B) II only
(C) III only
(D) I and II only
(E) II and III only

9. Consider the following code segment.

```
int x;
x = 53;
if (x > 10)
{
    System.out.print("A");
}
if (x > 30)
{
    System.out.print("B");
}
else if (x > 40)
{
    System.out.print("C");
}
if (x > 50)
{
    System.out.print ("D");
}
if (x > 70)
{
    System.out.print ("E");
}
```

What is the output when the code is executed?

(A) A
(B) D
(C) ABD
(D) ABCD
(E) ABCDE

GO ON TO THE NEXT PAGE.

10. Consider the following code segment:

```
int j;
int k;
for (j = -2; j <= 2; j = j + 2)
{
    for (k = j; k < j + 3; k++)
    {
        System.out.print(k + " ");
    }
}
```

What is the output when the code is executed?

(A) -2 -1 0

(B) -2 -1 0 1 2

(C) 0 1 2 0 1 2 0 1 2

(D) -2 0 2

(E) -2 -1 0 0 1 2 2 3 4

11. Consider the following method.

```
public void mystery (int  count, String s)
{
    if  (count  <=  0)
    {
        return;
    }
    if  (count % 3 == 0)
    {
        System.out.print(s + "--" + s);
    }
    else if (count % 3 == 1)
    {
        System.out.print(s + "-" + s);
    }
    else
    {
        System.out.print(s);
    }
    mystery(count - 1, s);
}
```

What is outputted by the call mystery(5, "X")?

(A) XX-XX--XXX-X

(B) XX-XX-XX-XX

(C) XXX--XX-X-XX--XXX

(D) XX-XXX--XXX-XX

(E) XXXXX

GO ON TO THE NEXT PAGE.

Questions 12–13 refer to the following classes and method descriptions.

Class `Table` has a method, `getPrice`, which takes no parameters and returns the price of the table.

Class `Chair` also has a method, `getPrice`, which takes no parameters and returns the price of the chair.

Class `DiningRoomSet` has a constructor which is passed a `Table` object and an `ArrayList` of `Chair` objects. It stores these parameters in its private data fields `myTable` and `myChairs`.

Class `DiningRoomSet` has a method, `getPrice`, which takes no parameters and returns the price of the dining room set. The price of a dining room set is calculated as the sum of the price of its table and all of its chairs.

12. What is the correct way to define the signature of the constructor for the `DiningRoomSet` class?

(A) `public void DiningRoomSet(Table t, ArrayList, chairs)`
(B) `public DiningRoomSet(Table t, ArrayList<Chair> chairs)`
(C) `public void DiningRoomSet(Table t, ArrayList Chair Chairs)`
(D) `public DiningRoomSet(Table t, ArrayList Chair Chairs)`
(E) `public DiningRoomSet(Table t, Chair Chairs)`

13. What is the correct way to implement the getPrice method of the `DiningRoomSet` class?

(A)
```
public double getPrice(Table t, ArrayList chairs)
{
        return t.getPrice() + chairs.getPrice();
}
```
(B)
```
public double getPrice(Table t, ArrayList chairs)
{
        return myTable.getPrice() + myChairs.getPrice();
}
```
(C)
```
public double getPrice()
{
        return myTable.getPrice() + myChairs.getPrice();
}
```
(D)
```
public double getPrice()
{
        double result  = myTable.getPrice();
        for (int k = 0; k < myChairs.size() - 1; k++)
        {
                result += ((Chair)myChairs.get(k)).getPrice();
        }
        return result;
}
```
(E)
```
public double getPrice()
{
        double result = myTable.getPrice();
        for (int k = 0; k <  myChairs.length - 1; k++)
        {
                result += ((Chair)myChairs[k]).getPrice();
        }
        return result;
}
```

GO ON TO THE NEXT PAGE.

14. Consider the following output:

```
6   5   4   3   2   1
5   4   3   2   1
4   3   2   1
3   2   1
2   1
1
```

Which of the following code segments produces the above output when executed?

(A)
```java
for  (int j = 6;  j  <  0;  j--)
{
  for (int k = j; k > 0; k--)
  {
      System.out.print(k  +  "    ");
  }
  System.out.println(" ");
}
```

(B)
```java
for (int j = 6; j >= 0; j--)
{
  for (int k = j; k >= 0; k--)
  {
      System.out.print(k + " ");
  }
  System.out.println(" ");
}
```

(C)
```java
for (int j = 0; j < 6; j++)
{
  for (int k = 6 - j; k > 0; k--)
  {
      System.out.print(k + "   ");
  }
  system.out.println(" ");
}
```

(D)
```java
for (int j = 0; j < 6; j++)
{
  for (int k = 7 - j ; k > 0 ; k--)
  {
      System.out.print(k + " ");
  }
  System.out.println(" ");
}
```

(E)
```java
for (int j = 0; j < 6; j++)
{
  for (int k = 6  -  j ; k >= 0; k--)
  {
      System.out.print(k + " ");
  }
  System.out.println(" ");
}
```

GO ON TO THE NEXT PAGE.

15. Consider the following code segment.

```
List<Integer> list = new ArrayList<Integer>();
list.add(new Integer(7));
list.add(new Integer(6));
list.add(1, new Integer(5));
list.add(1, new Integer(4));
list.add(new Integer(3));
list.set(2, new Integer(2));
list.add(1, new Integer(1));
System.out.println(list);
```

What is printed as a result of executing this code segment?

(A) [1, 4, 2, 7, 6, 3]
(B) [7, 1, 4, 2, 6, 3]
(C) [7, 2, 5, 4, 3, 1]
(D) [7, 6, 2, 4, 3, 1]
(E) [7, 1, 2]

16. Consider the following declarations.

```
public class Animal
{
    String makeSound()
    {
        // Implementation not shown
    }
    String animalType()
    {
        // Implementation not shown
    }
}
public static class Dog extends Animal
{
    public String makeSound(Animal a)
    {
        // Implementation not shown
    }
}
```

Which of the following methods must be included in the declaration of the Dog class in order for the class to successfully compile?

I.   public String makeSound()
II. public String animalType()
III. public String animalType(Animal b)

(A) I only
(B) II only
(C) I and II only
(D) II and III only
(E) None

GO ON TO THE NEXT PAGE.

17. Consider the following two classes.

```
public class Fish
{
  public String endoskeleton = "bone";

  public void action()
  {
      System.out.println("splash splash");
  }
}

public class Shark extends Fish
{
  public void action()
  {
      System.out.println("chomp chomp");
  }

  public String endoskeleton = "cartilage";
}
```

Which of the following is the correct output after the following code segment is executed?

```
Fish Bob = new Shark();
System.out.println(Bob.endoskeleton);
Bob.action();
```

(A) bone
    chomp chomp
(B) bone
    splash splash
(C) cartilage
    splash splash
(D) cartilage
    chomp chomp
(E) cartilage
    splash splash
    chomp chomp

GO ON TO THE NEXT PAGE.

Questions 18–19 refer to the following incomplete method.

The following `insertSort` method sorts the values in an integer array, `sort`, in ascending order.

```
1    public static void insertSort(int[] sort)
2       {
3          for (int index = 1;index < sort.length;index++)
4          {
5             int temp = sort[index];
6             while (index > 0 && sort[index - 1] > temp)
7                {
8          /* missing code */
9                }
10      sort[index] = temp;
11         }
12      }
```

18. Which of the following can be used to replace /* *missing code* */ so that the `insertSort` method will execute properly?

(A) `sort[index] = sort[index - 1];`
     `index++;`

(B) `sort[index - 1] = sort[index];`
     `index--;`

(C) `sort[index] = sort[index + 1];`
     `index++;`

(D) `sort[index] = sort[index - 1];`
     `index--;`

(E) `sort[index] = sort[index + 1];`
     `index--;`

19. Assuming that the /* *missing code* */ is implemented properly, what change can be made to the code in order for the array to be sorted in descending order?

(A) Replace Line 6 with: `while (index < 0 && sort[index - 1] > temp)`
(B) Replace Line 6 with: `while (index < 0 && sort[index - 1] < temp)`
(C) Replace Line 6 with: `while (index > 0 && sort[index - 1] < temp)`
(D) Replace Line 3 with: `for (int index = sort.length - 1;index > 0;index--)`
(E) Replace Line 3 with: `for (int index = 1;index > 0;index--)`

20. Which of the following arrays would be sorted the slowest using insertion sort?

(A) `[3 4 6 2 7 3 9]`
(B) `[3 2 5 4 6 7 9]`
(C) `[9 7 6 5 4 3 2]`
(D) `[2 3 4 5 6 7 9]`
(E) `[9 3 2 4 5 7 6]`

GO ON TO THE NEXT PAGE.

Questions 21–23 refer to the following incomplete class declaration used to represent fractions with integer numerators and denominators.

```java
public class Fraction
{
    private int numerator;
    private int denominator;

    public Fraction()
    {
        numerator = 0;
        denominator = 1;
    }

    public Fraction(int n, int d)
    {
        numerator = n;
        denominator = d;
    }

    // postcondition: returns the
    //     numerator
    public int getNumerator()
    {   /* implementation not shown */  }

    // postcondition: returns the
    //     denominator
    public int getDenominator()
    {   /* implementation not shown*/   }

    // postcondition: returns the greatest
    // common divisor of x and y
    public int gcd(int x, int y)
    {   /* implementation not shown*/    }

    // postcondition: returns the Fraction
    //     that is the result of multiplying
    //     this Fraction and f

    public Fraction multiply(Fraction f)
    {   /* implementation not shown */  }
    // ... other methods not shown
}
```

GO ON TO THE NEXT PAGE.

21. Consider the method `multiply` of the `Fraction` class.

```
// postcondition: returns the Fraction
//         that is the result of multiplying
//         this Fraction and f
public Fraction multiply(Fraction f)
{   /* missing code */   }
```

Which of the following statements can be used to replace /* *missing code* */ so that the `multiply` method is correctly implemented?

```
I.    return Fraction(
         numerator * f.getNumerator(),
         denominator * f.getDenominator());
II.   return new Fraction(
         numerator * f.numerator,
         denominator * f.denominator());
III.  return new Fraction(
         numerator * f.getNumerator(),
         denominator * f.getDenominator());
```

(A) I only
(B) II only
(C) III only
(D) I and III only
(E) II and III only

22. Consider the use of the `Fraction` class to multiply the fractions $\frac{3}{4}$ and $\frac{7}{19}$. Consider the following code:

```
Fraction fractionOne;
Fraction fractionTwo;
Fraction answer;
fractionOne = new Fraction(3, 4);
fractionTwo = new Fraction(7, 19);
/* missing code */
```

Which of the following could be used to replace /* *missing code* */ so that the answer contains the result of multiplying fractionOne by fractionTwo?

```
(A) answer = fractionOne * fractionTwo
(B) answer = multiply(fractionOne,fractionTwo);
(C) answer = fractionOne.multiply(fractionTwo);
(D) answer = new Fraction(fractionOne,fractionTwo);
(E) answer = (fractionOne.getNumerator() * fractionTwo.getNumerator()) /
         (fractionOne.getDenominator() * fractionTwo.getDenominator());
```

GO ON TO THE NEXT PAGE.

23. The following incomplete class declaration is intended to extend the `Fraction` class so that fractions can be manipulated in reduced form (lowest terms).

Note that a fraction can be reduced to lowest terms by dividing both the numerator and denominator by the greatest common divisor (gcd) of the numerator and denominator.

```
public class ReducedFraction extends Fraction
{
    private int reducedNumerator;
    private int reducedDenominator;
    // . . . constructors and other methods not shown
}
```

Consider the following proposed constructors for the `ReducedFraction` class:

```
I.  public ReducedFraction( )
    {
      reducedNumerator = 0;
      reducedDenominator = 1;
    }
II. public ReducedFraction(int n, int d)
    {
      numerator = n;
      denominator = d;
      reducedNumerator = n / gcd(n, d);
      reducedDenominator = d / gcd(n, d);
    }
III. public ReducedFraction(int n, int d)
    {
      super(n, d);
      reducedNumerator = n / gcd(n, d);
      reducedDenominator = d / gcd(n, d);
    }
```

Which of these constructor(s) would be legal for the `ReducedFraction` class?

(A) I only
(B) II only
(C) III only
(D) I and III only
(E) II and III only

GO ON TO THE NEXT PAGE.

24. Consider `s1` and `s2` defined as follows.

```
String s1 = new String("hello");
String s2 = new String("hello");
```

Which of the following is/are correct ways to see if `s1` and `s2` hold identical strings?

```
I.   if (s1 == s2)
        /* s1 and s2 are identical */
II.  if (s1.equals(s2))
        /* s1 and s2 are identical */
III. if (s1.compareTo(s2) == 0)
        /* s1 and s2 are identical */
```

(A) I only
(B) II only
(C) I and III only
(D) II and III only
(E) I, II, and III

25. Consider the following variable and method declarations:

```
String s;
String t;
public void mystery (String a, String b)
{
    a = a + b;
    b = b + a;
}
```

Assume that `s` has the value `"Elizabeth"` and `t` has the value `"Andrew"` and `mystery (s, t)` is called. What are the values of `s` and `t` after the call to `mystery`?

	s	t
(A)	Elizabeth	Andrew
(B)	ElizabethAndrew	AndrewElizabeth
(C)	ElizabethAndrew	AndrewElizabethAndrew
(D)	ElizabethAndrew	ElizabethAndrewAndrew
(E)	ElizabethAndrewElizabeth	AndrewElizabethAndrew

GO ON TO THE NEXT PAGE.

26. Consider the following incomplete and *incorrect* class and interface declarations:

```
public class Comparable Object
{
    public int compareTo(Object o)
    {
        //method body not shown
    }
//other methods and variables not shown
}
public class Point extends ComparableObject
{
    private int x;
    private int y;
    public boolean compareTo(Point other)
    {
        return (x == other.x &&
                y == other.y);
    }
    // . . . constructors and other methods
    //    not shown
}
```

For which of the following reasons is the above class structure incorrect?

I.   Objects may not access private data fields of other objects in the same class.
II. The `ComparableObject` class requires that `compareTo` be passed as an `Object` rather than a `Point`.
III. The `ComparableObject` class requires that `compareTo` return an `int` rather than a `boolean`.

(A) I only
(B) III only
(C) I and III only
(D) II and III only
(E) None, the above class declarations are correct.

GO ON TO THE NEXT PAGE.

27. Consider the following abstraction of a `for` loop where <1>, <2>, <3>, and <4> represent legal code in the indicated locations:

```
for (<1>; <2>; <3>)
{
    <4>
}
```

Which of the following `while` loops has the same functionality as the above `for` loop?

(A)
```
<1>;
while (<2>)
{
    <3>;
    <4>
}
```

(B)
```
<1>;
while (<2>)
{
    <4>
    <3>;
}
```

(C)
```
<1>;
    while (!<2>)
{
    <3>;
    <4>
}
```

(D)
```
<1>;
while (!<2>)
{
    <4>
    <3>;
}
```

(E)
```
<1>;
<3>;
while (<2>)
{
    <4>
    <3>;
}
```

28. Consider the following expression:

```
a / b + c - d % e * f
```

Which of the expressions given below is equivalent to the one given above?

(A) `((a / b) + (c - d)) % (e * f)`
(B) `((((a / b) + c) - d) % e) * f`
(C) `((a / b) + c) - (d % (e * f))`
(D) `(a / ((b + c) - d) % e) * f`
(E) `((a / b) + c) - ((d % e) * f)`

GO ON TO THE NEXT PAGE.

29. Assume that a program declares and initializes x as follows:

```
String[] x ;
x = new String[10] ;
initialize(x);              // Fills the array x with
                            // valid strings each of
                            // length 5
```

Which of the following code segments correctly traverses the array and prints out the first character of all ten strings followed by the second character of all ten strings, and so on?

```
  I. int i;
     int j;
     for (i = 0 ; i < 10 ; i++)
         for (j = 0 ; j < 5 ; j++)
             System.out.print(x[i].substring(j, j + 1));
 II. int i;
     int j;
     for (i = 0 ; i < 5 ; i++)
         for (j = 0 ; j < 10 ; j++)
             System.out.print(x[j].substring(i, i + 1));
III. int i ;
     int j ;
     for (i = 0 ; i < 5 ; i++)
         for (j = 0 ; j < 10 ; j++)
             System.out.print(x[i].substring(j, j + 1));
```

(A) I only
(B) II only
(C) I and II only
(D) II and III only
(E) I, II, and III

30. Consider the following declaration and assignment statements:

```
int a = 7;
int b = 4;
double c;
c = a / b;
```

After the assignment statement is executed, what's the value of c?

(A) 1.0
(B) 1.75
(C) 2.0
(D) An error occurs because c was not initialized.
(E) An error occurs because a and b are integers and c is a double.

GO ON TO THE NEXT PAGE.

31. Consider the following code segment:

```
int x;
x = /* initialized to an integer */
if (x % 2 == 0 && x / 3 == 1)
    System.out.print("Yes");
```

For what values of x will the word "Yes" be printed when the code segment is executed?

(A) 0

(B) 4

(C) Whenever x is even and x is not divisible by 3

(D) Whenever x is odd and x is divisible by 3

(E) Whenever x is even and x is divisible by 3

32. Consider the following incomplete class definition:

```
public class SomeClass
{
    private String myName;
    // postcondition: returns myName
    public String getName( )
    { /* implementation not shown */ }
    // postcondition: myName == name
    public void setName(String name)
    { /* implementation not shown */ }
    // ... constructors, other methods
    //     and private data not shown
}
```

Now consider the method swap, not part of the SomeClass class.

```
// precondition: x and y are correctly
//     constructed
// postcondition: the names of objects
//     x and y are swapped
public void swap (SomeClass x, SomeClass y)
{
    /* missing code */
}
```

GO ON TO THE NEXT PAGE.

Which of the following code segments can replace /* *missing code* */ so that the method swap works as intended?

```
I.   SomeClass temp;
     temp = x;
     x = y;
     y = temp;
II.  String temp;
     temp = x.myName;
     x.myName = y.myName;
     y.myName = temp;
III. String temp;
     temp = x.getName();
     x.setName(y.getName());
     y.setName(temp);
```

(A) I only
(B) III only
(C) I and III only
(D) II and III only
(E) I, II, and III

33. A bookstore wants to store information about the different types of books it sells.

For each book, it wants to keep track of the title of the book, the author of the book, and whether the book is a work of fiction or nonfiction.

If the book is a work of fiction, then the bookstore wants to keep track of whether it is a romance novel, a mystery novel, or science fiction.

If the book is a work of nonfiction, then the bookstore wants to keep track of whether it is a biography, a cookbook, or a self-help book.

Which of the following is the best design?

(A) Use one class, `Book`, which has three data fields: `String title`, `String author`, and `int bookType`.
(B) Use four unrelated classes: `Book`, `Title`, `Author`, and `BookType`.
(C) Use a class `Book` which has two data fields: `String title`, `String author`, and a subclass: `BookType`.
(D) Use a class `Book` which has two data fields: `String title`, `String author`, and six subclasses:
    `RomanceNovel`, `Mystery`, `ScienceFiction`, `Biography`, `Cookbook`, and `SelfHelpBook`.
(E) Use a class `Book` which has two data fields: `String title`, `String author`, and two subclasses:
    `FictionWork` and `NonFictionWork`. The class `FictionWork` has three subclasses, `RomanceNovel`,
    `Mystery`, and `ScienceFiction`. The class `NonFictionWork` has three subclasses: `Biography`,
    `Cookbook`, and `SelfHelpBook`.

GO ON TO THE NEXT PAGE.

34. Consider the following code:

```
public int mystery(int x)
{
    if (x == 1)
        return <missing value>;
    else
        return(2 * mystery(x - 1)) + x;
}
```

Which of the following can be used to replace <missing value> so that mystery (4) returns 34 ?

(A) 0

(B) 1

(C) 2

(D) 3

(E) 4

35. Consider the following code segment:

```
int [ ] X;
int [ ] Y;
int k;
X = initializeX();        // returns a valid
                          // initialized int [ ]
Y = initializeY();        // returns a valid
                          // initialized int [ ]
for (k = 0;
    k < X.length && X[k] == Y[k];
    k++)
{
    /* some code */
}
```

Assuming that after X and Y are initialized, X.length == Y.length, which of the following must be true after executing this code segment?

(A) k < X.length

(B) k < X.length && X[k] == Y[k]

(C) k < X.length && X[k] != Y[k]

(D) k >= X.length || X[k] == Y[k]

(E) k >= X.length || X[k] != Y[k]

36. Which of the following would *not* cause a run-time exception?

(A) Dividing an integer by zero

(B) Using an object that has been declared but not instantiated

(C) Accessing an array element with an array index that is equal to the length of the array

(D) Attempting to create a substring beginning at a negative index

(E) Attempting to call a method with the wrong number of arguments

GO ON TO THE NEXT PAGE.

37. Assume that a and b are properly initialized variables of type Double.

    Which of the following is an equivalent expression to:

    ```
    a.doubleValue()    != b.doubleValue()
    ```

    (A) `a != b`
    (B) `a.notEquals(b)`
    (C) `!(a.doubleValue() .equals(b.doubleValue()))`
    (D) `!(a.compareTo(b))`
    (E) `a.compareTo(b) != 0`

38. Which of the following would be the LEAST effective way of ensuring reliability in a program?

    (A) Encapsulating functionality in a class by declaring all data fields to be public
    (B) Defining and following preconditions and postconditions for every method
    (C) Including assertions at key places in the code
    (D) Using descriptive variable names
    (E) Indenting code in a consistent and logical manner

39. Consider a dictionary that has 1,024 pages with 50 words on each page.

    In order to look up a given target word, a student is considering using one of the following three methods:

    Method 1

    Use a binary search technique to find the correct page (comparing the target word with the first word on a given page). When the correct page is found, use a sequential search technique to find the target word on the page.

    Method 2

    Use a sequential search technique to find the correct page (comparing the target word with the first word on a given page). When the correct page is found, use another sequential search technique to find the target word on the page.

    Method 3

    Use a sequential search technique on all of the words in the dictionary to find the target word.

    Which of the following best characterizes the greatest number of words that will be examined using each method?

	Method 1	Method 2	Method 3
(A)	10	50	1,024
(B)	55	512	2,560
(C)	55	537	25,600
(D)	60	1,074	1,074
(E)	60	1,074	51,200

GO ON TO THE NEXT PAGE.

40. Consider the following recursive method.

```java
public static int mystery(int m)
{
    if (m == 0)
    {
        return 0;
    }
    else
    {
        return 4 + mystery(m - 2);
    }
}
```

Assuming that j is a positive integer and that m = 2j, what value is returned as a result of the call `mystery(j)`?

(A) 0
(B) m
(C) 2m
(D) j
(E) 2j

END OF SECTION I

IF YOU FINISH BEFORE TIME IS CALLED,
YOU MAY CHECK YOUR WORK ON THIS SECTION.

DO NOT GO ON TO SECTION II UNTIL YOU ARE TOLD TO DO SO.

COMPUTER SCIENCE A
SECTION II
Time—1 hour and 30 minutes
Number of Questions—4
Percent of Total Grade—50%

Directions: SHOW ALL YOUR WORK. REMEMBER THAT PROGRAM SEGMENTS ARE TO BE WRITTEN IN JAVA™.

Notes:

- Assume that the classes listed in the Java Quick Reference have been imported where appropriate.

- Unless otherwise noted in the question, assume that parameters in method calls are not null and that methods are called only when their preconditions are satisfied.

- In writing solutions for each question, you may use any of the accessible methods that are listed in classes defined in that question. Writing significant amounts of code that can be replaced by a call to one of these methods will not receive full credit.

FREE-RESPONSE QUESTIONS

1. In a certain school, students are permitted to enroll in one elective class from a list of electives offered. Because there are a limited number of spaces in each class for students, and because some electives are more popular than others, a lottery system was devised by the school to assign students to electives.

   Each student lists three choices for electives. The school orders the students randomly and assigns each student to the first available elective in the student's list of three choices. If none of the three choices is available (because those electives are fully enrolled), the school does not assign the student to an elective.

   After the school attempts to assign all of the students to electives, it produces a list of students it was unable to assign.

   For example, suppose there are six electives available to students: Astronomy, Ballroom Dance, Basket Weaving, Constitutional Law, Marine Biology, and Programming.

   The following table shows the name, maximum enrollment, and current enrollment for six electives after 64 students have been successfully assigned to electives:

Elective Name	Maximum Enrollment	Current Enrollment
Astronomy	12	12
Ballroom Dance	20	3
Basket Weaving	15	14
Constitutional Law	10	7
Marine Biology	10	10
Programming	18	18

GO ON TO THE NEXT PAGE.

Note that three electives, Astronomy, Programming, and Marine Biology, are fully enrolled and are no longer options for students.

Now suppose that the following students need to be assigned to electives:

Student	First Choice `getChoice (0)`	Second Choice `getChoice (1)`	Third Choice `getChoice (2)`
Andrew	Programming	Marine Biology	Ballroom Dance
David	Constitutional Law	Basket Weaving	Programming
Elizabeth	Marine Biology	Programming	Astronomy
Ethan	Basket Weaving	Marine Biology	Astronomy
Katharine	Programming	Basket Weaving	Marine Biology

Andrew's first and second choices are fully enrolled, but his third choice has openings. Andrew will be enrolled in Ballroom Dance.

David's first choice has openings. David will be enrolled in Constitutional Law.

All three of Elizabeth's choices are fully enrolled. Elizabeth will remain unassigned to an elective.

Ethan's first choice has one opening left. Ethan will be enrolled in Basket Weaving. Note that Basket Weaving is now fully enrolled.

All three of Katharine's choices are now fully enrolled. Katharine will remain unassigned to an elective.

In this problem, the school is modeled by the class `School`. Students and electives are modeled by the classes `Student` and `Elective`, respectively.

The `School` class includes the following methods and private data:

- `studentList`—This `ArrayList` holds the list of students in the order in which the students should be scheduled.

- `electiveList`—This `ArrayList` holds the electives that students may choose.

- `getElectiveByName`—This method returns the `Elective` in `electiveList` with the given name.

- `assignElectivesToStudents`—This method encapsulates the functionality of assigning students (if possible) their first, second, or third elective choice.

- `studentsWithoutElectives`—This method returns an `ArrayList` containing students that have not been assigned an elective.

GO ON TO THE NEXT PAGE.

```
public class School
{
    private ArrayList<Student> studentList;
    // each element is an instance of a
    // Student representing one student
    // at the school; students are in
    // the order they should be scheduled

    private ArrayList<Elective> electiveList;
    // each element is an instance of an
    // Elective representing one elective
    // offered at the school

    // precondition: name is the name of an
    //          Elective in electiveList
    // postcondition: returns the Elective
    //          in electiveList with the given
    //          name
    private Elective getElectiveByName (String name)
    { /* to be implemented in part (a) */ }
    // postcondition: returns the size
    //     of electiveList
    private int getElectiveListSize()
    {
        return electiveList.size();
    }
    private int getStudentListSize()
    {
        return studentList.size();
    }

    // postcondition: All Students in
    //          studentList have been either
    //          assigned their first available
    //          elective choice or not assigned;
    //          All Electives in electiveList have
    //          been updated appropriately as
    //          Students are assigned to them
    public void assignElectivesToStudents()
    { /* to be implemented in part (b) */ }

    // postcondition: returns a list of
    //          those Students who have not been
    //          assigned an Elective
    public ArrayList<Student>
        studentsWithoutElectives()
    { /* to be implemented in part (c) */}

    // ... constructors, other methods,
    //          and other private data not shown
}
```

GO ON TO THE NEXT PAGE.

The Student class includes the following methods and private data:

- getChoice—This method returns the name of the given elective choice of the student. The first elective choice has index 0, the second has index 1, and the third has index 2.

- hasElective—This method returns true if the student has been assigned an elective; it returns false otherwise.

- assignElective—This method assigns the given elective to this student.

```
public class Student
{
    // precondition: 0 <= index < 3
    // postcondition: returns the name
    //         of the given elective choice
    public String getChoice(int index)
    { /* code not shown */}

    // postcondition: returns true if
    //         an Elective has been assigned
    //         to this Student
    public boolean hasElective()
    { /* code not shown */ }

    // precondition: e is not null
    // postcondition: e has been assigned
    //         to this Student; e has not been
    //         modified
    public void assignElective(Elective e)
    { /* code not shown */ }

    // ... constructors, other methods,
    //     and other private data not shown
}
```

The Elective class includes the following methods:

- getName—This method returns the name of this elective.

- getMaxClassSize—This method returns the maximum number of students that can be assigned to this elective.

- getClassSize—This method returns the number of students that have been assigned to this elective.

- addStudent—This method assigns the given student to this elective.

GO ON TO THE NEXT PAGE.

```
public class Elective
{
    private String name;
    private in maxClassSize;
    private int classSize;
    private ArrayList studentList = new ArrayList();

    // postcondition: returns the name
    //      of this Elective
    public String getName()
    { /* code not shown */ }

    // postcondition: returns the
    //         maximum number of Students
    //         that can be added to this
    //         Elective
    public int getMaxClassSize()
    { /* code not shown */ }

    // postcondition: returns the
    //         number of Students that have
    //         been added to this Elective;
    //         0 < = getClassSize ( ) < =
    //         getMaxClassSize ( )
    public int getClassSize()
    { /* code not shown */ }

    // precondition: getClassSize ( ) <
    //         getMaxClassSize ( ); s is not null
    // postcondition: s has been added to
    //         this Elective; getClassSize ( ) has
    //         been increased by 1
    public void addStudent(Student s)
    { /* code not shown */ }

    // constructors, other methods, and other private data not shown
}
```

(a) Write the `School` method `getElectiveByName`. Method `getElectiveByName` should return the `Elective` in `electiveList` that has the given name.

Complete method `getElectiveByName` below.

```
// precondition: name is the name of an
//             Elective in electiveList
// postcondition: returns the Elective in
//             electiveList with the given name
private Elective getElectiveByName(String name)
```

(b) Write the `School` method `assignElectivesToStudents`. Method `assignElectivesToStudents` should assign electives to students as described at the beginning of this question.

In writing method `assignElectivesToStudents`, you may use the `private` helper method `getElectiveByName` specified in part (a). Assume that `getElectiveByName` works as specified, regardless of what you wrote in part (a). Solutions that reimplement functionality provided by this method, rather than invoking it, will not receive full credit.

Complete method `assignElectivesToStudents` below

```
// postcondition: All Students in
//                studentList have been either
//                assigned their first available
//                elective choice or not assigned;
//                All electives in electiveList have
//                been updated appropriately as
//                Students are assigned to them
public void assignElectivesToStudents()
```

GO ON TO THE NEXT PAGE.

(c) Write the `School` method `studentsWithoutElectives`. Method `studentsWithoutElectives` should return `ArrayList` of all Students in `studentList` who do not have an `Elective` assigned to them.

Complete method `studentsWithoutElectives` below

```
// postcondition: returns a list of those
//         Students who have not been assigned
//         an Elective
public ArrayList studentsWithoutElectives()
```

GO ON TO THE NEXT PAGE.

2. Consider a deck of *n* cards where *n* is even and each card is uniquely labeled from 1 to *n*.

A *shuffle* is performed when the deck is divided into two stacks and the stacks are interlaced so that a new stack is formed by alternately taking cards from each stack.

For instance, a deck of ten cards is in order when the card labeled 0 is on the top of the deck and the card labeled 9 is on the bottom of the deck.

Dividing the deck in half produces two stacks of cards—one stack with cards 0 through 4, the other with cards 5 through 9. Interlacing the stacks produces a deck in the following order:

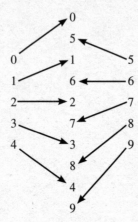

The number of times needed to shuffle the deck until it returns to its original order is called the *reorder count*. Note that the reorder count for a deck of ten cards is six:

Shuffle number

Original	1	2	3	4	5	6
0	0	0	0	0	0	0
1	5	7	8	4	2	1
2	1	5	7	8	4	2
3	6	3	6	3	6	3
4	2	1	5	7	8	4
5	7	8	4	2	1	5
6	3	6	3	6	3	6
7	8	4	2	1	5	7
8	4	2	1	5	7	8
9	9	9	9	9	9	9

GO ON TO THE NEXT PAGE.

A deck is modeled by the following incomplete declaration of the `Deck` class:

```
public class Deck
{
    private int [ ] cards;

    public Deck(int numCards)
    { /* code not shown */ }

    public boolean inOrder()
    { /* to be implemented in part (a) */ }

    public void shuffle()
    { /* to be implemented in part (b) */ }

    public int reorderingCount()
    { /* to be implemented in part (c) */ }
}
```

(a) Write the `Deck` method `inOrder`. Method `inOrder` should return true if the cards in the `deck` are in numerical order from 0 to `cards.length` $-$ 1 and should return false otherwise. Cards are in numerical order if cards [k] = = k for all $0 <= k <$ cards.length.

Complete method inOrder below.

```
        // precondition: For all k such that
        //              0 <= k < cards.length,
        //              0 <= cards [k] < cards.length and
        //              each card [k] is unique
        // postcondition: returns true if
        //              cards [k] = = k for all
        //              0 <= k < cards.length; returns
        //              false otherwise
        public boolean inOrder()
```

GO ON TO THE NEXT PAGE.

(b) Write the `Deck` method `shuffle`. This method should divide the deck into two equal stacks and interlace them evenly as described at the beginning of this question.

Complete method `shuffle` below.

```
// postcondition: the deck is shuffled by
//                dividing the deck into two equal stacks
//                that are evenly interlaced
public void shuffle()
```

GO ON TO THE NEXT PAGE.

(c) Write the `Deck` method `reorderCount`. Method `reorderCount` should return the number of shuffles necessary to return the deck to its original order.

In writing method `reorderCount`, you may use the methods `inOrder` and shuffle as specified in parts (a) and (b). Assume that `inOrder` and shuffle work as specified, regardless of what you wrote in parts (a) and (b). Solutions that reimplement functionality provided by these methods, rather than invoking them, will not receive full credit.

Complete method `reorderCount` below.

```
// postcondition: returns the number of
//          shuffles necessary to return the cards
//          in the deck to their original numerical
//          order such that inOrder ( ) = = true; the
//          cards in the deck are in their original
//          numerical order
public int reorderCount ()
```

GO ON TO THE NEXT PAGE.

3. Consider the design of an electronic cookbook modeled with the following class declarations:

```
public class Cookbook

{

    private ArrayList recipeList;  // each entry is an instance of a Recipe representing one recipe in the cook-
book
```

```
    /* precondition: numPeople > 0

     * postcondition: All recipes in recipeList have been converted to serve numPeople number of people

    */

    public void standardize(int numPeople)

    { /* code not shown */ }
```

```
    // ... constructors, other methods, and other private data not shown
}
```

```
public class Ingredient
{
    private String name;  // the name of this ingredient
    private double amount;  // the amount of this ingredient needed in the recipe
```

```
    // @returns the amount of this ingredient needed in the recipe
    public double getAmount()
    { /* code not shown */ }
```

```
    /** precondition: amt > 0.0
     * postcondition: amount has been set // to amt
    */
    public void setAmount (double amt)
    { /* code not shown */ }
```

```
    /* precondition: newNumber > 0
     * postcondition: numberServed has been set to newNumber
    */
    public void setNumberServed(int newNumber)
    { /* code not shown */ }
```

```
    // ... constructors and other methods not shown
```

```
}
```

GO ON TO THE NEXT PAGE.

(a) A recipe in the cookbook is modeled by the class `Recipe` with the following data and operations:

Data

- the name of the recipe
- the list of ingredients used in the recipe
- the description of the preparation process for the recipe
- the number of people served by the recipe

Operations

- create a recipe with a given name and number of people served
- add an ingredient to the recipe
- set the description of the preparation process for the recipe
- return the name of the recipe
- return the list of ingredients
- return the number of people served by the recipe
- scale the recipe to serve a given new number of people by changing the amount of each ingredient appropriately

Write the definition of the class `Recipe`, showing the appropriate data definitions and constructor and method signatures. You should *not* write the implementations of the constructor or methods for the `Recipe` class.

(b) Using the signature you wrote in part (a), write the implementation for the method that scales the recipe to serve a given new number of people.

In writing this method, you may call any of the methods in the `Recipe` class (as you defined it in part (a)) or in the `Ingredient` class. Assume that these methods work as specified.

(c) Write the `Cookbook` method `standardize` as described at the beginning of the question.

In writing this method, you may call any of the methods in the `Recipe` class (as you defined it in part (a)). Assume that these methods work as specified.

Complete method `standardize` below.

```
// precondition: numPeople > 0
// postcondition: All recipes in
//            recipeList have been scaled to
//            serve numPeople number of people
public void standardize(int numPeople)
```

GO ON TO THE NEXT PAGE.

4. Consider a school that contains x number of students that all start their first period class in one of n classrooms. This scenario can be represented using three classes. The School class contains an array of all the Classrooms in the school. The Classroom class has fields for the teacher in charge of the room teacherName and an array of all the Students in the classroom Students. The Student class has a field for the name of the student studentName and the ID number of the student studentID.

The School class contains a method findStudent that takes a teacher's name and a student ID as arguments and returns the name of the student. The method utilizes a sequential search algorithm to find the correct classroom and a binary search algorithm to find the correct student. If the student is not found in the classroom of which the given teacher is in charge, the method returns "Student Not Found."

Write the complete School, Classroom, and Student classes, including any instance variables, constructors, and necessary methods. You may assume that the student ID numbers in each classroom are sorted in ascending order.

STOP

END OF EXAM

Practice Test 2:
Answers and
Explanations

PRACTICE TEST 2 ANSWER KEY

1.	C	21.	C
2.	A	22.	C
3.	C	23.	D
4.	C	24.	D
5.	E	25.	A
6.	B	26.	E
7.	A	27.	B
8.	B	28.	E
9.	C	29.	B
10.	E	30.	A
11.	A	31.	B
12.	B	32.	B
13.	D	33.	E
14.	C	34.	C
15.	B	35.	E
16.	E	36.	E
17.	A	37.	E
18.	D	38.	A
19.	C	39.	E
20.	C	40.	C

PRACTICE TEST 2 EXPLANATIONS

Section I: Multiple-Choice Questions

1. **C** This question tests how well you understand assigning values to variables and following the steps of the code. When `trial()` is called, a is assigned to the integer value of 10 and b is assigned to the integer value of 5. Next `doubleValues()` is called with a and b as inputs c and d. The method `doubleValues()` multiplies the input values c and d by 2 and prints them out. Thus, the value of c is 10 * 2 = 20 and the value of d is 5 * 2 = 10. Because `System.out.print()` does not print any line breaks or spaces, the resulting print is "2010." While c and d have been reassigned new values, these values exist only within the `doubleValues()` call, so the values of a and b are unchanged. After the `doubleValues()` method is completed, the `trial()` method then prints the values of b and then a, printing 510. Once again, no spaces or line breaks are printed, so, combined together, what is printed from calling `trial()` is 2010510. Therefore, the correct answer is (C).

2. **A** The method `mystery(int a, int b)` takes as input integers a and b with the precondition that a > b > 0. Plug in x = 5 and y = 2. These values are passed as parameters to make a = 5 and b = 2. Set d = 0. Now go to the for loop, initializing c = a = 5. Since it is still the case that c > b, execute the for loop. Execute d = d + c by setting d = 0 + 5 = 5. Decrease c by 1 to get c = 4. Since c > b, execute the for loop again. Execute d = d + c by setting d = 5 + 4 = 9. Decrease c by 1 to get c = 3. Since it is still the case that c > b, execute the for loop again. Execute d = d + c by setting d = 9 + 3 = 12. Decrease c by 1 to get c = 2. Since it is no longer the case that c > b, stop executing the for loop. Return d = 12. Now go through the choices and eliminate any that don't describe a return of 12. Choice (A) is the sum of all integers greater than y but less than or equal to x. The sum of all integers greater than 2 but less than or equal to 5 is 3 + 4 + 5 = 12, so keep (A). Choice (B) is the sum of all integers greater than or equal to y but less than or equal to x. The sum of all integers greater than or equal to 2 but less than or equal to 5 is 2 + 3 + 4 + 5 = 14, so eliminate (B). Choice (C) is the sum of all integers greater than y but less than x. The sum of all integers greater than 2 but less than 5 is 3 + 4 = 7, so eliminate (C). Choice (D) is the sum of all integers greater than or equal to y but less than x. The sum of all integers greater than or equal to 2 but less than 5 is 2 + 3 + 4 = 9, so eliminate (D). Choice (E) is the sum of all integers less than y but greater than or equal to x. However, there are infinitely many integers less than 2 and infinitely many integers greater than or equal to 5, so this return would require an infinite loop. Eliminate (E). Only one answer remains. The correct answer is (A).

3. **C** The question asks for what is printed by the call `mystery(3)`. In the call, 3 is taken as a parameter and assigned to n. The integer k is then initialized in the for loop and set equal to 0. Since k < n, execute the for loop. Call `mystery(0)`, while keeping your place in the call of `mystery(3)`. Again, k is initialized in the for loop and set equal to 0. In this call, since n = 0, it is not the case that k < n, so do not execute the for loop. This completes the call of `mystery(0)`, so return to

mystery(3). The next command is System.out.print(k). Since k = 0, the first character printed is 0. Look to see whether any choices can be eliminated. However, all choices begin with 0, so no choices can be eliminated. Continue with the method call. Since this is the last command of the for loop, increment k to get k = 1. Since it is still the case that k < n, execute the for loop again. Call mystery(1), again keeping your place in the call of mystery(3). Again, k is initialized in the for loop and set equal to 0. In this call, since n = 1, it is the case that k < n, so execute the for loop. Call mystery(k), which is mystery(0). As seen above, mystery(0) prints nothing, so execute the next line in mystery(1), which is System.out.print(k). Since k = 0, print 0. Eliminate (A), since the second character printed is not 0. Increment k to get k = 1. Since it is no longer the case that k < n, do not execute the for loop again and end this call of mystery(1). Return to the original call of mystery(3), where k = 1 and System.out.print(k) is the next statement. Print 1. All remaining choices have 1 as the third character, so do not eliminate any choices. This is the end of the for loop, so increment k to get k = 2. Since n = 3, it is still the case that k < n, so execute the for loop. Call mystery(2), while holding your place in mystery(3). Again, k is initialized in the for loop and set equal to 0. In this call, since n = 2, it is the case that k < n, so execute the for loop. Call mystery(0), which prints nothing. Execute System.out.print(k) to print 0. Eliminate (B), since the next character is not 0. Increment k to get k = 1. Since k < n, execute the for loop. Call mystery(1), which, as described above, prints 0. All remaining choices have 0 as the next character, so don't eliminate any choices. The next command in mystery(2) is System.out.print(k), so print 1. Again, keep all the remaining choices. In mystery(2), increment k to get k = 2. Since n = 2, it is no longer the case that k < n, so stop executing the for loop. End mystery(2) and return to mystery(3), where k = 2 and the next command is System.out.print(k), so print 2. Again, keep all remaining choices. Increment k to get k = 3. Since it is no longer the case that k < n, stop executing the for loop. The method call is complete for mystery(3), so there will be no more printed characters. Eliminate (D) and (E), which have further characters printed.

In other words, the calling sequence looks like this

```
Function Call                        Prints
mystery(3)
   mystery(0)
   System.out.print(0)                 0
   mystery(1)
      mystery(0)
      System.out.print(0)              0
   System.out.print(1)                 1
   mystery(2)
      mystery(0)
      System.out.print(0)              0
      mystery(1)
         mystery(0)
         System.out.print(0)           0
      System.out.print(1)              1
   System.out.print(2)                 2
```

The correct answer is (C).

4. **C** `SelectionSort` walks through the array to find the smallest element in the part of the array not yet sorted. It then swaps that smallest element with the first unsorted element.

Start with the original array of values.

| 4 | 10 | 1 | 2 | 6 | 7 | 3 | 5 |

The smallest element is 1. Swap that with the first unsorted element, 4. The array now looks like this.

| 1 | 10 | 4 | 2 | 6 | 7 | 3 | 5 |

This is not a choice, so continue. The smallest element in the unsorted part of the array (from 10 to 5) is 2. Swap that with the first unsorted element, 10.

| 1 | 2 | 4 | 10 | 6 | 7 | 3 | 5 |

This is still not a choice, so continue this process. The smallest element in the unsorted part of the array (from 4 to 5) is 3. Swap that with the first unsorted element, 4.

| 1 | 2 | 3 | 10 | 6 | 7 | 4 | 5 |

This is (C), so stop here. If you're interested, here are the complete moves for selection sort.

| 1 | 2 | 3 | 4 | 6 | 7 | 10 | 5 |

| 1 | 2 | 3 | 4 | 5 | 7 | 10 | 6 |

| 1 | 2 | 3 | 4 | 5 | 6 | 10 | 7 |

| 1 | 2 | 3 | 4 | 5 | 6 | 7 | 10 |

The correct answer is (C).

5. **E** Execute the commands. The integer `k` and the integer array `A` are initialized. The array `A` is given length 7. Thus, the array, `A`, has seven elements with indexes from 0 to 6. Execute the first for loop. Set `k = 0`. Since `k < A.length`, execute the for loop, which sets `A[0]` equal to `A.length – k = 7 – 0 = 7`. Increment `k` to get `k = 1`. Since `1 < 7`, execute the for loop, which sets `A[1]` equal to `A.length – k = 7 – 1 = 6`. Increment `k` to get `k = 2`. Since `2 < 7`, execute the for loop, which sets `A[2]` equal to `A.length – k = 7 – 2 = 5`. Increment `k` to get `k = 3`. Since `3 < 7`, execute the for loop, which sets `A[3]` equal to `A.length – k = 7 – 3 = 4`. Increment `k` to get `k = 4`. Since `4 < 7`, execute the for loop, which sets `A[4]` equal to `A.length – k = 7 – 4 = 3`. Increment `k` to get `k = 5`. Since `5 < 7`, execute the for loop, which sets `A[5]` equal to `A.length – k = 7 – 5 = 2`. Increment `k` to get `k = 6`. Since `6 < 7`, execute the for loop, which sets `A[6]` equal to `A.length – k = 7 – 6 = 1`. Increment `k` to get `k = 7`. Since it is not the case that `7 < 7`, stop executing the for loop. Therefore, the array has the values

| 7 | 6 | 5 | 4 | 3 | 2 | 1 |

The second for loop puts the value of the kth element of the array into the (k + 1)st element. Be careful!

A quick glance might lead you to believe that each value is shifted in the array one spot to the right, giving an answer of (D). However, a step-by-step analysis demonstrates that this will not be the case. The for loop sets k = 0. Since 0 < A.length - 1, execute the for loop. The command in the for loop is A[k+1] = A[k]. Since k = 0, set A[1] = A[0] = 7. Increment k to get k = 1. Since it is still the case that k < A.length - 1, execute the for loop. Since k = 1, set A[2] = A[1] = 7. Continue in this manner. Since A.length - 1 = 7 - 1 = 6, only execute the for loop through k = 5. Each execution of the for loop is shown below.

```
k    Assignment      A[]
0    A[1] = A[0]     7 7 5 4 3 2 1
1    A[2] = A[1]     7 7 7 4 3 2 1
2    A[3] = A[2]     7 7 7 7 3 2 1
3    A[4] = A[3]     7 7 7 7 7 2 1
4    A[5] = A[4]     7 7 7 7 7 7 1
5    A[6] = A[5]     7 7 7 7 7 7 7
```

The final values contained by A are 7 7 7 7 7 7 7. The correct answer is (E).

6. **B** Choices (C), (D), and (E) are syntactically invalid according to the given class definitions. In (C), p is used as a PostOffice object rather than an array of PostOffice objects. Choice (D) treats getMail and getBox as static methods without invoking them from an object. Choice (E) creates a new Mail object attempting to use a Mail constructor. Even if such a constructor were available, there would be no way for the constructor to know about p, the array of PostOffices.

Choices (A) and (B) differ only in the indexes of the array and methods. There are two clues in the question that indicate that (B) is the correct answer. First, p is declared as an array of 10 PostOffices. This means that p[10] would raise an ArrayListOutOfBoundsException. Remember that p[9] actually refers to the 10th post office, since array indexes begin with 0. Second, the comments in the class definitions for the getBox and getMail methods indicate that the parameter they take is zero-based. Therefore, they should be passed an integer one less than the number of the box or piece of mail needed. For either reason, eliminate (A). The correct answer is (B).

7. **A** In the method printEmptyBoxes, the loop variable k refers to the index of the post office and the loop variable x refers to the index of the box within the post office. Choice (A) is correct. It checks to see if the box is assigned and if it does not have mail using the appropriate methods of the Box class. It then prints out the box number of the box. Choice (B) is similar to (A) but incorrectly interchanges x and k. Eliminate (B). Choice (C) omits the call to the method getBox. Therefore, it attempts to call the getBoxNumber() method of the PostOffice object p[k]. Since PostOffice objects do not have a getBoxNumber() method, this would result in a compile error. Eliminate (C). Choice (D) is similar to (C) but interchanges x and k. Eliminate (D). Choice (E) prints the

value of k, which is the index of the post office rather than the index of the box. Eliminate (E). The correct answer is (A).

8. **B**   There are four possibilities for the values of a and b. Either both a and b are true, both a and b are false, a is true and b is false, or a is false and b is true.

Analyze the possibilities in a table.

a (initial value)	b (initial value)	a = a && b (final value)	b = a || b (final value)
true	true	true	true
true	false	false	false
false	true	false	true
false	false	false	false

Remember when calculating b = a || b that a has already been modified. Therefore, use the final, rather than the initial, value of a when calculating the final value of b.

Go through each statement. Statement I says that the final value of a is equal to the initial value of a. This is not the case in the second row of the table, so Statement I is not always true. Eliminate any choice that includes it: (A) and (D). Statement II says that the final value of b is equal to the initial value of b. This is true in each row and Statement II is always true, so eliminate the choice that does not include it: (C). Statement III says that the final value of a is equal to the initial value of b. This is not the case in the third row of the table, so Statement III is not always true. Eliminate any choice that includes it: (E). The correct answer is (B).

9. **C**   The best way to solve this problem is to look at each if statement individually. The integer x is initialized and then set equal to 53. The next statement is an if statement with the condition (x > 10). Since 53 > 10, execute the statement, System.out.print("A"), and print A. The next statement is an if-else statement, this one having the condition (x > 30). Since 53 > 30, execute the if statement, System.out.print("B"), and print B. Even though 53 > 40, because the statement is an else statement, it cannot be executed if the original if statement was executed. Therefore, do not execute the else statement, and do not print C. The next statement is another if statement, this one having the condition (x > 50). Since 53 > 50, execute the statement, System.out.print("D"), and print D. The next statement is another if statement, this one having the condition (x > 70). Since it is not the case that 53 > 70, do not execute the statement. There is no further code to execute, so the result of the printing is ABD. The correct answer is (C).

10. **E**   This problem tests your ability to work with nested for loops. Although it appears complicated at first glance, it can easily be solved by systematically walking through the code.

Be sure to write the values of the variables j and k down on paper; don't try to keep track of j and k in your head. Use the empty space in the question booklet for this purpose.

Code	j	k	Output
Set j to the value -2.	-2		
Test the condition: j <= 2? Yes.	-2		
Set k to the value that j has.	-2	-2	
Test the condition: k < j + 3? Yes.	-2	-2	
Output k.	-2	-2	-2
Update k: k++	-2	-1	-2
Test the condition: k < j + 3? Yes.	-2	-1	-2
Output k.	-2	-1	-2 -1
Update k: k++	-2	0	-2 -1
Test the condition: k < j + 3? Yes.	-2	0	-2 -1
Output k.	-2	0	-2 -1 0
Update k: k++	-2	1	-2 -1 0
Test the condition: k < j + 3? No.	-2	1	-2 -1 0
Update j: j = j + 2	0	1	-2 -1 0
Test the condition: j <= 2? Yes	0	1	-2 -1 0
Set k to the value that j has.	0	0	-2 -1 0
Test the condition: k < j + 3? Yes.	0	0	-2 -1 0
Output k.	0	0	-2 -1 0 0

At this point, stop because (E) is the only choice that starts -2 -1 0 0. However, repeating this process will result in the correct output of -2 -1 0 0 1 2 2 3 4. The correct answer is (E).

11. **A** To solve this problem, first note that count % 3 is equal to the remainder when count is divided by 3. Execute the method call mystery(5, "X"), taking count = 5 and s = "X" as parameters. Because it is not the case that 5 <= 0, do not execute the first if statement.

Because 5 % 3 = 2, calling mystery(5, "X") will execute the else statement, printing X. Then, it will call mystery(4, "X"), and return. Because 4 % 3 = 1, calling mystery(4, "X") will execute the else if statement, printing X-X, call mystery(3, "X"), and return. At this point, (C) and (E) can be eliminated. Because 3 % 3 = 0, calling mystery(3, "X") will execute the if statement, printing X–X, call mystery(2, "X"), and return. Note that you can stop at this point because (B) and (D) can be eliminated. If you're interested, here is the remainder of the execution. Because 2 % 3 = 2, calling mystery(2, "X") will execute the else statement, printing X, call mystery(1, "X"), and return. Because 1 % 3 = 1, calling mystery(1, "X") will execute the else if statement, printing X-X, call mystery(0, "X"), and return. Finally, calling mystery(0, "X") will simply return because count is less than or equal to zero. Putting it all together, mystery(5, "X") prints

XX-XX--XXX-X

The correct answer is (A).

12. **B** The only information that you need to solve this problem is the first sentence in the description of the constructor. Class `DiningRoomSet` has a constructor, which is passed a `Table` object and an `ArrayList` of `Chair` objects. Because you are writing a constructor, you can immediately eliminate (A) and (C), which are void methods. Constructors never return anything, so there is never a need to specify a void return. Choice (E) is incorrect because the constructor is passed a `Table` object and a `Chair` object, not a `Table` object and an `ArrayList` of `Chair` objects. Choice (D) is incorrect because the second parameter has two types associated with it. It should have only one type: `ArrayList`. Choice (B) is correct.

13. **D** The best way to solve this problem is to eliminate choices. Choices (A) and (B) are incorrect because the class description states that the `getPrice` method of the `DiningRoomSet` class does not take any parameters. Choice (C) can be eliminated because the private data field `myChairs` is not a `Chair`; it is an `ArrayList`. Therefore, it does not have a `getPrice` method. This leaves (D) and (E). You need to know that `ArrayLists` are accessed using the get method while arrays are accessed using the `[]` notation. `MyChairs` is an `ArrayList`, so the correct answer is (D).

14. **C** To solve this type of problem, use information about the output and the loops to eliminate incorrect choices. Then, if necessary, work through the code for any remaining choices to determine the correct answer. There are six lines of output. By examining the outer loop of each of the choices, you can eliminate (B) because it will traverse the loop seven times, and during each traversal at least one number will be printed. You can also eliminate (A) because the outer loop will never be executed. The initial value of j is 6, but the condition `j < 0` causes the loop to terminate immediately. The remaining choices have the same outer loop, so turn your attention to the inner loop. Eliminate (D) because the first time through the loop, a 7 will be printed—clearly not the correct output. Finally, eliminate (E) because the condition of the inner loop, `k >= 0`, will cause a 0 to be printed at the end of each line. This leaves (C), which is indeed the correct answer.

15. **B** This problem tests your knowledge of the methods of the ArrayList class. The following table shows the contents of list after each line of code.

Code	Contents of list	Explanation
list = new ArrayList();	[]	A newly created ArrayList is empty
list.add(new Integer(7));	[7]	Adds 7 to the end of list
list.add(new Integer(6));	[7, 6]	Adds 6 to the end of list
list.add(1, new Integer(5));	[7, 5, 6]	Inserts 5 into list as position 1, shifting elements to the right as necessary
list.add(1, new Integer(4));	[7, 4, 5, 6]	Inserts 4 into list as position 1, shifting elements to the right as necessary
list.add(new Integer(3));	[7, 4, 5, 6, 3]	Adds 3 to the end of list

`list.set(2, new Integer(2));`	`[7, 4, 2, 6, 3]`	Replaces the number at position 2 in the list with 2
`list.add(1, new Integer(1));`	`[7, 1, 4, 2, 6, 3]`	Inserts 1 into list at position 1, shifting elements to the right as necessary

The next command is to print list. Therefore, the correct answer is (B).

16. **E** Although the `Dog` class extends `Animal`, Java does not require `Dog` to have any specific methods. New methods will be unique to `Dog` objects (and those of its subclasses, when applicable) and methods inherited from `Animal` can be invoked as normal.

The correct answer is (E).

17. **A** This question is testing your understanding of static and dynamic types.

```
Fish Bob = new Shark();
```

This line creates the `Bob` variable with the static type of `Fish` and the dynamic type of `Shark`.

```
System.out.println(Bob.endoskeleton);
```

This line prints the `endoskeleton` field of the variable `Bob`. When looking up a field, the static type is used so "bone" is printed.

```
Bob.action();
```

This line executes the method `action()`. When looking up a method, the dynamic type is used so "chomp chomp" is printed. The correct answer is (A).

18. **D** The insertion sort algorithm creates a sorted array by sorting elements one at a time.

The for loop of the code shows that the elements are being sorted from left to right. To determine the position of the new element to be sorted, the value of the new element must be compared with the values of the sorted elements from right to left. This requires `index--` in the while loop, not `index++`. Choices (A) and (C) are wrong.

In order to place the new element to be sorted in its correct position, any sorted elements larger than the new element must be shifted to the right. This requires `sort[index] = sort[index -1]`. Choices (B) and (E) are wrong. The correct answer is (D).

19. **C** In order for the array to be sorted in descending order, you will need to make a change. Plug each answer choice into the array to see which is correct. In (A) and (B), as the index will never be less than 0, the contents of the while loop will never be executed. Choice (C) is the correct answer as it changes the condition of finding the position of the new element from being less than the compared element to greater. In (D), altering the for loop this way would lead to the elements being sorted from right to left but still in ascending order. In (E), the index is initialized at 1 and decremented while index > 0, so it will execute the for loop only once. The correct answer is (C).

20. **C** The rate at which insertion sort runs depends on the number of comparisons that are made. The number of comparisons is minimized with an array with elements that are already sorted in ascending order and maximized with an array with elements that are sorted in descending order. The array in (C) is sorted in reverse order and will require the most comparisons to sort. The correct answer is (C).

21. **C** All three responses look very similar, so look carefully at the difference. Statement I is missing the keyword `new`, which is needed to create a new object. Eliminate any choice that includes Statement I: (A) and (D). Statements II and III differ in that Statement II uses `f.numerator` and `f.denominator` while Statement III uses `f.getNumerator()` and `f.getDenominator()`. Since the integers `numerator` and `denominator` are private while the methods `getNumerator()` and `getDenominator()` are public, the methods must be called by another object. Therefore, Statement II is not valid. Eliminate any choice that includes it: (B) and (E). The correct answer is (C).

22. **C** Go through the choices one at a time. Choice (A) is incorrect because the multiplication operator, `*`, is not defined to work on `Fraction` objects. Eliminate (A). Choice (B) is incorrect because the multiply method takes only one parameter and it is not correctly invoked by a `Fraction` object. Eliminate (B). Choice (C) correctly calls the `multiply()` method as through a fraction object, taking the other fraction as a parameter. Keep (C). Choice (D) attempts to create a new `Fraction` object but incorrectly constructs it by passing two `Fraction` objects rather than two integers. Eliminate (D). Finally, while (E) calculates the value of the result of the multiplication, the "/" operator assigns integer types, which cannot be applied to `answer`, which is an object of type `Fraction`. Eliminate (E). The correct answer is (C).

23. **D** Go through each statement one at a time. Constructor I is legal. This default constructor of the `ReducedFraction` class will automatically call the default constructor of the `Fraction` class and the private data of both classes will be set appropriately. Eliminate any choice that does not include Constructor I: (B), (C), and (E). Because Constructor II is not included in the remaining choices, do not worry about analyzing it. Constructor III is also legal. The call `super(n, d)` invokes the second constructor of the `Fraction` class which sets the private data of the `Fraction` class appropriately. The private data of the `ReducedFraction` class is then set explicitly in the `ReducedFraction` constructor. Note that if the call `super(n, d)` were not present, Constructor III would still be legal. However, it would create a logical error in the code as the default constructor of the Fraction class would be invoked and the private data of the Fraction class would not be set appropriately. Eliminate (A), which does not include Constructor III. Only one choice remains, so there is no need to continue. However, to see why Constructor II is illegal, remember that derived classes may not access the private data of their super classes. In other words, the constructor for a `ReducedFraction` may not directly access numerator and denominator in the Fraction class. The correct answer is (D).

24. **D** Go through each statement one at a time. Statement I is incorrect. "==" checks object references as opposed to their contents. This is an important distinction as two different objects may hold the same data. Eliminate (A), (C), and (E), which contain Statement I. Both of the remaining choices contain Statement II, so don't worry about analyzing it. Statement III is correct. The compareTo() method of the String class returns 0 if the two String objects hold the same strings. Eliminate (B), which does not include Statement III. Only one choice remains, so there is no need to continue. However, you should see why Statement II is also correct. The equals method of the String class returns true if the two String objects hold the same strings. The correct answer is (D).

25. **A** The values of s and t are not changed in mystery(). Even though s and t are both parameters of the method, only the instance variables a and b are changed. Thus, the original Strings s and t are unaffected by any action in mystery(). The correct answer is (A).

26. **E** Though these two classes are related through an inheritance relationship, there is no rule in Java that requires this structure to share methods and/or data. Therefore, there are no requirements on either class. The correct answer is (E).

27. **B** An example will help clarify this question.

Consider the following for loop:

```
for (int k = 0; k < 3; k++)
{
        Systemout.println(k);
}
```

This prints out the integers 0 to 2, one number per line. Matching int k = 0 to <1>; k < 3 to <2>; k++ to <3> and System.out.println(k); to <4>, go through each choice one at a time and determine whether each has the same functionality.

Choice (A) initializes k and assigns it the value 0. Then it tests to determine whether k < 3. This is true, so execute the while loop. The next command is k++, so increase k by 1 to get k = 0 + 1 = 1. Now execute System.out.println(k) to print 1. However, the first number printed in the original was 0, so this is incorrect. Eliminate (A).

Choice (B) initializes k and assigns it the value 0. Then it tests to determine whether k < 3. This is true, so execute the while loop. Now execute System.out.println(k) to print 0. The next command is k++, so increase k by 1 to get k = 0 + 1 = 1. Go back to the top of the while loop. Since k = 1, it is still the case that k < 3, so execute the while loop. Now execute System.out.println(k) to print 1. The next command is k++, so increase k by 1 to get k = 1 + 1 = 2. Go back to the top of the while loop. Since k = 2, it is still the case that k < 3, so execute the while loop. Now execute System.out.println(k) to print 2. The next command is k++, so increase k by 1 to get k = 2 + 1 = 3. Go back to the top of the while loop. Since k = 3, it is no longer the case that k < 3, so stop executing the while loop. The result of the program is printing the integers 0 to 2, one number per line, so keep (B).

Choice (C) initializes k and assigns it the value 0. Then it tests the condition !(k < 3). Since it is the case that k < 3, the statement (k < 3) has the boolean value true making the boolean value of !(k < 3) false. Thus the while loop is not executed. Since the while loop is not executed, nothing is printed. Eliminate (C).

Choice (D) has the same initialization statement and while loop condition as choice (C), so nothing is printed by this choice either. Eliminate (D).

Choice (E) initializes k and assigns it the value 0. The next command is k++, so increase k by 1 to get k = 0 + 1 = 1. Then it tests to determine whether k < 3. This is true, so execute the while loop. Execute System.out.println(k) to print 1. However, the first number printed in the original was 0, so this is incorrect. Eliminate (E).

The correct answer is (B).

28. **E** This question tests your knowledge of operator precedence. In Java, multiplication, division, and modulus are performed before addition and subtraction. If more than one operator in an expression has the same precedence, the operations are performed left-to-right. Parenthesizing the expression one step at a time

```
        a / b + c - d % e * f
  →    (a / b) + c - d % e * f
  →    (a / b) + c - (d % e) * f
  →    (a / b) + c - ((d % e) * f)
  →    ((a / b) + c) - ((d % e) * f)
```

The correct answer is (E).

29. **B** Come up with a sample array of 10 strings with length 5. Let String[] x be {"gator", "teeth", "ducky", "quack", "doggy", "woofs", "kitty", "meows", "bears", "growl"}. The code must print the first letter of all 10 strings, followed by the second letter of all 10 strings, and so on. Therefore, it must print

```
        gtdqdwkmbgaeuuooieer...
```

Go through each segment one at a time.

Segment I initializes i and j with no values. The outer for loop sets i = 0, and the inner for loop sets j = 0. The instruction of the inner for loop is System.out.print(x[i].substring(j, j + 1). The substring(a, b) method of the String class returns a string made up of all the characters starting with the index of the a through the index of b - 1. Therefore, x[i].substring(j, j + 1) returns the characters of x[i] from index j through index (j + 1) - 1. Since (j + 1) - 1 = j, it returns all the characters from indexes j through j—a single character string made up of the character at index j. Therefore, if i = 0 and j = 0, System.out.print(x[i].substring(j, j + 1) returns the character at index 0 of the string at index 0. This is the "g" from "gator". This is what should be printed, so continue. The inner for loop increments j to get j = 1. Since j < 5, the loop is executed again, printing the character at index 1 of the string at index 0. This is the character "a" from "gator". However, the character "t" from "teeth" should be the next character printed, so Segment I does not execute as intended. There is no need to continue with Segment I, but note that it will eventually print all of the characters of the first string followed by all of the characters of the second string, and so on. Eliminate (A), (C), and (E), which include Segment I.

Both remaining choices include Segment II, so don't worry about checking this one. Instead, analyze Segment III.

Segment III initializes i and j with no values. The outer for loop sets i = 0, and the inner for loop sets j = 0. The instruction of the inner for loop is System.out.print(x[i].substring(j, j + 1). As discussed above, when i = 0 and j = 0, this command returns the character at index 0 of the string at index 0, which is the "g" from "gator". This is what should be printed, so continue. The inner for loop increments j to get j = 1. Since j < 5, the loop is executed again, printing the character at index 1 of the string at index 0. This is the character "a" from "gator". Again, the character "t" from "teeth" should be the next character printed, so Segment III does not execute as intended. There is no need to continue with Segment III, but note that it will attempt to print the first 10 characters of the first 5 strings. Since each String contains only 5 characters, an IndexOutOfBoundsException will be thrown when j = 5 and the program attempts to print the character at index 5. Eliminate (D), which includes Segment III.

Only one answer remains, so there is no need to continue. However, to see why Segment II is correct, note that it is similar to Segment I, but it reverses the roles of i and j. The command System.out.print(x[j].substring(i, i + 1)) prints the character at index j of the string at index i. The inner for loop increments the index of the String array before the outer loop increments the index of the character in each String. Therefore, Segment II correctly prints out the first character of all 10 strings followed by the second character of all 10 strings, and so on. The correct answer is (B).

30.　**A**　Begin with (D) and (E), which discuss whether an error would occur. Because c is initialized with the command in the third line, double c;, eliminate (D). It is perfectly legal to assign a value of type int to a variable of type double in an expression, so eliminate (E). However, certain rules apply when evaluating the expression. In the expression c = a / b; a and b are both integers. Therefore, the / operator represents integer division. The result of the division is truncated by discarding the fractional component. In this example, 7 / 4 has the value 1—the result of truncating 1.75. When assigning an integer to a variable of type double, the integer value is converted to its equivalent double value. Therefore, the correct answer is (A).

31.　**B**　For the code to print the word Yes two conditions must be true. The remainder must be zero when x is divided by 2. In other words, x must be divisible by 2, that is, even. The value after truncating the result when x is divided by 3 must be 1. In other words, $1 \le x / 3 < 2$. The second condition is more narrow than the first. The only integers that fulfill the second condition are 3, 4, and 5. Of those, only 4 is even and therefore also fulfills the first condition. Therefore, the correct answer is (B).

32. **B** Go through each statement one at a time. Segment I is incorrect because all parameters in Java are passed by value. After a method returns to its caller, the value of the caller's parameters are not modified. The strings will not be swapped. Eliminate (A), (C), and (E), which include Segment I. Since both remaining choices include Segment III, don't worry about it. Segment II is incorrect because `myName` is a private data field of the `SomeClass` class and may not be accessed by the `swap` method. Note that the question specifically states that the `swap` method is not a method of the `SomeClass` class. Eliminate (D), which includes Segment II. Only one choice remains, so there is no need to continue. To see that Segment III correctly swaps the names of the objects, note that it calls the public methods `setName()` and `getName()` rather than the private `String my-Name`. Because the references of the instance object variables are the same as the references of the class object variables, modifying the data of the instance variables also changes the data of the class variable. The correct answer is (B).

33. **E** The way to approach this type of design problem is to look for HAS-A and IS-A relationships among the distinct pieces of data. A book HAS-A title and author. The title and author should be data fields of the `Book` class, either as `Strings` or as their own unrelated classes. This information is not enough to answer the question though. Looking for the IS-A relationships, a mystery IS-A work of fiction which IS-A book. Therefore, it makes good design sense for these three items to be separate classes. Specifically, `Mystery` should be a subclass of `FictionWork`, which should be a subclass of `Book`. Similarly, `RomanceNovel` and `ScienceFiction` should be subclasses of `FictionWork` and `Biography`, `Cookbook`, and `SelfHelpBook` should be subclasses of `NonFictionWork`, which should be a subclass of `Book`. Only (E) meets all of these design criteria.

34. **C** In order to solve this recursive problem, work backward from the base case to the known value of `mystery(4)`.

Let y represent the <missing value>. Note that `mystery(1) = y`. Now calculate `mystery(2)`, `mystery(3)`, and `mystery(4)` in terms of y.

```
mystery(2) = 2 * mystery(1) + 2
           = 2 * y + 2
mystery(3) = 2 * mystery(2) + 3
           = 2 * (2 * y + 2) + 3
           = 4 * y + 4 + 3
           = 4 * y + 7
mystery(4) = 2 * mystery(3) + 4
           = 2 * (4 * y + 7) + 4
           = 8 * y + 14 + 4
           = 8 * y + 18
```

Because `mystery(4)` also equals 34, set 8 * y + 18 = 34 and solve for y.

8 * y + 18 = 34
8 * y = 16
y = 2

The correct answer is (C).

35. **E** The for loop terminates when the condition is no longer true. This can happen either because k is no longer less than `X.length` or because `X[k]` does not equal `Y[k]`. Choice (E) states this formally. Another way to approach the problem is to use DeMorgan's Law to negate the condition in the for loop. Recall that DeMorgan's Law states that

```
! (p && q) is equivalent to !p || !q
```
Negating the condition in the for loop gives

```
  ! (k < X.length && X[k] == Y[k])
=> !(k < X.length) || !(X[k] == Y[k])
=> k >= X.length || X[k] != Y[k]
```
This method also gives (E) as the correct answer.

36. **E** Choices (A), (B), (C), and (D) are examples of an `ArithmeticException`, a `nullPointer-Exception`, an `ArrayIndexOutOfBoundsException`, and an `IndexOutOfBoundsException`, respectively. Be careful! While (E) may appear to be an example of an `IllegalArgumentException`, it is actually an example of an error that is caught at compile time rather than at runtime. An `IllegalArgumentException` occurs when a method is called with an argument that is either illegal or inappropriate—for instance, passing −1 to a method that expects to be passed only positive integers. Therefore, the correct answer is (E).

37. **E** First note that a and b are of type `Double`, not of type `double`. This distinction is important. The type `double` is a primitive type; the type `Double` is a subclass of the `Object` class that implements the `Comparable` interface. A `Double` is an object wrapper for a `double` value. Go through each choice one at a time. Choice (A) is incorrect. It compares a and b directly rather than the `double` values inside the objects. Even if a and b held the same value, they might be different objects. Eliminate (A). Choice (B) is incorrect. The `Double` class does not have a `notEquals` method. Eliminate (B). Choice (C) is incorrect, because `a.doubleValue()` returns a double. Since `double` is a primitive type, it does not have any methods. Had this choice been `!(a.equals(b))`, it would have been correct.

The expression `a.compareTo(b)` returns a value less than zero if `a.doubleValue()` is less than `b.doubleValue()`, a value equal to zero if `a.doubleValue()` is equal to `b.doubleValue()`, and a value greater than zero if `a.doubleValue()` is greater than `b.doubleValue()`. Choice (D) is incorrect because the `compareTo` method returns an int rather than a boolean. Choice (E) is correct. Since `compareTo()` returns 0 if and only if the two objects hold the same values, it will not return 0 if the values are different. The correct answer is (E).

38. **A** While "encapsulating functionality in a class" sounds like (and is) a good thing, "declaring all data fields to be public" is the exact opposite of good programming practice. Data fields to a class should be declared to be private in order to hide the underlying representation of an object. This, in turn, helps increase system reliability. Choices (B), (C), (D), and (E) all describe effective ways to ensure reliability in a program. The correct answer is (A).

39. **E** Go through each method one at a time. Method 1 examines at most 10 words using a binary search technique on 1,024 pages to find the correct page. Remember, the maximum number of searches using binary search is $\log_2(n)$ where n is the number of entries. It then searches sequentially on the page to find the correct word. If the target word is the last word on the page, this method will examine all 50 words on the page. Therefore, Method 1 will examine at most 60 words. Eliminate (A), (B), and (C), which don't have 60 for Method 1. The two remaining choices both have the same number for Method 2, so worry only about Method 3. Method 3 sequentially searches through all of the words in the dictionary. Because there are 51,200 words in the dictionary and the target word may be the last word in the dictionary, this method may have to examine all 51,200 words in order to find the target word. Eliminate (D), which does not have 51,200 for Method 3. Only one choice remains, so there is no need to continue. However, note that Method 2 first uses a sequential search technique to find the correct page. If the target word is on the last page, this method will examine the first word on all 1,024 pages. Then, as with Method 1, it may examine as many as all 50 words on the page to find the target word. Therefore, Method 2 will examine at most 1,074 words. The correct answer is (E).

40. **C** Pick a positive value of j. The question says that j is a positive integer. A recursive method is easiest if it takes fewer recursions to get to the base case, so try j = 1. If j = 1, then m = 2j = 2(1) = 2. Determine the return of `mystery(2)`. Since it is not the case that m = 0, the if condition is false, so execute the else statement, which is to return 4 + `mystery(m - 2)`. Since m – 2 = 2 – 2 = 0, `mystery(2)` returns 4 + `mystery(0)`. Determine the return of `mystery(0)`. In `mystery(0)`, m = 0, so the if condition is true, which causes the method to return 0. Therefore, `mystery(0)` returns 0, and `mystery(2)` returns 4 + `mystery(0)` = 4 + 0 = 4. Go through each choice and eliminate any that are not 4. Choice (A) is 0, so eliminate (A), (B) is m, which is 2, so eliminate (B). Choice (C) is 2m, which is 2(2) = 4, so keep (C). Choice (D) is j, which is 1, so eliminate (D). Choice (E) is 2j, which is 2(1) = 2, so eliminate (E). Only one choice remains. The correct answer is (C).

Section II: Free-Response Questions

1. (a)   Sample Answer #1

```
private Elective getElectiveByName (String name)
{
  for (int eIndex = 0; eIndex < this.getElectiveListSize(); eIndex++)
  {
    Elective e = electiveList.get(eIndex);
    String eName = e.getName();
    if (name.equals(eName))
        return e;
  }
  return null;
}
```

Sample Answer #2

```
private Elective getElectiveByName (String name)
{
  int index;
  for (int eIndex; getElectiveList)
  {
    Elective e = electiveList.get(eIndex);
    String eName = e.getName();
    if (name.equals(eName))
        index = eIndex;
  }
  return electiveList.get(index);
}
```

Sample Answer #3

```
private Elective getElectiveByName (String name)
{
  int eIndex = 0;
  while (eIndex < this.getElectiveListSize())
  {
    Elective e = electiveList.get(eIndex);
    String eName = e.getName();
    if (name.equals(eName))
        Return e;
    eIndex++
  }
  return null;
}
```

The goal of the method is to return the Elective with the name matching the parameter. Go through electiveList using either a while loop, for loop, or enhanced-for loop. At each index of electiveList, the method must determine whether the name of the Elective matches the parameter String name. Remember that since name is a private variable, it cannot be called by another class, so the public method getName() must be used. Also, when comparing Strings, the == operator cannot be used, because this operator tests whether the objects are the same rather than whether two objects have the same value. To test whether two objects have the same value, the `equals()` method of the `String` class must be used. Once a match is found, there is no need to continue execution of the method, so the `Elective` with the matching name can be returned. Because a precondition indicates there will be a match, this return statement will be reached. However, the compiler will not recognize this. In order to avoid a compile-time error, there must be a return statement in a non-conditional statement, so add a `null` return (or any other return). An alternative method is to record the index of the match. After searching all indexes, return the `Elective` at the recorded index of `electiveList`.

(b) Sample Answer #1

```
public void assignElectivesToStudents()
{
    for (int sIndex = 0; sIndex < this.getStudentListSize(); sIndex++)
    {
        Student s = studentList.get(sIndex);
        int choice = 0;
        while (choice < 3 && !s.hasElective())
        {
            String name = s.getChoice(choice);
            Elective e = getElectiveByName(name);
            if (e.getClassSize() < e.getMaxClassSize())
            {
                e.addStudent(s);
                s.assignElective(e);
            }
            choice += 1;
        }
    }
}
```

Sample Answer #2

```
public void assignElectivesToStudents()
{
    for (int sIndex: this.getStudentListSize())
    {

        for (int choice = 0; choice < 3; choice++)
        {
            String name = studentList.get(sIndex).getChoice(choice);
            Elective e = getElectiveByName(name);
            if (e.getClassSize() < e.getMaxClassSize() &&
                            !studentList.get(sIndex).hasElective())
            {
                e.addStudent(studentList.get(sIndex));
                s.assignElective(e);
            }
        }
    }
}
```

The method must assign each student to his or her first available choice of elective. Go through all the students, in order, using a for loop, an enhanced for loop, or a while loop. For each student, go through the student's three choices, in order, using another loop (which also could be any of the three listed above). For each choice, use the `getElectiveByName()` method from part (a) to find the matching `Elective` object, and assign the student to the class if there is room in the class (i.e., the class size is less than the max class size) and the student remains unassigned to an elective (i.e., the student's `hasElective()` method returns false). A student must be assigned to an elective using the `assignElective()` and the student must be added to the Elective's student list using the elective's `addStudents()` method.

(c) Sample Answer:

```java
public ArrayList studentsWithoutElectives()
{
  ArrayList<Student> result = new ArrayList<Student>();
  for (int sIndex = 0; sIndex < this.getStudentListSize(); sIndex++)
  {
    Student s = studentList.get(sIndex);
    if (!s.hasElective())
        result.add(s);
  }
  return result;
}
```

The goal of the method is to go through each student and return an ArrayList of students who have been unassigned. First create an empty `ArrayList` of `Student` objects to be returned. Go through the school's student list using a for loop, an enhanced for loop, or a while loop. At each index, if the student at that index is unassigned (i.e., if the `hasElective()` method returns `false`), add the student to the `ArrayList`. After the end, return the `ArrayList`.

2. (a) Sample Answer #1

```java
public boolean inOrder()
{
  for (int k = 0; k < cards.length; k++)
  {
    if (cards[k] != k)
        return false;
  }
  return true;
}
```

Sample Answer #2

```
public boolean inOrder()
{
  boolean temp = true;
  int k = 0;
  while (k < cards.length && temp)
  {
      if (cards[k] != k)
          temp =  false;
      k++;
  }
  return temp;
}
```

Sample Answer #3

```
public boolean inOrder()
{
  boolean temp = true;
  for (int k : cards)
  {
      if (!(cards[k] == k))
          temp =  false;
  }
  return temp;
}
```

The goal of the method is to determine whether the deck is in order and return the appropriate boolean. Because the cards in a deck of length *n* are numbered 0 through n - 1, an ordered deck will have all the values matching their indexes. Go through each card in the deck one at a time using a for loop, an enhanced-for loop, or a while loop. A deck is ordered only if *all* the card values match their indexes. If even one card value does not match the index, the method must return false. Therefore, the return false statement can be made immediately upon finding the card that doesn't match the index. If false is never returned in the for loop, then true must be returned. As an alternative, create a boolean outside the loop set to true. Set it to false if any card is found for which the value does not match the index. Then return the boolean after the loop.

(b)   **Sample Answer #1**

```
public void shuffle()
{
  int[] newCards = new int[cards.length];
  for(int k = 0; k < cards.length/2; k++)
  {
      newCards[k*2] = cards[k];
      newCards[k*2+1] = cards[cards.length/2+k];
  }
  cards = newCards;
}
```

Sample Answer #2

```
public void shuffle()
{
  int[] newCards = new int[cards.length];
  for(int k : newCards)
  {
    if (k%2 == 0)
        newCards[k] = cards[k/2];
    else
        newCards[k] = cards[cards.length/2+k/2];
  }
  cards = newCards;
}
```

Sample Answer #3

```
public void shuffle()
{
  int[] front = new int[cards.length/2];
  for (int k = 0; k < front.length; k++)
    front[k] = cards[k];
  int[] back = new int[cards.length/2];
  for (int k = 0; back.length; k++)
    back[k] = cards[back.length + k];
  int[] newCards = new int[cards.length]
  int j = 0;
  while(j < newCards.length)
  {
    if (k % 2 == 1)
        newCards[k] = back[cards.length/2];
    else
        newCards[k] = front[k/2];
  }
  cards = newCards;
}
```

The goal of this method is to rearrange the values in cards according to the method described in the question. To do this, the deck must be split into a front half and a back half; then the cards must alternate, beginning with the front half. One possible approach is to directly separate the deck, as is done in Sample Answer #3. This is not necessary, though, as long as you place the first card of the deck in index 0 of the shuffled deck, the first card of the second half in index 1, the second card of the first half in index 2, the second card of the second half in index 3, and so on. A new deck of the same length as the original deck must be created. Copy the card from the original deck into the new deck, using one of the methods described above. The return is void, so the deck represented by the int array cards must be assigned the values of the new deck.

(c)   Sample Answer #1

```
public int reorderingCount()
{
  int count = 0;
  while (!inOrder() || count == 0)
  {
     shuffle();
     count += 1;
  }
  return count;
}
```

Sample Answer #2

```
public int reorderingCount()
{
  Shuffle();
  int count;
  for (count = 1; !inOrder(); count++)
     shuffle();
  return count;
}
```

The goal of the method is to shuffle the deck repeatedly until it is back in its original order, and return the number of times it was shuffled. Create a counter by initializing an int and setting it equal to zero. Make sure to shuffle at least once. Use a for or while loop to do repeated shuffles until it is back in order, incrementing the counter at each shuffle, including the first. The loop must stop when the deck is back in order, so it must continue while inOrder() is false. After it is back in order, the loop must terminate, and the counter variable must be returned by the method.

3.   (a)

```
public class Recipe
{
  private String name;
  private ArrayList<Ingredient> ingredientList;
  private String preparationProcess;
  private int numberServed;
  public ArrayList<Ingredient> getIngredientList()
     { /* implementation not needed */ }
  public Recipe(String recipeName, int numServed)
     { /* implementation not needed */ }
  public void addIngredient(Ingredient newIngredient)
     { /* implementation not needed */ }
  public void setPreparationProcess(String newPreparationProcess)
     { /* implementation not needed */ }
  public String getName()
     { /* implementation not needed */ }
  public int getNumberServed()
     { /* implementation not needed */ }
  public void scale(int newNumberServed)
     { /* implementation not needed */ }
}
```

Be sure to list all the needed variables with the appropriate data types as described in the question. Both the name of the recipe and the description of the preparation process are text, so use String types. The list of ingredients will need to be of a variable size, so use an `ArrayList`. Use an int for the `numberServed`. Also be sure to list out the method signatures as described in the question. To create a recipe with a given name and number of people served, use a constructor method with String and int parameters. To add an ingredient, use a method that takes an ingredient as a parameter. Since this method will alter the already existing ingredients list within the `Recipe` object rather than create a new list, the return should be void. Similarly, the method to set the description will alter an already existing data within the `Recipe` object, so take a String parameter and have a void return. To return the name of the recipe, number of people served, or the list of ingredients, take no parameters and return the appropriate data type. The method to scale the amount based on a new number of people served must take the new number of people served as a parameter and alter already existing `Ingredient` objects and the `NumberServed` integer so it should have a void return.

(b) Sample Answer #1

```
public void scale(int newNumberServed)
{
  double oldAmount;
  double newAmount;
  for (int k = 0; k < ingredientList.size; k++)
  {
      Ingredient ingred = (Ingredient) ingredientList.get(k);
      oldAmount = ingred.getAmount();
      newAmount = newNumberServed * (oldAmount / numberServed);
      ingred.setAmount(newAmount);
  }
  numberServed = newNumberServed;
}
```

Sample Answer #2

```
public void scale(int newNumberServed)
{

  for (int k : ingredientList)
  {
      double oldAmount = (Ingredient) ingredientList.get(k).getAmount();
      double newAmount = newAmount = (oldAmount * newNumberServed) /
numberServed;
      ingredientList.get(k).setAmount(newAmount);
  }
  numberServed = newNumberServed;
}
```

There are two goals for this recipe. One is to change the number of people served by the recipe. This can be achieved by one command: setting the class variable for the number of people served equal to the parameter. However, this should be done at the end of the method, so that the original number of people served can be used. The other goal is to scale the amount of each ingredient to the new number of people. Go through each ingredient in ingredientList using a for loop, an enhanced for loop, or a while loop. For each ingredient, record the original amount. Get the new amount by using an appropriate scaling. To determine how to do this, use a proportion: $\dfrac{oldAmount}{newAmount} = \dfrac{numberServed}{newNumberServed}$. To find an expression for newAmount, cross-multiply to get newAmount * numberServed = oldAmount * newNumberServed. Divide both sides by number-Served to get newAmount = (oldAmount * newNumberServed) / numberServed. (An alternative but equivalent formula is shown in Sample Answer # 1.) Use the setAmount() method of the ingredient, passing newAmount as a parameter to update the amount of the ingredient. Finally, end the loop and set the number served to the new amount as discussed above.

(c)   Sample Answer #1

```
public void standardize(int numPeople)
{
  double oldAmount;
  double newAmount;
  for (int j = 0; j < recipeList.size(); j++)
  {
    for (int k = 0; k < recipeList.size(); k++)
    {
        Ingredient ingred = (Ingredient) recipeList.
        get(j).get
        IngredientList().get(k);
        oldAmount = ingred.getAmount();
        newAmount = numPeople / oldAmount;
        ingred.setAmount(newAmount);
    }
    recipeList.get(j).setNumberServed(numPeople);
  }
}
```

Sample Answer #2

```
public void standardize(int numPeople)
{
  int j = 0
  while (j < recipeList.size())
  {
    for (int k: recipeList.size())
    {
        (Ingredient) recipeList.get(j).getIngredientList().get(k).
ingred.scale(newAmount);
    }
    j++;
  }
}
```

The goal of the method is to apply the setAmount() method to all recipes using a predetermined number of people. Take the number of people as a parameter. Because the method is intended to alter already existing objects rather than create new objects, the return should be void. Go through each recipe using a for loop, an enhanced-for loop, or a while loop. For each recipe, use an inner loop of any of the three types to go through each ingredient and scale it to the new amount. This can be done in a similar method to what was done in part (b) or can be done simply by using the scale method.

4.

```
public class School
{
  private ArrayList<Classroom> classrooms;
  public School(ArrayList<Classroom> schoolRooms)
  {
    classrooms = SchoolRooms;
  }
  public String findStudent(String teacher, int IDnumber)
  {
    for (int k = 0; k < classrooms.size(); k++)
    {
        if (classrooms.get(k).getTeacherName().equals(teacher))
        {
            int low = 0;
            int high = classrooms.get(k).getStudents().size() - 1;
            while (low <= high)
            {
                int middle = (low + high) / 2;
                if (IDnumber < classrooms.get(k).getStudents().
get(middle).getStudentID())
                {
                    high = middle - 1;
```

```
                        }
                        else if (IDnumber >
classrooms.get(k).getStudents().get(middle).getStudentID())
                        {
                                low = middle + 1;
                        }
                        else
                        {
                                return classrooms.get(k).getStudents().
get(middle).getStudentName();
                        }
                }
            }
        }
        return "Student Not Found";
    }
}


public class Classroom
{
  private String teacherName;
  private ArrayList<Student> Students;
  public Classroom(String teacher, ArrayList<Student> theStudents)
  {
      teacherName = teacher;
      Students = theStudents;
  }
  public String getTeacherName()
  {
      return teacherName;
  }
  public ArrayList<Student> getStudents()
  {
      return Students;
  }
}


public class Student
{
  private String studentName;
  private int studentID;
  public Student(String name, int ID)
  {
      studentName = name;
      studentID = ID;
  }
  public int getStudentID()
  {
      return studentID;
  }
  public String getStudentName()
  {
      return studentName;
  }
}
```

The question specifies that there must be three classes: `School`, `Classroom`, and `Student`. Create a class definition for each, including a constructor taking the required data fields as parameters. `School` must take `ArrayList<Classroom>` `schoolRooms`, `Classroom` must take `String` `teacherName` and `ArrayList<Student>` `theStudents`, and `Student` must take `String` `name` and `int` `ID`. The only method specified by the question is `findStudent` in the `School` class. However, the description of this method indicates that it will require information from `Classroom` and `Student` objects. Since, on the AP Exam, all variables should be specified as private, this will require the use of public methods in the `Classroom` and `Student` classes. The variables in `Classroom` are `teacherName` and `students`, so create a `getTeacherName()` method returning a `String` with the same value as `teacherName` and a `getStudents` to return the `ArrayList` `Students`. The variables in `Student` are `studentID` and `studentName`, so create a `getStudentID()` method returning an integer equal to `studentID` and a `getStudentName()` method returning a String with the same value as `studentName`.

To create the `findStudent` method, the question specifies that it must take a String for teacher name and an integer for student ID as parameters. The question also specifies that a sequential search must be used to find the classroom based on teacher name. A sequential search can be most easily accomplished using a for loop or an enhanced for loop (though a while loop is also possible). Search through the entire list of classrooms, one at a time, to determine whether the teacher parameter matches the `teacherName` in the `Classroom`. To do this, be sure to get the `getTeacherName()` method of the `Classroom` object, since `teacherName` is a private variable. Also, be sure to use the `equals()` method of the String class, since the `==` operator returns true only if the String objects are the same name rather than if they have the same value. If a match is found, search the classroom for the student using `ID`. The question specifies that a binary search must be used. Use a standard binary search. If a match is found, return the name of the student using the `getStudentName()` method of the `Student` object. If no match is found, nothing will be returned by the searches. Outside the two searches, return "`Student Not Found`" as specified by the question.

Practice Test 3

AP® Computer Science A Exam

SECTION I: Multiple-Choice Questions

DO NOT OPEN THIS BOOKLET UNTIL YOU ARE TOLD TO DO SO.

At a Glance

Total Time
1 hour 30 minutes
Number of Questions
40
Percent of Total Score
50%
Writing Instrument
Pencil required

Instructions

Section I of this examination contains 40 multiple-choice questions. Fill in only the ovals for numbers 1 through 40 on your answer sheet.

Indicate all of your answers to the multiple-choice questions on the answer sheet. No credit will be given for anything written in this exam booklet, but you may use the booklet for notes or scratch work. After you have decided which of the suggested answers is best, completely fill in the corresponding oval on the answer sheet. Give only one answer to each question. If you change an answer, be sure that the previous mark is erased completely. Here is a sample question and answer.

Sample Question Sample Answer

Chicago is a
(A) state
(B) city
(C) country
(D) continent
(E) county

Use your time effectively, working as quickly as you can without losing accuracy. Do not spend too much time on any one question. Go on to other questions and come back to the ones you have not answered if you have time. It is not expected that everyone will know the answers to all the multiple-choice questions.

About Guessing

Many candidates wonder whether or not to guess the answers to questions about which they are not certain. Multiple-choice scores are based on the number of questions answered correctly. Points are not deducted for incorrect answers, and no points are awarded for unanswered questions. Because points are not deducted for incorrect answers, you are encouraged to answer all multiple-choice questions. On any questions you do not know the answer to, you should eliminate as many choices as you can, and then select the best answer among the remaining choices.

GO ON TO THE NEXT PAGE.

Java Quick Reference

Class Constructors and Methods	Explanation
String Class	
`String(String str)`	Constructs a new `String` object that represents the same sequence of characters as `str`
`int length()`	Returns the number of characters in a `String` object
`String substring(int from, int to)`	Returns the substring beginning at index `from` and ending at index `to - 1`
`String substring(int from)`	Returns `substring(from, length())`
`int indexOf(String str)`	Returns the index of the first occurrence of `str`; returns −1 if not found
`boolean equals(String other)`	Returns `true` if `this` is equal to `other`; returns `false` otherwise
`int compareTo(String other)`	Returns a value <0 if `this` is less than `other`; returns zero if `this` is equal to `other`; returns a value of >0 if `this` is greater than `other`
Integer Class	
`Integer(int value)`	Constructs a new `Integer` object that represents the specified `int` value
`Integer.MIN_VALUE`	The minimum value represented by an `int` or `Integer`
`Integer.MAX_VALUE`	The maximum value represented by an `int` or `Integer`
`int intValue()`	Returns the value of this `Integer` as an `int`
Double Class	
`Double(double value)`	Constructs a new `Double` object that represents the specified `double` value
`double doubleValue()`	Returns the value of this `Double` as a `double`
Math Class	
`static int abs(int x)`	Returns the absolute value of an `int` value
`static double abs(double x)`	Returns the absolute value of a `double` value
`static double pow(double base, double exponent)`	Returns the value of the first parameter raised to the power of the second parameter
`static double sqrt(double x)`	Returns the positive square root of a `double` value
`static double random()`	Returns a `double` value greater than or equal to `0.0` and less than `1.0`
ArrayList Class	
`int size()`	Returns the number of elements in the list
`boolean add(E obj)`	Appends `obj` to end of list; returns `true`
`void add(int index, E obj)`	Inserts `obj` at position index (`0 <= index <= size`), moving elements at position `index` and higher to the right (adds 1 to their indices) and adds 1 to size
`E get(int index)`	Returns the element at position `index` in the list
`E set(int index, E obj)`	Replaces the element at position `index` with `obj`; returns the element formerly at position `index`
`E remove(int index)`	Removes element from position `index`, moving elements at position `index + 1` and higher to the left (subtracts 1 from their indices) and subtracts 1 from size; returns the element formerly at position `index`
Object Class	
`boolean equals(Object other)`	
`String toString()`	

GO ON TO THE NEXT PAGE.

COMPUTER SCIENCE A

SECTION I

Time—1 hour and 30 minutes

Number of Questions—40

Percent of total exam grade—50%

Directions: Determine the answer to each of the following questions or incomplete statements, using the available space for any necessary scratchwork. Then decide which is the best of the choices given and fill in the corresponding oval on the answer sheet. No credit will be given for anything written in the examination booklet. Do not spend too much time on any one problem.

Notes:

- Assume that the classes listed in the Quick Reference have been imported where appropriate.
- Assume that declarations of variables and methods appear within the context of an enclosing class.
- Assume that method calls that are not prefixed with an object or class name and are not shown within a complete class definition appear within the context of an enclosing class.
- Unless otherwise noted in the question, assume that parameters in the method calls are not `null` and that methods are called only when their preconditions are satisfied.

1. Consider the following method.

```
public static int mystery(int a, int b)
{
    if (a <= 0)
        return b;
    else
        return mystery(a - 2, b);
}
```

What value is returned by the call `mystery(12, 5)`?

(A) 5
(B) 6
(C) 12
(D) 60
(E) 1565

GO ON TO THE NEXT PAGE.

2. Consider the following instance variable and method.

```
private int[] numList;

//Precondition: numList contains a list of int values in no particular order

public int mystery(int n)
{
    for (int k = 0; k <= numList.length - 1; k++)
    {
        if (n <= numList[k])
            return k;
    }
    return numList.length;
}
```

Which of the following statements is most accurate about `numList` following the execution of the following statement?

```
int j = mystery(number);
```

(A) The greatest value in `numList` is at index j.

(B) The greatest value in `numList` that is less than `number` is at index j.

(C) All values in `numList` from index 0 to j–1 are greater than or equal to `number`.

(D) All values in `numList` from index 0 to j–1 are less than `number`.

(E) All values in `numList` from index j to `numList.length-1` are greater than `number`.

GO ON TO THE NEXT PAGE.

Questions 3–4 refer to the following incomplete class declaration for a new data type called a `Quack`.

```
Public class Quack
{
    ArrayList<Object> myData;

    // Constructor initializes myData
    public Quack()
    {   /* implementation not shown */   }

    // Quack.
    public void enquack(Object x)
    {   /* implementation not shown */  }

    // if front is true, returns the object at the front end of the Quack;  otherwise returns the object at the back end of the
    // Quack.  Assumes the Quack is not empty.
    public Object dequack(boolean front)
    {   /* implementation not shown */   }

    // Returns true if the Quack has no objects; otherwise returns false.
    public boolean isEmpty()
    {   /* implementation not shown /*   }

    <designation> ArrayList myData;

    // ... other methods and data not shown
```

3. Which of the following is the best choice for `<designation>` and the best reason for that choice?

   (A) `<designation>` should be `private` so that programs using a `Quack` will not be able to modify `myData` by using methods `enquack` and `dequack`, thereby preserving the principle of data stability.

   (B) `<designation>` should be `private` so that programs using a `Quack` can modify `myData` only by using methods such as `enquack` and `dequack`, thereby preserving the principle of information hiding.

   (C) `<designation>` should be `private` as an indication to programs using a `Quack` that `myData` can be modified directly but that it is *better* to modify `myData` only by using methods such as `enquack` and `dequack`, thereby preserving the principle of maximum information dissemination.

   (D) `<designation>` should be `public` because programs using a `Quack` need to know how the `Quack` class has been implemented in order to use it.

   (E) `<designation>` should be `public`. Otherwise, only objects constructed from derived subclasses of a `Quack` will be able to modify the contents of a `Quack`.

4. Which of the following is an effective return statement for `isEmpty` as described in the incomplete declaration above?

   (A) `return (myData.length == 0)`
   (B) `return (size() == 0)`
   (C) `return (myData.size() == 0);`
   (D) `return (myData.length() == 0)`
   (E) `return (myData.size == 0)`

GO ON TO THE NEXT PAGE.

5. Consider the following method definition.

```
public static int mystery(int n)
{
    if (n <= 1)
        return 2;
    else
        return 1 + mystery(n - 3);
}
```

Which of the following lines of code can replace the line in mystery containing the recursive call so that the functionality of mystery does not change?

(A) `return 1 + ((n + 2) / 3);`

(B) `return 1 + ((n + 3) / 2);`

(C) `return 2 + ((n + 1) / 3);`

(D) `return 2 + ((n + 2) / 3);`

(E) `return 3 + ((n + 1) / 2);`

GO ON TO THE NEXT PAGE.

Questions 6–7 refer to the following incomplete class declaration.

```
public class DistanceTracker
{
    private int kilometers;
    private int meters;

    /* Constructs a DistanceTracker object
     * @param k the number of kilometers
     * Precondition: k ≥ 0
     * @param m the number of meters
     * Precondition: 0 ≤ m < 1000
     */
    public DistanceTracker (int k, int m)
    {
        kilometer = k;
        meters = m;
    }
    /* @return the number of kilometers
     */
    public int getKilometers()
    { /* implementation not shown */}
    /* @return the number of meters
     */
    public int getMeters()
    { /* implementation not shown */}
        /* Adds k kilometers and m meters
         * @param k the number of kilometers
         * Precondition: k ≥ 0
         *@param m the number of meters
     * Precondition: m ≥ 0
     */
    public void addDistance(int k, int m)
    {
        kilometers += k;
        meters += m;
        /* rest of method not shown */
    }
//Rest of class not shown
}
```

6. Which of the following code segments can be used to replace /* rest of method not shown */ so addDistance will correctly increase the distance?

(A) `kilometers += meters / 1000`
    `meters = meters % 1000`

(B) `kilometers += meters % 1000`
    `meters = meters / 1000`

(C) `meters += kilometers % 1000`

(D) `kilometers += meters % 1000`

(E) `meters = meters % 1000`

GO ON TO THE NEXT PAGE.

7. Consider the following incomplete class declaration.

```
public class DistanceTrackerSet
{
    Distance Tracker[] set;
    /*Declaration method not shown*/

    public  DistanceTracker total()
    {
        DistanceTracker temp = new DistanceTracker(0, 0);
    for (int k = 0; k < set.length; k++)
        {
            /* missing code */
        }
        return temp;
    }
/*Other methods not shown*/
}
```

Assuming set is properly initialized with DistanceTracker objects and all needed classes are properly imported, which of the following can be used to replace /* missing code */ so that the method returns a DistanceTracker object with the total of all distances stored in set?

(A) temp.addDistance(temp[k].kilometers, temp[k].meters);

(B) set[k].addDistance(temp[k].getKilometers(), temp[k].getMeters());

(C) set[k].addDistance();

(D) temp += temp.addDistance();

(E) temp.addDistance(temp[k].getKilometers(), temp[k].getMeters());

8. Consider the following method.

```
public List<Integer> nums() {
    List<Integer> values = new ArrayList<Integer>() ;
    for (int i = 0; i < 50; i = i + 5)
        if (i % 4 == 1)
            values.add(i) ;
    return value ;
}
```

What will return of nums() contain?

(A) [5, 45]

(B) [5, 25, 45]

(C) [0, 20, 40]

(D) [5, 9, 13, 17, 21, 25, 29, 33, 37, 41, 45]

(E) [0, 5, 10, 15, 20, 25, 30, 35, 40, 45]

GO ON TO THE NEXT PAGE.

9. Consider the following incomplete method `mystery`.

```
public static boolean mystery(boolean a, boolean b, boolean c)
{
    return <expression>;
}
```

What should `<expression>` be replaced with so that `mystery` returns `true` when exactly two of its three parameters are true; otherwise `mystery` returns `false`?

(A) ```
(a && b && !c) ||
(a && !b && c) ||
(!a && b && c)
```

(B) ```
(a && b && !c) &&
(a && !b && c) &&
(!a && b && c)
```

(C) ```
(a || b || !c) &&
(a || !b || c) &&
(!a || b || c)
```

(D) ```
(a && b) ||
(a && c) ||
(b && c)
```

(E) ```
(a || b) &&
(a || c) &&
(b || c)
```

10. Consider the following code segment.

```
int x;
x = 5 - 4 + 9 * 12 / 3 - 10;
```

What is the value of x after the code segment is executed?

(A) 13

(B) 27

(C) 30

(D) -57

(E) -10

11. What is the best way to declare a variable `myStrings` that will store 50 `String` values if each `String` will be no longer than 25 characters?

(A) `ArrayList <String> myStrings[String[50]];`

(B) `ArrayList <String> myStrings = new String[50];`

(C) `ArrayList <String> myStrings = new String[25];`

(D) `String [] myStrings = new String [50, 25];`

(E) `String [] myStrings = new String [50];`

GO ON TO THE NEXT PAGE.
```

12. Consider the following code segment.

```
List <Integer> scores= new ArrayList<Integer>();
scores.add(93);
scores.add(97);
scores.add(84);
scores.add(91);
scores.remove(2);
scores.add(1, 83);
scores.set(3, 99);
System.out.println(scores);
```

What is the output of the code segment?

(A) [83, 93, 99, 91]
(B) [93, 83, 91, 99]
(C) [83, 94, 91, 99]
(D) [93, 83, 97, 99]
(E) The code throws an `ArrayIndexOutofBoundsException`.

13. Consider the following precondition, postcondition, and signature for the `getDigit` method.

```
// precondition: n >= 0
//               whichDigit >= 0
// postcondition: Returns the digit of n in
//               the whichDigit position
//               when the digits of n are
//               numbered from right to
//               left starting with zero.
//               Returns 0 if whichDigit >=
//               number of digits of n.
int getDigit (int n, int whichDigit)
```

Consider also the following three possible implementations of the `getDigit` method.

```
I.   if (whichDigit == 0)
       return n % 10;
     else
       return getDigit(n / 10, whichDigit - 1) ;
II.  return (n / (int) Math.pow(10, whichDigit) )  % 10;
III. for (int k = 0; k < whichDigit; k++)
       n /= 10;
     return n % 10;
```

Which implementation(s) would satisfy the postcondition of the `getDigit` method?

(A) I and II only
(B) I and III only
(C) II and III only
(D) I, II, and III
(E) None of the above

GO ON TO THE NEXT PAGE.

14. Consider an array of integers.

    4   10   1   2   6   7   3   5

    Assume that `SelectionSort` is used to order the array from smallest to largest values.

    Which of the following represents the state of the array immediately after the first iteration of the outer for loop in the `SelectionSort` process?

    (A) 1   4   10   2   3   6   7   5
    (B) 1   2   4   6   10   7   3   5
    (C) 1   10   4   2   6   7   3   5
    (D) 4   3   1   5   6   7   10   2
    (E) 5   3   7   6   2   1   10   4

15. Assume that a program declares and initializes v as follows.

    ```
    String [] v;
    v = initialize () ;          // Returns an array of
                                 // length 10 containing
                                 // ten valid strings
    ```

    Which of the following code segments correctly traverses the array *backwards* and prints out the elements (one per line)?

    ```
    I.  for (int k = 9; k >= 0; k--)
            System.out.println(v[k]) ;
    II. int k = 0;
        while (k < 10)
        {
            System.out.println(v[9 - k]);
            k++;
        }
    III. int k = 10;
        while (k >= 0)
        {
            System.out.println(v[k]);
            k-- ;
        }
    ```

    (A) I only
    (B) II only
    (C) I and II only
    (D) II and III only
    (E) I, II, and III

GO ON TO THE NEXT PAGE.

16. Consider the following method.

```
/**Precondition: @param set  an ArrayList that contains distinct integers
*@param n an int value
*/
public int mystery(List<Integer> set, int n)
{
    for (int k = 0; k < set.length(); k++)
    {
        if (set.get(k) > n)
        {
            return (set.remove(k) + mystery(set, n));
        }
    }
    return 0;
}
```

What is returned by the method call `mystery(set, n)`?

(A) 0

(B) The number of elements of set that are greater than n

(C) The sum of the elements of set that are greater than n

(D) The sum of the elements of set that are less than n

(E) The sum of the elements of set that are less than or equal to n

GO ON TO THE NEXT PAGE.

17. Consider the following two-dimensional array.

```
[ [0, 0, 0 ,0]
  [0, 1, 0, 0]
  [0, 1, 2, 0]
  [0, 1, 2, 3] ]
```

Which of the following methods returns this two-dimensional array?

(A) `public int[][] nums()`
```
    {
      int[][] temp = new int[4][4];
      for (int j = 0; j < 4; j++)
      {
         for (int k = 0; k < 4; k ++)
         {
                temp[j][k] = j;
         }
      }
      return temp;
    }
```

(B) `public int[][] nums()`
```
    {
      int[][] temp = new int[4][4];
      for (int j = 0; j < 4; j++)
      {
         for (int k = 0; k < 4; k ++)
         {
                temp[j][k] = k;
         }
      }
      return temp;
    }
```

(C) `public int[][] nums()`
```
    {
      int[][] temp = new int[4][4];
      for (int j = 0; j < 4; j++)
      {
         for (int k = j; k < 4; k ++)
         {
                temp[j][k] = k;
         }
      }
      return temp;
    }
```

GO ON TO THE NEXT PAGE.

```
(D)  public int[][] nums()
     {
       int[][] temp = new int[4][4];
       for (int j = 0; j < 4; j++)
       {
           for (int k = 0; k <= j; k ++)
           {
                   temp[j][k] = j;
           }
       }
       return temp;
     }
(E)  public int[][] nums()
     {
       int[][] temp = new int[4][4];
       for (int j = 0; j < 4; j++)
       {
           for (int k = 0; k <= j; k ++)
           {
                   temp[j][k] = k;
           }
       }
       return temp;
     }
```

GO ON TO THE NEXT PAGE.

18. A children's club classifies members based on age according to the table below:

Years	Classification
Under 3	Infant
3 to 7 inclusive	Pee-Wee
8 to 13 inclusive	Cub
Over 14	Leader

Which of the following methods will correctly take the integer parameter age and return the String Classification?

(A)
```java
public String Classification(int age)
{
    String temp;
    if (age < 3)
        temp = "Infant";
    if (age <= 7)
        temp = "Pee-Wee";
    if (age <= 13)
        temp = "Cub";
    if (age >= 14)
        temp = "Leader";
    return temp;
}
```

(B)
```java
public String Classification(int age)
{
    String temp;
    if (age < 3)
        temp = "Infant";
    if (3 <= age <= 7)
        temp = "Pee-Wee";
    if (8 <= age <= 13)
        temp = "Cub";
    if (age >= 14)
        temp = "Leader";
    return temp;
}
```

(C)
```java
public String Classification(int age)
{
    String temp;
    if (age < 3)
        temp = "Infant";
    else if (age <= 7)
        temp = "Pee-Wee";
    else if (age <= 13)
        temp = "Cub";
    else if (age > 14)
        temp = "Leader";
    return temp;
}
```

GO ON TO THE NEXT PAGE.

```
(D)  public String Classification(int age)
     {
         String temp;
         if (age < 3)
            temp = "Infant";
         else if (age < 7)
            temp = "Pee-Wee";
         else if (age < 13)
            temp = "Cub";
         else if (age > 14)
            temp = "Leader";
         return temp;
     }
(E)  public String Classification(int age)
     {
         String temp;
         if (age < 3)
             temp = "Infant";
         if (age < 7)
             temp = "Pee-Wee";
         if (age < 13)
             temp = "Cub";
         if (age > 14)
             temp = "Leader";
         return temp;
     }
```

GO ON TO THE NEXT PAGE.

Questions 19–20 refer to the method `getGap` with line numbers added for reference. Method `getGap` is intended to find the maximum difference between the indexes of any two occurrences of `num` in the array `arr`. The method `getGap` does not work as intended.

For example, if the array `arr` contains [8, 7, 5, 5, 4, 3, 2, 7, 1, 2, 7], the call `getGap(arr, 7)` should return 9, the difference between the indexes of the first and last occurrence of 7.

`/**Precondition: arr contains at least two occurrences of num */`

```
1:      public int getGap(int[] arr, int num)
2:      {
3:          int index1 = -1;
4:          int index2 = -1;
5:          for (int k = 0; k < arr.length; k++)
6:          {
7:              if (arr[k] == num)
8:              {
9:                  if (index1 == -1)
10:                 {
11:                     index1 = k;
12:                     index2 = k;
13:                 }
14:                 else
15:                 {
16:                     index1 = index2;
17:                     index2 = k;
18:                 }
19:             }
20:         }
21:         return (index2 - index1);
22:     }
```

19. The method `getGap` does not work as intended. Which of the following best describes the return of the method `getGap` ?

    (A) The difference between the indexes of the last two occurrences of `num` in `arr`
    (B) The minimum difference between the indexes of any two occurrences of `num` in `arr`
    (C) The difference between the first two occurrences of `num` in `arr`
    (D) The length of the array `arr`
    (E) The number of occurrences of `num` in `arr`

20. Which of the following changes should be made to `getGap` so that the method will work as intended?

    (A) Delete the statement at line 4.
    (B) Delete the statement at line 11.
    (C) Delete the statement at line 12.
    (D) Delete the statement at line 16.
    (E) Delete the statement at line 17.

GO ON TO THE NEXT PAGE.

Questions 21–23 refer to the following incomplete class declaration used to represent calendar dates.

```
Public class Date
{
    private int month;
        // represents month 0–11
    private int day;
        // represents day of the month
        // 0-31
    private int year;
        // represents the year

    // constructor sets the private data
    public Date (int m, int d, int y)
    { /* implementation not shown */ }

    // postconditions: returns the month
    public int getMonth()
    { /* implementation not shown */ }

    // postcondition: return the day
    public int getDay()
    { /* implementation not shown */ }

    // postcondition: returns the year
    public int getYear()
    { /* implementation not shown */ }

    // postcondition: returns the number of
    //               days which, when
    //               added to this Date,
    //               gives newDate
    public int daysUntil (Date newDate)
    { /* implementation not shown */ }

    // postcondition: returns true if
    //               the month, day, and
    //               year of this Date are
    //               are equal to those of
    //               other; otherwise
    //               returns false
    public boolean equals (Date other)
    { /* implementation not shown */ }

    // ... other methods not shown
```

21. Consider the method equals of the `Object` class.

    Which of the following method signatures is appropriate for the `equals` method?

    (A) `public boolean equals (Object other)`
    (B) `public int equals (Object other)`
    (C) `public boolean equals (Date other)`
    (D) `public int equals (Date other)`
    (E) `public boolean equals (Date d1, Date d2)`

GO ON TO THE NEXT PAGE.

22. Which of the following code segments could be used to implement the `equals` method of the `Date` class so that the `equals` method works as intended?

```
I.    if (month == other.month)
        if (day == other.day)
            if (year == other.year)
                return true;
      Return false;
II.   if (month == other.getMonth() &&
            day == other.getDay() &&
            year == other.getYear())
        return true;
      else
        return false;
III.  return !((getMonth()  != other.getMonth())  ||
          (getDay()  != other.getDay())  ||
          (getYear() != other.getYear())) ;
```

(A) I only
(B) II only
(C) I and II only
(D) II and III only
(E) I, II, and III

23. During the testing of the `Date` class, it is determined that the class does not correctly handle leap years—although it handles non-leap years correctly.

In which method of the `Date` class is the problem most likely to be found?

(A) The `Date` constructor
(B) The `getMonth` method
(C) The `getDay` method
(D) The `daysUntil` method
(E) The `equals` method

GO ON TO THE NEXT PAGE.

24. Consider the following methods:

```
public static void mystery()
{
    int [] A;
    A = initialize ();
        // returns a valid initialized
        // array of integers
    for (int k = 0; k < A.length / 2; k++)
        swap (A[k], A[A.length - k - 1]);
}

public static void swap (int x, int y)
{
    int temp;
    temp = x;
    x = y;
    y = temp;
}
```

Which of the following best characterizes the effect of the for loop in the method mystery?

(A) It sorts the elements of A.
(B) It reverses the elements of A.
(C) It reverses the order of the first half of A and leaves the second half unchanged.
(D) It reverses the order of the second half of A and leaves the first half unchanged.
(E) It leaves all of the elements of A in their original order.

GO ON TO THE NEXT PAGE.

25. Consider the following code segment:

```
int [][] A = new int [4][3] ;
for (int j = 0; j < A[0].length; j++)
    for (int k = 0; k < A.length; k++)
        if (j == 0)
            A[k][j] = 0;
        else if (k % j == 0)
            A[k][j] = 1;
        else
            A[k][j] = 2;
```

What are the contents of A after the code segment has been executed?

(A) 0 0 0 0
     1 1 1 1
     1 2 1 2
(B) 0 1 1 1
     0 2 2 2
     0 1 2 1
(C) 0 0 0
     1 1 2
     1 1 1
     1 1 2
(D) 0 1 1
     0 2 1
     0 2 2
     0 2 1
(E) 0 1 1
     0 1 2
     0 1 1
     0 1 2

26. Consider the following method:

```
/** @param num an int value such that num >= 0
 */
public void mystery(int num)
{
    System.out.print(num % 100);
    if ((num / 100) != 0)
    {
        mystery(num / 100);
    }
    System.out.print(num % 100);
}
```

Which of the following is printed as a result of the call mystery(456789)?

(A) 456789
(B) 896745
(C) 987654
(D) 456789896745
(E) 896745456789

GO ON TO THE NEXT PAGE.

27. Consider the following method:

```
public static int mystery(int x, int y)
{
    if (x > 0)
        return x;
    else if (y > 0)
        return y;
    else
        return x / y;
}
```

In accordance with good design and testing practices, which of the following is the best set of test cases (x, y) for the method mystery?

(A) (3, 4), (-3, 4), (-3, -4)
(B) (3, 4), (-3, 4), (-3, -4), (-3, 0)
(C) (3, 4), (3, -4), (-3, -4), (-3, 0)
(D) (3, 4), (3, -4), (-3, -4), (-3, 4), (-3, 0)
(E) (3, 4), (2, 5), (3, -4), (-3, 0), (4, 0), (0, 0)

28. Consider the following method.

```
/** Precondition: numList is not empty
 */
private int mystery(int[] numList)
{
    int n = numList[numList.length-1];
    for (int k : numList)
    {
     if (n > k)
        {
          n = k;
        }
    }
    return n;
}
```

Which of the following best describes the return of mystery?

(A) The largest value in the array numList
(B) The least value in the array numList
(C) The index of the largest value in the array numList
(D) The index of the least value in the array numList
(E) The number of indexes whose values are less than numList[n]

GO ON TO THE NEXT PAGE.

29. Consider the following method.

```
public int[] editArray(int[] arr, int oldNum, int newNum)
{
    /* missing code */
    return arr;
}
```

The method above is intended to replace any instance of oldNum in arr with any instances of newNum. Which of the following can be used to replace /* missing code */ to replace any values of old in the array with values of newNum?

(A)
```
for (int k = 0; k < arr.length; k++)
{
    if (arr[k] = oldNum)
    {
        arr[k] == newNum;
    }
}
```

(B)
```
for (int k = 0; k < arr.length; k++)
{
    if (arr[k] == oldNum)
    {
        arr[k] = newNum;
    }
}
```

(C)
```
while (arr[k] == oldNum)
{
    arr[k] = newNum
}
```

(D)
```
for (int k = 0; k < arr.length; k++)
{
    arr[k] == newNum;
}
```

(E)
```
while (int k = 0; k < arr.length; k++)
{
    if (arr[k] = oldNum)
    {
        arr[k] == newNum;
    }
}
```

GO ON TO THE NEXT PAGE.

30. Consider the following two classes.

```java
public class SalesPerson
{
    public void sale()
    {
        System.out.print("greet ");
        pitch();
    }
    public void pitch()
    {
        System.out.print("pitch ");
    }

}

public class CommissionedSalesPerson extends SalesPerson
{
    public void sale()
    {
        super.sale();
        System.out.print("record ");
    }
    public void pitch()
    {
        super.pitch();
        system.out.print("close ");
    }

}
```

The following code segment is found in a class other than `SalesPerson`.

```java
SalesPerson vincent = new CommissionedSalesPerson();
vincent.sale();
```

Which of the following is the best description of the functionality of this code segment?

(A) `greet pitch`
(B) `greet pitch close`
(C) `greet pitch record`
(D) `greet pitch record close`
(E) `greet pitch close record`

GO ON TO THE NEXT PAGE.

31. Consider the following declaration of a class that will be used to represent dimensions of rectangular crates.

```
public class Crate
{
    private int length;
    private int width;
    private int height;

    public Crate(int x, int y, int z)
    {
        length = x;
        width = y;
        height = z;
    }

    //other methods not shown
}
```

The following incomplete class declaration is intended to extend the Crate class so that the color of the crate can be specified.

```
public class ColoredCrate extends Crate
{
    private String color;
    //Constructors not shown
    //Other methods not shown
}
```

Which of the following possible constructors for ColoredCrate would be considered legal?

```
I.   public ColoredCrate(int a, int b, int c, String crateColor)
     {
         length = a;
         width = b;
         height = c;
         color = crateColor;
     }
II.  public ColoredCrate(int a, int b, int c, String crateColor)
     {
         super (a, b, c)
         color = crateColor;
     }
III. public ColoredCrate()
     {
         color = "";
     }
```

(A) I only
(B) III only
(C) I and II only
(D) I and III only
(E) II and III only

GO ON TO THE NEXT PAGE.

32. Consider the following three proposed implementations of method `reverse`, intended to return an `ArrayList` of the objects in reversed order:

I.
```java
public static ArrayList<Object> reverse (ArrayList<Object> q)
{
        ArrayList<Object> s = new ArrayList<Object>();
        while (q.size() != 0)
                s.add(0, q.remove(0));
        return s;
}
```

II.
```java
public static ArrayList<Object> reverse (ArrayList<Object> q)
{
        ArrayList<Object> s = new ArrayList<Object>();
        for (int k = 0; k < q.size(); k++)
                s.add(0, q.remove(0));
        return s;
}
```

III.
```java
public static ArrayList<Object> reverse (ArrayList<Object> q)
{
        Object obj;
        if (q.size() != 0)
        {
                obj = q.remove(0);
                q = reverse(q);
                q.add(obj);
        }
        return q;
}
```

Which of the above implementations of method `reverse` work as intended?

(A) I only

(B) III only

(C) I and II only

(D) I and III only

(E) I, II, and III

GO ON TO THE NEXT PAGE.

33. Consider the following code segment.

```
List<Integer> values = new ArrayList<Integer>();
values.add(5);
values.add(3);
values.add(2);
values.add(2);
values.add(6);
values.add(3);
values.add(9);
values.add(2);
values.add(1);
for (int j = 0; j < values.size(); j++)
{
    if (values.get(j).intValue() == 2)
    {
        values.remove(j);
    }
}
```

What will values contain as a result of executing this code segment?

(A) [5, 3, 2, 2, 6, 3, 9, 2, 1]
(B) [5, 3, 2, 6, 3, 9, 1]
(C) [5, 3, 6, 3, 9, 1]
(D) [2, 2, 2, 5, 3, 6, 3, 9, 1]
(E) The code throws an `ArrayIndexOutOfBoundsException`.

GO ON TO THE NEXT PAGE.

34. Consider the class `Data` partially defined below. The completed `max1D` method returns the maximum value of b, a one-dimensional array of integers. The completed `max2D` method is intended to return the maximum value c, a two dimensional array of integers.

```
public class Data
{
    /** Returns the maximum value of one-dimensional array b */
    public int max1D(int[] b)
    { /* implementation not shown */}
    /** Returns the maximum value of two-dimensional array c */
    public int max2D(int[] c)
    {
        int max;
        /* missing code */
        returns max
    }
    /* other methods of Data class not shown*/
}
```

Assume that `max1D` works as intended. Which of the following can replace /* *missing code* */ so that `max2D` works as intended?

I.
```
for (int[] row: c)
{
    max = max1D(row);
}
```
II.
```
max = max1D(c[0]);
for (int k = 1; k <= c.length; k++)
{
    max = max1D(c[k]);
}
```
III.
```
max = max1D(c[0]);
for (int[] row: c)
{
    if (max < maxID(row))
    {
        max = max1D(row);
    }
}
```

(A) I only
(B) III only
(C) I and II only
(D) II and III only
(E) I, II, and III

GO ON TO THE NEXT PAGE.

35. Consider the following instance `variable`, `numList`, and incomplete method, `countZeros`. The method is intended to return an integer array count such that for all k, `count[k]` is equal to the number of elements equal to 0 from `numList[0]` through `numList[k]`. For example, if `numList` contains the values {1, 4, 0, 5, 0, 0}, the array `countZeros` contains the values {0, 0, 1, 1, 2, 3}.

```
public int[] countZeros(int[] numList)
{
    int[] count = new int[numList.length];
    for (int k : count)
    {
        count[k] = 0;
    }
    /* missing code */
    return count;
}
```

The following two versions of   /* *missing code* */ are suggested to make the method work as intended.

Version 1
```
    for (int k = 0;  k <= numList.length; k++)
    {
        for (int j = 0; j <= k; j++)
        {
            if  (numList[j] == 0)
            {
                count[k] = count[k] + 1;
            }
        }
    }
```

Version 2
```
    for (int k = 0; k < numList.length; k++)
    {
        if  (numList[k] = 0)
        {
            count[k] = count[k - 1] + 1;
        }
        else
        {
            count[k] = count[k - 1];
        }
    }
```

Which of the following statements is true?

(A) Both Version 1 and Version 2 will work as intended, but Version 1 is faster than Version 2.
(B) Both Version 1 and Version 2 will work as intended, but Version 2 is faster than Version 1.
(C) Version 1 will work as intended, but Version 2 causes an `ArrayIndexOutOfBoundsException`.
(D) Version 2 will work as intended, but Version 1 causes an `ArrayIndexOutOfBoundsException`.
(E) Version 1 and Version 2 each cause an `ArrayIndexOutOfBoundsException`.

GO ON TO THE NEXT PAGE.

36. A real estate agent wants to develop a program to record information about apartments for rent. For each apartment, she intends to record the number of bedrooms, number of bathrooms, whether pets are allowed, and the monthly rent charged. Which of the following object-oriented program designs would be preferred?

    (A) Use a class `Apartment` with four subclasses: `Bedrooms`, `Bathrooms`, `PetsAllowed`, and `Rent`.

    (B) Use four classes: `Bedrooms`, `Bathrooms`, `PetsAllowed`, and `Rent`, each with subclass `Apartment`.

    (C) Use a class `Apartment` with four instance variables `int bedrooms`, `int bathrooms`, `boolean petsAllowed`, and `double rent`.

    (D) Use five unrelated classes: `Apartment`, `Bedrooms`, `Bathrooms`, `PetsAllowed`, and `Rent`.

    (E) Use a class `Apartment`, with a subclass `Bedrooms`, with a subclass `Bathrooms`, with a subclass `PetsAllowed`, with a subclass `Rent`.

37. Consider the following declarations:

```
public class Book
{
    boolean hasMorePagesThan(Book b);
    //other methods not shown
}
Public class Dictionary extends Book
{
    //other methods not shown
}
```

    Of the following method headings of `hasMorePagesThan`, which can be added to `Dictionary` so that it will satisfy the `Book` superclass?

    I.   `int hasMorePagesThan(Book b)`
    II. `boolean hasMorePagesThan(Book b)`
    III. `boolean hasMorePagesThan(Dictionary d)`

    (A) I only
    (B) I and II only
    (C) II only
    (D) II and III only
    (E) I, II, and III

GO ON TO THE NEXT PAGE.

38. Consider the following method.

```
/**Precondition: set does not contain any negative values
 */
public int mystery(int[] set, int max)
{
    int m = 0;
    int count = 0;
    for (int n = 0; n < set.length && set[n] < max; n++)
    {
        if (set[n] >= m)
        {
            m = set[n]; //Statement A
        }
        count++; //Statement B
    }
    return count;
}
```

Assume that mystery is called and is executed without error. Which of the following are possible combinations of the number of the value of max, the number of times Statement A is executed, and the number of times Statement B is executed?

	Value of max	Executions of Statement A	Executions of Statement B
I	8	2	3
II	3	7	5
III	7	0	4

(A) I only
(B) III only
(C) I and II only
(D) I and III only
(E) I, II, and III

GO ON TO THE NEXT PAGE.

39. The following method is intended to return an array that inserts an integer m at index n, pushing the values of all indexes after n to the index one higher. For example, if the index arr is

4	2	1	3

and the command arr = insert(arr, 5, 2) is called, the method is intended to return

4	2	5	1	3

```
1        public int[] insert(int[] arr, int m, int n)
2        {
3              int[] temp = new int[arr.length+1];
4              for (int k  = 0; k < arr.length; k++)
5              {
6                    if (k < n)
7                    {
8                          temp[k] = arr[k];
9                    }
10                   else
11                   {
12                         temp[k + 1] = arr[k];
13                   }
14             }
15             temp[m] = n;
16             return temp;
17       }
```

The method insert does not work as intended. Which of the following changes will cause it to work as intended?

(A) Change Line 6 to if (k > n)
(B) Change Line 6 to if (k <= n)
(C) Change Line 12 to temp[k] = arr[k + 1];
(D) Change Line 15 to temp[n] = m;
(E) Change Line 16 to return arr;

GO ON TO THE NEXT PAGE.

40. If X, Y, and Z are integer values, the boolean expression

      `(X > Y)  && (Y > Z)`

can be replaced by which of the following?

(A) `X > Z`

(B) `(X < Y) || (Y < Z)`

(C) `(X <= Y) || (Y <= Z)`

(D) `!((X < Y) || (Y < Z))`

(E) `!((X <= Y) || (Y <= Z))`

END OF SECTION I

**IF YOU FINISH BEFORE TIME IS CALLED,
YOU MAY CHECK YOUR WORK ON THIS SECTION.**

DO NOT GO ON TO SECTION II UNTIL YOU ARE TOLD TO DO SO.

COMPUTER SCIENCE A
SECTION II
Time—1 hour and 30 minutes
Number of Questions—4
Percent of Total Grade—50

Directions: SHOW ALL YOUR WORK. REMEMBER THAT PROGRAM SEGMENTS ARE TO BE WRITTEN IN JAVA™.

Notes:

- Assume that the classes listed in the Java Quick Reference have been imported where appropriate.

- Unless otherwise noted in the question, assume that parameters in method calls are not null and that methods are called only when their preconditions are satisfied.

- In writing solutions for each question, you may use any of the accessible methods that are listed in classes defined in that question. Writing significant amounts of code that can be replaced by a call to one of these methods will not receive full credit.

FREE-RESPONSE QUESTIONS

1. A monochrome (black-and-white) screen is a rectangular grid of pixels that can be either white or black. A pixel is a location on the screen represented by its row number and column number.

   Consider the following proposal for modeling a screen and its pixels.

   A black pixel on the screen is modeled by an object of type `Pixel`. The `Pixel` class includes the following private data and methods:

   - `row`—this `int` holds the row number of this pixel
   - `col`—this `int` holds the column number of this pixel
   - `Pixel` constructor—this constructor creates a `Pixel` based on the given row and column
   - `getRow`—this method returns the row number of this pixel
   - `getCol`—this method returns the column number of this pixel

```java
public class Pixel
{
    private int row;
    private int col;
    public Pixel (int r, int c)
    {row = r; col = c; }
    public int getRow ( )
    {return row; }
    public int getCol ( )
    { return col; }
}
```

GO ON TO THE NEXT PAGE.

A screen is modeled by an object of type Screen. Internally, the screen is represented by an array of linked lists of pixels. The index into the array represents the given row on the screen; the linked list at that element represents the *black* pixels at the various columns in order from smallest to largest column. *White pixels are not stored in the linked list.* A pixel not in the list is assumed to be white.

The Screen class includes the following private data and methods:

- `data`—The array of linked lists

- `pixelAt`—This method returns the pixel at the given location if it exists (i.e., is black) in this Screen. Otherwise, this method returns null.

- `pixelOn`—This method creates and stores a black Pixel at the appropriate place in the array of linked lists based on the given row and column number.

```
public class Screen
{
    private ArrayList<int>[] data;
    private int numCols;

    // postcondition: data is created with
    //                height elements;
    //                numCols is set to
    //                width
    public Screen (int width, int height)
    {  /* to be implemented in part  (a)  */

    // precondition: 0 <= row <=
    //               data.length-1;
    //               0 <= col <= numCols-1
    // postcondition: returns the pixel at
    //                the given row and col
    //                if it exists (black)
    //                or null if the pixel
    //                doesn't exist (white)
    public Pixel pixelAt (int row, int col)
    { /* to be implemented in part  (b)  */}

    // precondition: 0 <= row <=
    //               data.length-1;
    //               0 <= col <= numCols-1;
    //               the pixel at row,col
    //               does not exist
    //               in this Screen
    // postcondition: adds the pixel at
    //                the given row and col
    //                so that pixels in a
    //                given row of data are
    //                in increasing column
    //                order
    public void pixelOn (int row, int col)
    {  /*to be implemented in part (c) */ }

    // ... constructors, other methods,
    //     and other private data not shown
```

GO ON TO THE NEXT PAGE.

(a) Write the constructor for the `Screen` class. The constructor should initialize the private data of the `Screen` class as appropriate.

Complete the constructor for the Screen class below.

```
// postcondition: data is created with
//                height elements; numCols
//                is set to width
public Screen(int width, int height)
```

(b) Write the `Screen` method pixelAt. Method `pixelAt` that should return the pixel at the given row and column of the screen if that pixel exists (i.e., is black). Otherwise pixelAt should return null.

Complete method `pixelAt` below.

```
// precondition: 0 <= row <=
//                data.length-1;
//                0 <= col <= numCols-1
// postcondition: returns the pixel at
//                the given row and col
//                if it exists (black)
//                or null if the pixel
//                doesn't exist (white)
public Pixel pixelAt(int row, int col)
```

(c) Write the `Screen` method pixelOn. Method `pixelOn` should modify this `Screen` so that a pixel is stored at the given row and column.

Complete method `pixelOn` below.

```
// precondition: 0 <= row <=
//                data.length-1;
//                0 <= col <= <= numCols-1;
//                the pixel at row,col
//                does not exist
//                in this Screen
// postcondition: adds the pixel at
//                the given row and col
//                so that pixels in a
//                given row of a data are
//                in increasing column
//                order
public void pixelOn(int row, int col)
```

GO ON TO THE NEXT PAGE.

2. A toy collector is creating an inventory of her marble collection. A marble set specifies the color and number of a particular group of marbles from her collection. The declaration of the `MarbleSet` class is shown below.

```java
public class MarbleSet
{
    /** Constructs a new MarbleSet object */
    public MarbleSet(String color, int numMarbles)
    {   /* implementation not shown*/  }

    /** @return the color of the set of marbles
     */
    public String getColor()
    {   /* implementation not shown*/   }

    /** @return the number of marbles in the set
     */
    public int getNumber()
    { /* implementation not shown*/   }

    // There may be instance variables, constructors, and methods that are not shown.
}
```

The `MarbleCollection` class documents all sets of marbles in the collection. The declaration of the `MarbleCollection` class is shown below.

```java
public class MarbleCollection
{
    /** This is a list of all marble sets */
    private List<MarbleSet> sets;

    /** Constructs a new MarbleSet object */
    public MarbleCollection()
    {   sets = new ArrayList<MarbleSet>();         }

    /** Adds theSet to the marble collection
     * @param theSet the marble set to add to the marble collection
     */
    public void addSet(MarbleSet theSet)
    {   sets.add(theSet);      }

    /** @return the total number of marbles
     */
    public int getTotalMarbles()
    { /* to be implemented in part (a)*/        }
    /** Removes all the marble sets from the marble collection that have the same color as
     * marbleColor and returns the total number of marbles removed
     * @param marbleColor the color of the marble sets to be removed
     * @return the total number of marbles of marbleColor in the marble sets removed
     */
    public int removeColor(String marbleCol)
    { /* to be implemented in part (b)*/        }
```

GO ON TO THE NEXT PAGE.

(a) The `getTotalMarbles` method computes and returns the sum of the number of marbles. If there are no marble sets, the method returns 0.

```
Complete method  getTotalMarbles below
/** @return the sum of the number of marbles in all marble sets
 */
public int getTotalMarbles()
```

(b) The `removeColor` updates the marble collection by removing all the marble sets for which the color of the marbles matches the parameter `marbleCol`. The marble collection may contain zero or more marbles with the same color as the `marbleCol`. The method returns the number of marbles removed.

For example, after the execution of the following code segment

```
MarbleCollection m = new MarbleCollection();
m.addSet(new MarbleSet("red", 2);
m.addSet(new MarbleSet("blue", 3);
m.addSet(new MarbleSet("green", 3);
m.addSet(new MarbleSet("blue", 4);
m.addSet(new MarbleSet("red", 1);
```

the contents of the marble collection can be expressed with the following table.

"red"	"blue"	"green"	"blue"	"red"
2	3	3	4	1

The method call `m.removecolor("red")` returns 3 because there were two red marble sets containing a total of 3 marbles. The new marble collection is shown below.

"blue"	"green"	"blue"
3	3	4

The method call `m.removecolor("purple")` returns 0 and makes no modifications to the marble collection.

Complete the method `removeColor` below.

```
/** Removes all the marble sets from the marble collection that have the same
*color as  marbleColor and returns the total number of marbles removed
* @param marbleColor the color of the marble sets to be removed
* @return the total number of marbles of marbleColor in the marble sets removed
*/
    public int removeColor(String marbleCol)
```

GO ON TO THE NEXT PAGE.

3. A binary, or base two, integer is a number consisting of digits that are either 0 or 1. Digits in a binary integer are numbered from right to left starting with 0.

The decimal value of the binary integer is the sum of each digit multiplied by 2^d where d is the number of the digit.

For example, the decimal value of the binary integer 1011010 is

$$(0 * 2^0) + (1 * 2^1) + (0 * 2^2) + (1 * 2^3) + (1 * 2^4) + (0 * 2^5) + (1 + 2^6)$$

$$= 0 + 2 + 0 + 8 + 16 + 0 + 64$$

$$= 90$$

A decimal integer can be converted into its corresponding binary integer according to the following algorithm:

- Calculate the remainder when the decimal integer is divided by 2. This is the rightmost digit of the corresponding binary integer.

- Divide the decimal integer by 2 using integer division. If the result is 0, stop. Otherwise, repeat the algorithm using the new value of the decimal integer.

The digits produced will be in right-to-left order in the binary integer.

For instance, the decimal integer 90 can be converted into its corresponding binary integer as follows:

90 % 2 = 0	(the rightmost digit)
90 / 2 = 45 45 % 2 = 1	(the second digit from the right)
45 / 2 = 22 22 % 2 = 0	(the third digit from the right)
22 / 2 = 11 11 % 2 = 1	(the fourth digit from the right)
11 / 2 = 55 % 2 = 1	(the fifth digit from the right)
5 / 2 = 22 % 2 = 0	(the sixth digit from the right)
2 / 2 = 11 % 2 = 1	(the leftmost digit)
1 / 2 = 0	

Consider the design of a class that represents an arbitrary length non-negative binary integer.

The operations on this class include

- constructing an empty binary integer with value zero

- constructing a binary integer from an arbitrary non-negative decimal integer

- returning a binary integer that represents the result of adding another binary integer to this binary integer

- returning the result of converting this binary integer to a `String`

- returning a positive integer if this binary integer is less than another binary integer, zero if it is equal, and a negative integer if it is less

GO ON TO THE NEXT PAGE.

In addition, the binary integer class should fully implement the `Comparable` interface.

(a) Write the definition of a binary integer class called BinaryInt, showing the appropriate data definitions, constructors, and method signatures. You should *not* write the implementations of the constructor or any of the methods you define for the BinaryInt class.

(b) Using the signature you wrote in part (a), write the implementation for the operation that constructs a BinaryInt from an arbitrary decimal integer. In writing this method, you may call any of the methods in the BinaryInt class (as you defined it in part (a)). Assume that these methods work as specified.

(c) Using the BinaryInt class (as you defined it in part (a)), complete the following method, Test, that adds the following pairs of decimal integers in binary and outputs the larger of the two binary sums. Test is *not* a method of the binary integer class.

Pair 1: 2,314,279,623 and 3,236,550,123. Pair 2: 3,412,579,010 and 2,128,250,735.

In writing this method, you may call any of the methods BinaryInt (as you defined it in part (a)). Assume that these methods work as specified.

Complete method Test below.

```
public static void Test ()
```

GO ON TO THE NEXT PAGE.

4. A parabola is a graph defined by the equation $y = ax^2 + bx + c$, where a, b, and c are all integers and a is non-zero. The x-value of the axis of symmetry of a parabola is defined by the double $-b/2a$. A point is a pair of integer values, x and y. A point is defined to be on a parabola if it satisfies the equation of the parabola. Consider the examples in the table below:

Equation	Axis of symmetry ($-b/2a$)	Is point (4, 3) on parabola?
$y = 2x^2 - 6x - 5$	$-(-6)/2(2) = 1.5$	Yes, $3 = 2(4)^2 - 6(4) - 5$
$y = 4x^2 + 2x - 3$	$-2/2(4) = -0.25$	No, $3 \neq 4(4)^2 + 2(4) - 3$

The following code segment is from a method outside the class `Parabola` and demonstrates how the `Parabola` class can be used to represent the two equations above:

```
Parabola par1 = new Parabola(2, -6, -5);
double axis1 = par1.getAxis(); //assigns 1.5 to axis1
boolean onGraph1 = par1.isOnGraph(4, 3); //assigns true to onGraph1

Parabola par2 = new Parabola(4, 2, -2);
double axis2 = par2.getAxis(); //assigns -0.25 to axis2
boolean onGraph2 = par2.isOnGraph(4, 3); //assigns false to onGraph2
```

Write the `Parabola` class. The constructor class of `Parabola` must take three integer parameters that represent a, b, and c, successively. You may assume as a precondition that a be a non-zero integer. You must include a `getAxis` method that returns the x-coordinate of the axis of symmetry as a double and an `isOnGraph` method that takes a point represented by two integer parameters, x and y, and returns true if the point is on the `Parabola` and returns false if it is not. Your class methods must be able to return the values indicated in the examples above. You can ignore any overflow issues.

STOP

END OF EXAM

Practice Test 3:
Answers and
Explanations

PRACTICE TEST 3 ANSWER KEY

1.	A	21.	A
2.	D	22.	D
3.	B	23.	D
4.	C	24.	E
5.	C	25.	E
6.	A	26.	E
7.	E	27.	D
8.	B	28.	B
9.	A	29.	B
10.	B	30.	E
11.	E	31.	E
12.	D	32.	D
13.	D	33.	B
14.	C	34.	B
15.	C	35.	E
16.	C	36.	C
17.	E	37.	C
18.	C	38.	A
19.	A	39.	D
20.	D	40.	E

PRACTICE TEST 3 EXPLANATIONS

Section I: Multiple-Choice Questions

1. **A** This problem looks far more complicated than it is because the value of b never changes. The call of `mystery(12, 5)` will return `mystery(10, 5)`, since the value of a is 12, which is greater than 0. Similarly, the call of `mystery(10, 5)` will return `mystery(8, 5)`, which will return `mystery(6, 5)`, which will return `mystery(4, 5)`, which will return `mystery(2, 5)`, which will return `mystery(0, 5)`. In the call of `mystery(0, 5)`, a = 0, so it will return the value of b, which is 5. Regardless of the initial value of a, eventually a will be less than or equal to zero and the value of b will be returned by each call to mystery. The correct answer is (A).

2. **D** Use Trial and Error. For example, let `numList` = {3, 5, 8, 2, 1, 9} and `number` = 6. (Note that `numList` need not be in any particular order.) When `mystery` is called, `number` is stored as the parameter n, so n = 6. Enter the for loop. In the first iteration of the for loop, k = 0. The condition on the if statement is (n <= numList[k]). Since it is not the case that 6 <= numList[0] = 3, skip the if statement and end this iteration of the for loop. Increment k, so k = 1. Go to the if statement again. Since it is not the case that 6 <= numList[1] = 5, skip the if statement and end this iteration of the for loop. Increment k again, so k = 2. Go to the if statement. Since it is the case that 6 <= numList[2] = 8, execute the if statement and return the value of k, which is 2. Since `mystery(6)` returns 2, j = 2. Check each answer and eliminate any that are false. Remember that `numList` can be any list of integers, so if you generated a different set of numbers that are yielding different results, be sure to ask yourself whether it is possible to make each choice wrong.

    Choice (A) is incorrect. The value at index 2 is 8, which is not the greatest value.

    Choice (B) is incorrect. The greatest value in `numList` that is less than 6 is 5, which is not at index 2.

    Choice (C) is incorrect. All the values in `numList` from 0 to 2 – 1 = 1 are less than `number`, not greater.

    Choice (D) is true for this set of values, so keep (D).

    Choice (E) is incorrect. Some of the numbers from indexes 2 through 5 are greater than 6 but not all.

    Choice (D) is the only correct answer. Since the numbers are not in order, no assumption can be made about the indexes after j, but the indexes prior to j must contains lesser values in order for the if statement containing the return to not be executed.

3. **B** In general, data fields of a class are designated private in order to hide the implementation of the class. This ensures that the functionality of the class—as seen by the programmer using the class—does not change if the implementation changes. Choice (B) is correct.

    Choice (A) is incorrect. Methods of a class are able to access the private data of their class.

Choice (C) is incorrect. Data fields that are designated as private cannot be modified outside their class.

Choice (D) is incorrect. A program does not need to know how a class is implemented in order to use it.

Choice (E) is incorrect. The methods `enquack` and `dequack` are public and accessible to any program using the `Quack` class. These methods modify the contents of a `Quack`.

4. **C**   The `isEmpty` method has to return true if `myData` contains no elements and is false otherwise. If `myData` contains no elements, then the size is 0. The term `length` is used for arrays rather than ArrayLists, so eliminate (A) and (D). Since `size` is an `ArrayList` method rather than a variable, `size()` must be used instead of `size`, so eliminate (E). Also, since `size()` is an `ArrayList` method rather than a `Quack` method, the `ArrayList myData` must be referenced, so eliminate (B). The correct answer is (C).

5. **C**   The fastest way to solve this problem is to make a table of values for `mystery(n)` and see which gives answers that match those given by the original method. Start by letting n = 2. If n = 2, the if condition is not met, so the else is executed, which returns 1 + `mystery(n - 3)`. Since n − 3 = 2 − 3 = −1, `mystery(n - 3)` is `mystery(-1)`. In this case n = −1, so the if condition is met and mystery(−1) returns 2. Therefore, the original return, 1 + `mystery(n - 2)`, returns 1 + 2 = 3. Now compare that to the choices. Remember that integer division rounds to 0, so lop off any decimal. Choices (A) and (E) do not return 3, so eliminate them. Now try n = 3. Following the method just as above, the return of mystery (3) is also 3. Choices (B) and (D) do not return 3, so eliminate them, as well.

   Note that you can stop filling in answers for a particular choice as soon as one of the answers does not match the answer given by the original method.

n	Original	(A)	(B)	(C)	(D)	(E)
2	3	2	3	3	3	4
3	3	–	4	3	4	–

   After checking two values, only (C) provides answers that are the same as the original method. Choice (C) is correct.

6. **A**   The `addDistance` method adds the parameter k to the number of kilometers and m to the number of meters. This might appear to be sufficient, but every 1000 meters should be converted to 1 kilometer. Determine which answer choice correctly does this. Consider one possible case. Let kilometers = 3 and meters = 2300. Then 2300 meters should be converted to 2 kilometers and 300 meters, leaving an end result of `kilometers` = 5 and `meters` = 300. Eliminate any answer choice that doesn't give this result.

   Choice (A) adds `meters / 1000` to `kilometers`. Remember that integer division in Java is performed by dropping any remainder and rounding toward 0. Therefore, `meters / 1000 =`

2300 / 1000 = 2, so 2 is added to kilometers to get 5. This is correct, so far. The second statement sets meters equal to meters % 1000, which is the remainder when meters is divided by 1000. This sets meters = 300, which is also correct, so keep (A).

Choice (B) adds meters % 1000 to kilometers. Thus, kilometers = 3 + 300 = 303. Since this is not correct, eliminate (B).

Choice (C) adds kilometers % 1000 to meters. 3 % 1000 = 3, so meters would equal 2300 + 3 = 2303. This is not correct, so eliminate (C).

Choice (D) adds meters % 1000 to kilometers, so kilometers = 3 + 300 = 303, which is incorrect, so eliminate (D).

Choice (E) sets meters = meters % 1000 = 300, which is correct. However, it doesn't change the value of kilometers, which incorrectly remains 3, so eliminate (E).

Therefore, the correct answer is (A).

7. **E** Go through each answer choice one at a time.

Choice (A) may appear to be correct. However, remember that kilometers and meters are private variables (as are all variables in AP Computer Science). Therefore, they cannot be directly accessed by another class. Eliminate (A).

Choice (B) correctly accesses these variables by using the public getKilometers and getMeters methods. However, these values are added to set[k]. Therefore, this would simply double each of the distances without adding anything to temp. Since temp is the value that is returned, eliminate (B).

Choice (C) uses set[k].addDistance(). However, the method requires two integer parameters, so eliminate (C).

Eliminate (D) for the same reason.

Choice (E) correctly accesses kilometers and meters via getKilometers and getMeters from set[k]. These values are also correctly added to temp, the DistanceTracker to be returned, via its addDistance method. Therefore, the correct answer is (E).

8. **B** Follow the method coding, one line at a time. First create the empty ArrayList of type Integer called values. Now go through the for loop. First, let i = 0. Look at the condition in the if statement. i%4, i.e., the remainder when i is divided by 4, equals 0. Since this value does not meet the condition, do not execute the if statement. Since 0 is not in the ArrayList, eliminate any choices that include 0: (C) and (E). Now, add 5 to i to get i = 5. Since i%4 = 1, execute the statement and add 5 to the ArrayList. Now, add 5 again to get i = 10. Since i%4 = 2, do not execute the statement. Note that the value of i has skipped over 9, which is one of the integers in (D). Since i will never equal 9, eliminate (D). Add 5 again to get i = 15. Since i%4 = 3, do not execute the statement. Add 5 again to get i = 20. Since i%4 = 0, do not execute the statement. Now, add 5 to i to get i = 25.

Since i%4 = 1, execute the statement and add 25 to the ArrayList. Since 25 is not included in (A), eliminate this choice. The correct answer is therefore (B).

9. **A**   To have the correct return, <expression> must be true when exactly two of the boolean variables are true and exactly one is false. There are three possible ways for this to happen: if a and b are true but c is false, if a and c are true but b is false, and if b and c are true but a is false. Put these three into proper Java boolean terminology. In Java "and" is represented by &&, "or" is represented by ||, and "not" is represented by !. The first case, a and b are true but c is false, is expressed by a && b && !c. (Note that in logic, there is no distinction between "and" and "but.") The second case, a and c are true but b is false, is expressed by a && !b && c. The third case, b and c are true but a is false, is expressed by !a && b && c. Since <expression> should be true if *any* of these cases is true, these should be combined as an "or" statement: (a && b && !c) || (a && !b && c) || (!a && b && c). The correct answer is (A).

10. **B**   This problem tests your knowledge of operator precedence in expressions. Multiplication and division are performed before addition and subtraction operations that are at the same precedence level, which are performed in left-to-right order.

Apply these rules to the code segment in the question

```
x    = 5 – 4 + 9 * 12 / 3 – 10
     = 5 – 4 + (9 * 12) / 3 – 10
     = 5 – 4 + 108 / 3 – 10
     = 5 – 4 + (108 / 3) – 10
     = 5 – 4 + 36 – 10
     = (5 – 4) + 36 – 10
     = 1 + 36 – 10
     = (1 + 36) – 10
     = 37 – 10
     = 27
```

Choice (B) is correct.

11. **E**   String objects are dynamic in the sense that they do not have a maximum length (other than one imposed by a limit of available memory!), so the mention of this limit is just a red herring. Therefore, (C) and (D), which appear to refer to a 25-character String limit, can be eliminated immediately.

Choice (A) can be eliminated because it is not valid Java code.

Choice (B) can be eliminated because an array of Strings is being instantiated and then incorrectly assigned to an ArrayList object.

Choice (E) correctly declares and creates an array of 50 Strings. The correct answer is (E).

12. **D** Go through each line of coding one at a time. First, create the empty `ArrayList<Integer>` `scores`. Then, add the integer 93. The ArrayList is [93]. Then, add the integer 97. Since the add method with one parameter adds the integer parameter to the end of the list, the list is now [93, 97]. Similarly, add 84 to get [93, 97, 84], and add 91 to get [93, 97, 84, 91]. Now, remove the integer at index 2, and move the following elements to the left. Since the indexes start with 0, the index 2 refers to the 84. The list is now [93, 97, 91]. Now execute the `line scores.add(1, 83)`. When the add method has 2 parameters, the first parameter is the index to which the second parameter is inserted. Therefore, 83 is inserted at index 1, and, without deleting any items, all succeeding items are pushed to the right. Therefore, the list is now [93, 83, 97, 91]. Now, execute `scores.set(3, 99)`. The first parameter, 3, is the index to which the second parameter, 99, must replace the existing integer. Therefore, the list is now [93, 83, 97, 99]. `System.out.println(scores)` outputs this list. Therefore, the correct answer is (D).

13. **D** Implementation I is correct. This implementation recursively finds the correct digit by noting that the rightmost digit of n can be found by taking the remainder when n is divided by 10 (the base case). Other digits of n can be found by dividing n by 10 and finding the digit one place to the right (the recursive case). Eliminate any choice that does not include Implementation I: (C) and (E).

Implementation II is correct. The pow method calculates $10^{whichDigit}$. Dividing n by this number gives a number whose rightmost digit is the target digit. Taking the remainder of this number divided by 10 returns the correct digit. Eliminate any choice that does not include Implementation II: (B).

Implementation III is correct. The loop has the same effect as dividing n by $10^{whichDigit}$. The implementation then returns the correct digit by taking the remainder of this number divided by 10. Eliminate any choice that doesn't include Implementation III: (A).

The correct answer is (D).

14. **C** `SelectionSort` begins at index 0 and swaps that element with the least element in the rest of the array. The item in the rest of the array with the least value is 1 at index 2. Swap the 4 from index 0 with the 1 from index 2, and leave all other elements the same. The result is (C).

15. **C** Segment I is correct. This is the most straightforward way of traversing the array backward and printing out the values. The for loop causes k to take on values from 9 down to 0 and print out the kth element of v. Eliminate any choice that does not include Segment I: (B) and (D).

Segment II is also correct. Although k takes on values from 0 up to 9, the array index 9-k gives the correct indexes of 9 down to 0. Eliminate any choice that does not include Segment II: (A).

Segment III is incorrect. The first time through the loop, k will have a value of 10, which will raise an `ArrayIndexOutOfBounds` exception. Eliminate any choice that does include Segment III: (E).

Choice (C) is the correct answer.

16. **C** To answer this question, invent a set and an integer n. Let set = {4, 2, 5, 3, 1} and let n = 3. Now go through the method call. Begin with the for loop, which initializes k = 0. Since k is less than `set.length()` = 5, execute the for loop, which includes an if statement. The condition on the if is that `set.get(k) > n`. Remember that indexes begin with 0, so `set.get(k) = set.get(0)` = 4. This is greater than n = 3, so execute the if statement, which is to `return (set.remove(k) + mystery(set, n))`. The remove method of ArrayList not only removes the element but also returns it at the specified index. Therefore, this returns 4 + `mystery(set, 3)` with the new set: {2, 5, 3, 1}. Note that the return statement ends the execution of the method, so there will not be a need to continue with the for loop. However, in this case, it also calls the method recursively, so execute the new method call for `mystery(set, 3)`. Once again, start with the for loop, which initializes k = 0, which is less than `set.length()` = 4, so execute the for statement again. The condition on this if statement, this time, is not met since `set.get(k)` = 2 < n = 3. Increment k to get k = 1. Since this is less than 4, execute the for statement. This time, the if condition is met, since `set.get(1)` = 5 > 3, so execute the statement. Remove 5 from set but also return 5 + `mystery(set, 3)` with the new set being {2, 3, 1}. Insert this into the original return to get 4 + 5 + `mystery(set, 3)`. Execute the new method call. Once again, start with the for loop. k = 0 < `set.length()` = 3, so execute the for statement again. The condition on this if statement is not met since `set.get(k)` = 2 < n = 3. Increment k to get k = 1. This is also less than `set.length()` = 3, so continue the loop. The condition on this if statement is not met since `set.get(k)` = 3, which is equal to but not less than the value of n. Increment k to get k = 2. This is less than `set.length()` = 3, so continue. The condition on this if statement is not met since `set.get(k)` = 1 < n = 3. Increment k to get k = 3. Since this is not less than `set.length ()` = 3, terminate the for loop. Return 0 and insert this into the original return to get a return of 4 + 5 + 0 = 9. Now go through the answer choices and eliminate anything that is not 9.

Choice (A) is 0, so eliminate this choice.

Choice (B) is the number of elements greater than n. If n = 3 and there are two elements greater than 3, eliminate this choice.

Choice (C) is the sum of the elements greater than n. Since the elements greater than n are 4 and 5, which have a sum of 9, keep this choice.

Choice (D) is the sum of the elements that are less than n. The elements less than 3 are 2 and 1, which have a sum of 3, so eliminate this choice.

Choice (E) is the sum of the elements that are less than or equal to n. The elements less than or equal to 3 are 2, 3, and 1, which have a sum of 6, so eliminate this choice too. The correct answer is (C).

17.   **E**   Each of the answer choices creates a 4-by-4 two-dimensional array called `temp` and returns that array. The question, therefore, becomes which correctly fills the array. Choice (A) creates a for loop with initial value int j = 0. Since j <= 3, continue with the for loop to get to a new for loop with initial value int k = 0.

Since k < 4, continue with this for loop to reach the statement `temp[j][k] = j;` This assigns `temp[0][0]` = 0. Remember that all indexes begin with 0, so `temp[0][0]` refers to the first row, first column. This is the correct value for this element, so continue. Increment the value of k to get k = 1. This is still less than 4, so continue with this inner for loop. Assign `temp[j][k] = j`, so `temp[0][1]` = 0. Because this is the first row, second column, which contains a 0, continue. Increment the value of k again to get k = 2. This is still less than 4, so continue with this inner for loop. Assign `temp[j][k] = j`, so `temp[0][2]` = 0. Since this is the first row, third column, which contains a 0, continue. Increment the value of k again to get k = 3. This is still less than 4, so continue with this inner for loop. Assign `temp[j][k] = j`, so `temp[0][3]` = 0. Because this is the first row, fourth column, which contains a 0, continue. Increment the value of k to get k = 4. As this is not less than 4, end the inner for loop. Return to the outer for loop and increment j to get j = 1. Begin the inner for loop with initial value k = 0. Since this is less than 4, enter this for loop. Assign `temp[j][k] = j`, so `temp[1][0]` = 1. This element refers to the second row first column, which does not have a value of 1. This is incorrect, so eliminate (A). Go on to (B).

Similarly, (B) begins with the same for loop for the j values *and* the same for loop for the k values. Therefore, the statement `temp[j][k] = k` assigns `temp[0][0]` = 0 (since k is also 0). This is correct, so continue. Increment the value of k to get k = 1. Since this is less than 4, continue the inner for loop. Now, the statement `temp[j][k] = k` assigns `temp[0][1]` = 1. This is not the value in this position, so eliminate (B). Go on to (C).

Choice (C) has the same outer for loop, so initialize the value of j to be 0. The inner for loop initializes k = j, so k = 0. This is less than 4, so execute the statement. Thus, `temp[j][k] = k` assigns `temp[0][0]` = 0. As this is the correct value, continue. Increment k to get k = 1. Since this is less than 4, continue the inner for loop. Now, the statement `temp[j][k] = k` assigns `temp[0][1]` = 1. Since this is not the value in this position, eliminate (C). Go on to (D).

Choice (D) has the same outer for loop, so initialize the value of j to be 0. The inner for loop initializes k = 0. The condition on the inner for loop is k <= j. This is true, so enter the inner for loop. Execute `temp[j][k] = j` to get `temp[0][0]` = 0. Since this is the correct value, continue. Increment the value of k to get k = 1. As k is greater than j, end the inner for loop. Go back to the outer for loop and increment j to get j = 1. This is still less than 4, so continue with the outer for loop and go to the inner for loop, which gives k an initial value of 0. Because k is less than or equal to j, execute `temp[j][k] = j` to get `temp[1][0]` = 1. This is not the correct value, so eliminate (D).

Go to (E). Choice (E) has the same outer for loop, so give j initial value 0. Now, go to the inner for loop and give k initial value 0. The condition on the inner for loop is k is less than or equal to j.

This is true, so enter the inner for loop. Execute `temp[j][k] = j` to get `temp[0][0] = 0`. This is the correct value, so continue. Increment the value of `k` to get `k = 1`. Since `k` is greater than `j`, end the inner for loop. Go back to the outer loop and increment `j` to get `j = 1`. This is still less than 4, so continue with the outer for loop and go to the inner for loop, which gives `k` initial value 0. Since `k` is less than or equal to `j`, execute `temp[j][k] = k` to get `temp[1][0] = 0`. This is still the correct value, so continue. Increment the value of `k` to get `k = 1`. Since `k` is still less than or equal to `j`, continue the inner for loop and execute `temp[j][k] = k` to get `temp[1][1] = 1`. Once again, this is the correct value, so continue. Increment `k` to get `k = 2`, which is greater than the value of `j`, so end the inner for loop and return to the outer for loop. Increment `j` to get `j = 2`. Because this is less than 4, continue to the inner for loop. Initialize `k = 0`. Because `k` is less than or equal to `j`, execute `temp[j][k] = k` to get `temp[2][0] = 0`. This is the correct value, so continue. Increment `k` to get `k = 1`. Since `k` is less than or equal to `j`, execute `temp[j][k] = k` to get `temp[2][1] = 1`. This is the correct value, so continue. Increment `k` to get `k = 2`. Since `k` is less than or equal to `j`, execute `temp[j][k] = k` to get `temp[2][2] = 2`. This is the correct value, so continue. Increment `k` to get `k = 3`. Because this is greater than the value of `j`, end the inner for loop and return to the outer for loop. Increment `j` to get `j = 3`. Since this is less than 4, continue to the inner for loop, which gives `k` initial value 0. As `k` is less than or equal to `j`, execute `temp[j][k] = k` to get `temp[3][0] = 0`. This is the correct value, so continue. Increment the value of `k` to get `k = 1`. Since `k` is still less than or equal to `j`, continue the inner for loop and execute `temp[j][k] = k` to get `temp[3][1] = 1`. This is the correct value, so continue. Increment `k` to get `k = 2`. Because `k` is less than or equal to `j`, execute `temp[j][k] = k` to get `temp[3][2] = 2`. This is the correct value, so continue. Increment `k` to get `k = 3`. Since `k` is less than or equal to `j`, execute `temp[j][k] = k` to get `temp[3][3] = 3`. This is the correct value, so continue. Increment `k` to get `k = 4`. Because this is greater than `j`, end the inner for loop and return to the outer for loop. Increment `j` to get `j = 4`. Since this is not less than 4, end the outer for loop. Remember that type `int` is initialized by default as 0. Therefore, any element whose value has not been specifically assigned or modified has value 0. This is consistent with the given array. Therefore, (E) is correct.

18. **C**   Go through each answer choice one at a time.

Choice (A) creates an empty `String temp`. Then, if `age` is less than 3, `temp` is set equal to `"infant"`. This is correct. Then, if `age` is less than or equal to 7, the `temp` is set equal to `"Pee-Wee"`. This appears to be correct. However, this instruction will apply not only to those from 3 to 7 but also to those less than 3. Therefore, those less than 3 will be incorrectly labeled `"Pee-Wee"`. Therefore, eliminate (A).

Choice (B) also creates an empty `String temp`. Then, if `age` is less than 3, `temp` is set equal to `"Infant"`. This is correct. However, the next if condition, `(3 <= age <= 7)`, is not a valid statement formation in Java. Therefore, eliminate (B).

Choice (C) creates an empty `String temp`. Then, if `age` is less than 3, `temp` is set equal to `"Infant"`. This is correct. The next statement is an `else if (age <= 7)`. This may appear to be the same problem as (A). However, the else means that this instruction will not be executed if the original condition was met. Therefore, this statement does not apply to any age less than 3. Therefore, for the remaining ages that are less than or equal to 7, the String temp will be assigned the value "Pee-Wee". This is correct, so far. Next is another else if statement. Similarly, for all ages less than or equal to 7, this statement will not be executed. For the remaining ages that are less than or equal to 13, the String temp will be assigned the value "Cub". Then, there is another else if statement. Ignore all ages less than or equal to 13. If age is greater than or equal to 14, which is all remaining ages, then the String temp is assigned "Leader". This is correct. Finally, the method returns the correctly assigned String temp. This is correct. Check the two remaining answers to be sure.

Choice (D) begins like the other three. Empty String temp is created and if age is less than 3, temp set equal to "Infant". Next, there is an else if (age < 7). Because of the else, this is not correctly executed for ages less than 3. However, because the operator is < and not <=, it is not executed for those equal to 7. The table says that all those from 3 to 7 *inclusive* should be assigned to "Pee-Wee". Since those who are exactly 7 would not get this assignment, eliminate (D).

Choice (E) makes both the mistake of (A), not using the else, and the mistake of (D), not using <=. Therefore, eliminate (E).

The correct answer is (C).

19. **A** Consider the results of executing the example given. Let arr contain [8, 7, 5, 5, 4, 7, 2, 7, 1, 2, 7]. Call getGap(arr, 7). Set index1 and index2 equal to –1. Now execute the for loop. for(int k = 0; k < arr.length; k++) executes the for loop for each index of arr and calls that index k. Start with k = 0. The condition on the if statement is (arr[k] == num). Since arr[0] is equal to 8 and not 7, do not execute the if statement. The if statement is the entirety of the for loop, so go to k = 1. Because arr[1] = 7, execute the if statement, which begins with a new if statement with the condition (index1 == –1). This is true, so execute the if statement and ignore the else statement. Set index1 = 1 and index2 = 1. Now, increment k to get k = 2. Since arr[2] = 5, do not execute the if statement and increment to get k = 3. As arr[3] = 5, do not execute the if statement and increment to get k = 4. Because arr[4] = 4, do not execute the if statement and increment to get k = 5. Since arr[5] = 7, execute the if statement. Look at the condition of the inner if statement, (index1 == –1). This is now false, so execute the else statement. Set index1 equal to index2, which is 1. Then set index2 equal to k, which is 5. Now, go to k = 6. Since arr[6] = 2, do not execute the if statement and increment to get k = 7. Because arr[7] = 7, execute the if statement. Look at the condition of the inner if statement, (index1 == –1). This is false, so execute the else statement. Set index1 equal to index2, which is 5. Set index2 equal to k, which is 7. Now, go to k = 8. Since arr[8] = 1, do not execute the if statement and go to k = 9. As arr[9] = 2, do not execute the if statement and go to k = 10. Because arr[10] = 7, execute the if statement. Look at the condition of the inner if statement, (index1 == –1). Since this is false, execute the else statement. Set index1 equal to index2, which is 7. Then set index2 equal to k, which is 10. Now, go to

k = 11, which is equal to `arr.length`, so end the for loop. Now execute the return statement, which is `return (index2 - index1)`. This returns 10 − 7 = 3. Now go through the answer choices to see which are equal to 3. Choice (A) is the difference between the indexes of the last two occurrences of num. The last two occurrences of 7 are at index 7 and index 10. Since this difference is 3, keep this answer choice.

Choice (B) is the minimum difference between two occurrences of `num`. The least difference is between the 7's at indexes 5 and 7. Since the difference is 2, eliminate (B).

Choice (C) if the difference between the first two occurrences in `arr`. The first two occurrences are at index 1 and 5, which have a difference of 4, so eliminate (C).

Choice (D) is the length of the array `arr`, which is 11, so eliminate (D).

Choice (E) is the number of occurrence of `arr`, which is 4, so eliminate (E).

The correct answer is (A).

20. **D** The method is intended to determine the maximum difference between the indexes of any two occurrences of num in `arr`. In order for this to happen, `index1` must be the index of the first occurrence of `num` and `index2` must be the last occurrence. `Index1` is given the index of the first occurrence at line 11. `Index2` is given the index of the last occurrence at the final execution of line 17. This is correct. However, the reason the method does not work as intended is that the value of index1 is changed at line 16. Therefore, this statement should be deleted. The correct answer is (D).

21. **A** The `Object` class `equals` method is called with boolean return and Object parameter, so the call will have to use this exactly. The only choice that does this is (A).

22. **D** Only Segments II and III are correct.

Segment I calls variables `other.month`, `other.day`, and `other.year`. However, these variables are private and, thus, can be recognized only within `other`.

Segment II combines the three tests into one if statement condition and returns true if that condition is satisfied.

Segment III returns the opposite of checking if any one of the `month`, `day`, or `year` is not equal. This is an application of DeMorgan's Law. The correct answer is (D).

23. **D** The `daysUntil` method is the only method that needs to know about leap years in order to work properly. For example, the number of days between February 27 and March 2 is different according to whether or not the year is a leap year.

All of the other methods do not depend on whether the year is a leap year. The correct answer is (D).

24. **E** In Java, parameters methods are passed by value. Thus, the values of any arguments in the code that calls the method are not changed by calling the method.

In this question—despite its misleading name—the `swap` method does not change the arguments of the code that calls `swap`.

Because swap has no effect, (E) is correct: The elements of A are left in their original order.

25. **E** To solve this problem, first eliminate (A) and (B) as they represent two-dimensional arrays that have 3 rows and 4 columns, not 4 rows and 3 columns as indicated in the code segment.

Note that k iterates through the rows and j iterates through the columns.

Second, examine the value at `A[1][0]`. This value is set when k = 1 and j = 0. Because j has the value 0, `A[1][0]` should be set to 0. This eliminates (C).

Finally, examine the value at `A[1][1]`. This value is set when k = 1 and j = 1. Because k % j has the value 0, `A[1][1]` should be set to 1. This eliminates (D).

Choice (E) is correct.

26. **E** Execute the recursive call one step at a time. When `mystery(456789)` is called, the first executed line is `System.out.print(num % 100)`. In Java, the % symbol refers to the remainder when the first term is divided by the second. Since num = 456789, the remainder when dividing by 100 is the last two digits, 89. Therefore, the program will print 89. Eliminate any choice that does not print 89: (A), (C), and (D). Now go to the if statement, for which the condition is `(num / 100 != 0)`. Since 456789 / 100 = 4567 (rounding toward 0), execute the if statement, which is `mystery(num / 100)`, i.e., `mystery(4567)`. Execute this method call. The first executed line of `mystery(4567)` is `System.out.print(num % 100)`, i.e., `System.out.print(4567 % 100)`. Since the remainder of `4567 % 100` is 67, the program prints 67 and displays 8967. Now go to the if statement, which is `if (num / 100 != 0)`. Since 4567 / 100 (rounded toward 0) is 45, execute the if statement, `mystery(num / 100)`, i.e., `mystery(45)`. The first executed line of `mystery(45)` is `System.out.print(num % 100)`, i.e., `System.out.print(45 % 100)`. Since the remainder of 45 / 100 is 45, the program prints 45 and displays 896745. This is (B). Check to see whether anything else is printed. The if statement says `if (num / 100 != 0)`. Since 45 / 100 (rounding toward 0) is 0, don't execute the if statement. Go to the next statement, which is `System.out.print(num % 100)`. Since num % 100 is 45, print 45. More is printed than what is indicated by (B), so eliminate (B). The correct answer is (E). [Note that the program will complete the execution of `mystery(4567)` and print 67, then complete `mystery(456789)` and print 89, giving the output indicated by (E).]

27. **D**   A good set of test data exercises every conditional test in the code including cases that generate errors.

In the method mystery, a good set of test cases must include, at the minimum, data that allows each of the return statements to be executed.

x > 0 and y = <anything>

x <= 0 and y > 0

x <= 0 and y < 0

x <= 0 and y = 0 (the error condition)

Only (D) meets all four of these criteria.

28. **B**   Test the method using a particular array of integers. For example, consider the array {2, 3, 6, 0, 1}. Execute the method with this array as the parameter `numList`. Initialize n = `numList.length` − 1 = 5 − 1 = 4. Now go to the for loop, which is an enhanced-for loop. Go through each index of `numList` and one at a time, assign each index to k. Let k = 0. The condition on the if statement is (`numList[n]` > `numList[k]`). Since `numList[4]` = 1 is not greater than `numList[0]` = 2, skip the if statement. Increment k to get k = 1. Go to the if statement. Since `numList[4]` = 1 is not greater than `numList[1]` = 3, skip the if statement. Increment k to get k = 2. Go to the if statement. Since `numList[4]` = 1 is not greater than `numList[2]` = 6, skip the if statement. Increment k to get k = 2. Go to the if statement. Since `numList[4]` = 1 is greater than `numList[3]` = 0, execute the if statement. Set n = k = 3.

Increment k to get k = 4. Go to the if statement. Since `numList[4]` = 1 is not greater itself, skip the if statement. Since that is the last index of `numList`, end the for loop. Now return `numList[n]` = `numList[3]` = 0. This is not the largest value in the array, so eliminate (A). This is the least value in the array, so keep (B). This is not the index of the largest value in the array, so eliminate (C). This is not the index of the least value in the array, so eliminate (D). This is not the number of indexes whose values are less than `numList[n]`, so eliminate (E). The correct answer is (B).

29. **B**   Go through each choice one at a time and determine whether each will give the intended result: replacing any instances of `oldNum` with instances of `newNum`. Choice (A) may look good initially. However, the condition of the if statement uses the assignment "=" rather than the boolean "==". Similarly, the if statement itself uses the boolean rather than the assignment. Therefore, this is not proper syntax. Eliminate (A).

Choice (B) uses a for loop to go through each index of `arr`. Then, if the value at any index is equal to `oldNum`, it is changed to `newNum`. Keep this choice.

Choice (C) uses a while loop that terminates at the first index for which the value is not `oldNum`. Since there may be some instances later, this is not correct. Eliminate (C).

Choice (D) uses a for loop to go through each index of arr but changes all values to new rather than using a conditional statement. Eliminate (D).

Similar to (D), (E) uses a while loop that terminates at the first instance of an index whose value is not old. Eliminate (E). Therefore, the correct answer is (B).

30. **E**   The SalesPerson vincent is a CommissionedSalesPerson, so follow the coding of the CommissionedSalesPerson. Execute Vincent.sale() by following the Commissioned-SalesPerson method sale(). Since the first command is System.out.print("greet"), the output must begin with this word. The next command is pitch(). Even though it is called by the superclass, since vincent is a CommissionedSalesPerson, default to the Commissioned-SalesPerson pitch() method. The first command is super.pitch(). Now go to SalesPerson pitch(), which has one command: System.out.print("pitch"), so the second word of the output must be pitch. Now complete the execution of CommissionedSalesPerson pitch(), which includes one additional command: System.out.print("close"). Since the next word of the output must be "close", eliminate (A), (C), and (D). Now complete the execution of the CommissionedSalesPerson sale() method, which has one remaining command: System.out.print("record"). Since the next and final word of the output must be "record", eliminate (B). The correct answer is (E).

31. **E**   Go through each of the possible constructors and determine whether each is legal. Constructor I takes three integers and a String as parameters. It then assigns the three integers to height, width, and length, respectively. However, these are private variables in another class, even one which inherits from the superclass. Only public or protected variables can be inherited. Therefore, this is illegal. Eliminate any choices that include Constructor I: (A), (C), and (D). Constructor II also takes three integers and a String as parameters. It correctly assigns the integers to the private variables using the constructor method. It then assigns the String to color, which is part of, and therefore accessible by, the subclass. Therefore, this is legal. Eliminate any choice that does not include Constructor II: (B). Only one choice remains. To see why Constructor III is legal, realize that a constructor need not give each variable a value to be legal. The correct answer is (E).

32. **D**   Consider each possible reverse method. Test using an array integer with elements 1, 2, and 3. The end result should be 3, 2, and 1. Start with Method I, which takes the ArrayList<Object> q as a parameter. It creates a new ArrayList<Object> s. Go to the while loop. The condition is that q.size() != 0. Since the size of q is 3, enter the while loop. The lone statement in the while loop is s.add(0, q.remove(0)). This assigns the object returned by q.remove(0) to s at index 0. The method call q.remove(0) removes the Object at index 0, moving all objects at later indexes to the left in order to fill in the gap and return the removed object. In this case, the object at index 0 of q is the Integer 1. This object is removed from q, leaving the list with two Objects: 2 and 3. The Integer 1 is also added to the list s at index 0, leaving s as a list with one Object: 1. Now, q.size() = 2. Since it is still not 0, execute the while loop again. Remove the Object of q at index 0, leaving it with one Object: 3. Add the removed object to the s at index 0, moving Objects at later indexes

to the right, leaving it with two Objects: 2 and 1. Since `q.size()` now equals 1, execute the while loop again. Once again remove the object from q at 0 and add it to s at 0. Thus, the Integer Object 3 is removed from q, leaving it with no objects, and added to s, leaving it with 3 Objects: 3, 2, and 1. Since `q.size()` is now equal to 0, do not execute the while loop again. Return the `ArrayList` s, which is 3, 2, 1. Since this is the reverse of the original, I works as intended. Eliminate any choice that does not include Method I: (B).

Now look at Method II. This method creates a new `ArrayList<Object>` s. Go to the for loop. The for loop initializes k = 0. The condition is that k < `q.size()`. Since q is the Integers 1, 2, and 3, `q.size()` = 3, so execute the for loop. The lone command in the for loop is s.add(0, `q.remove(0)`). When there is only one parameter, the `add()` adds the Object parameter to the end. Therefore, this removes 1 from the list q and adds it to the list s. Thus, q has the Objects 2 and 3, and s has the Object 1. Increment k to get k = 1. Since `q.size()` is now 2, the for loop condition is still true, so execute the for loop. The command `s.add(0, q.remove(0))` removes the Object 2 from q and adds it to the end of s. Thus, the list q has the Object 3 and s has the Objects 1 and 2. Increment k to get k = 2. Since `q.size()` is now 1, the for loop condition is false. Do not execute the for loop again. Return s, which is 2 and 1. Since this is not the reversal of the original, eliminate any choice that includes Method II: (C) and (E).

Finally, look at Method III. This method creates an `Object` obj. The if statement has the condition that `q.size()` != 0. Since q is the list 1, 2, and 3, `q.size()` is 3 and the condition is true, execute the if statement. The first command is obj = `q.remove(0)`. This assigns the Object at index 0, the Integer 1, to obj and removes it from q. The next command is the recursive call `reverse(q)`. Execute the call for the `ArrayList<Object>` q with Integer Objects 2 and 3. Then a new Object obj is created that is independent from the old and exists only in this execution of reverse. Since `q.size()` is still not 0, execute the if statement. Execute the command obj = `q.remove(0)` by removing 2 from q and assign obj with 2. Now execute the recursive call `reverse(q)`. In this call, the `ArrayList` q contains only one element, the Integer 3. Now create new `Object` obj. Since `q.size()` is 1, execute the if statement. The command obj = `q.remove(0)` removes the Integer 3 from q and assigns it to obj, leaving q with no Objects. The recursive call `reverse(q)` uses the empty `ArrayList` q. This method call creates an `Object` obj. Since `q.size()` is 0, skip the if statement and execute the return statement by returning an empty `ArrayList`. Going back to the previous remove call, q is assigned this empty `ArrayList`. The next command is q.add(obj). Since, in this call, obj is 3, 3 is added to the end of q, resulting in the list with Integer 3. This list is returned to the previous call of the method. In this call, obj = 2. This obj is added to the end of the list, leaving the list with integers 3 and 2. This list is returned to the prior call. In this call obj = 1, so 1 is add to q to get a list with integers 3, 2, and 1. This list is returned. There is no prior call so the final return is a list with integers 3, 2, and 1. Since this is the reverse, this version of the method works as intended. Eliminate (A). The correct answer is (D).

33. **B** Go through each line of code one at a time. This will be especially important in this example since `remove()` method changes the indexes. First, create `values`, an empty ArrayList of Integers. Next add 5 to the list. Then, add 3 to the end. And then add 2 to the end. Next, add another 2 to the end. Then, add 6 to the end. And then add 3 to the end. Next, add 9 to the end. Then, add 2 to the end, and then add 1 to the end. The List now contains [5, 3, 2, 2, 6, 3, 9, 2, 1]. Now, go to the for loop. Initialize `j = 0`. Since `values.size()` returns the number of elements in the list, `values.size() = 9`. Since `j < values.size()`, execute the for loop. Since `values.get(j)` returns the element at index `j`, `value.get(j) = 5`. (Remember that the indexes begin with 0.) As this is not equal to 2, do not execute the instruction in the if statement. Now add 1 to `j` to get `j = 1`. This is still less than `values.size()`, so execute the for loop. This time, `value.get(j) = 3`. Since this is not equal to 2, do not execute the instruction in the if statement. Now add 1 to `j` to get `j = 2`. This is still less than `values.size()`, so execute the for loop. This time, `value.get(j) = 2`, so execute the instruction in the if statement. The statement `values.remove(j)` removes the element at index `j` and moves each of the following elements to the previous index. Therefore, the List now contains [5, 3, 2, 6, 3, 9, 2, 1]. Note that `values.size()` is now 8. Now add 1 to `j` to get `j = 3`. This is still less than `values.size()`, so execute the for loop. Execute `value.get(j)`. However, remember that the List has changed. The element that is at index 3 is no longer the second 2 but rather the 6. Since this is not equal to 2, do not execute the instruction in the if statement. Now add 1 to `j` to get `j = 4`. This is still less than `values.size()`, so execute the for loop. This time, `value.get(j) = 3`. Since this is not equal to 2, do not execute the instruction in the if statement. Add 1 to `j` to get `j = 5`. This is still less than `values.size()`, so execute the for loop. This time, `value.get(j) = 9`. Since this is not equal to 2, do not execute the instruction in the if statement. Add 1 to `j` to get `j = 6`. This is still less than `values.size()`, so execute the for loop. This time, `value.get(j) = 2`, so execute the instruction in the if statement. Remove the 2. The List now contains [5, 3, 2, 6, 3, 9, 1]. Note that `values.size()` is now 7. Add 1 to `j` to get `j = 7`. Since this is no longer less than `values.size()`, stop executing the for loop. The final version of the List is [5, 3, 2, 6, 3, 9, 1]. The correct answer is (B).

34. **B** Check Options I, II, and III one at a time. Option I uses the enhanced-for loop notation. Remember that two dimensional array c is actually an array of one dimensional arrays, i.e., an array of the rows of the two dimensional array. Therefore, `for(int[] row: c)` goes through each one dimensional array in the two dimensional array c and refers to it as the variable row. In the for loop, it sets the int `max` equal to the return of the `max1D(row)`, which is the maximum value of each row. However, since it automatically changes it, the result will simply be the maximum value of the last row rather than the maximum value of the two dimensional array. Therefore, Option I does not work as intended. Eliminate any answer that includes it: (A), (C), and (E). Now try Option II. Option II also automatically changes the value of `max` at every row. Therefore, it would also result in the `max` being set at the maximum value of the value row, rather than the maximum value of the whole two dimensional array. Eliminate any answer choice that includes Option II: (D). Only one choice remains. To see why Option III works, note that it sets the value of `max` at the maximum value of `c[0]`, which is the first row, and changes the value only if `max` is less than the maximum value of a particular row. Therefore, the correct answer is (B).

35. **E** Use the numList given as a test for each version. Try Version 1. The outer for loop initiates k = 0. The inner for loop initiates j = 0. Go to the if statement, which says if (numList[j] = 0). Since numList[0] is not 0, skip the if statement. Increment j to get j = 1. Because j > k, end the inner for loop and increment k to get k = 1. The inner for loop initiates j = 0. Go to the if statement, which says if (numList[j] = 0). As numList[0] is not 0, skip the if statement. Increment j to get j = 1. Since numList[1] is not 0, skip the if statement. Increment j to get j = 2. Since j > k, terminate the inner for loop and increment k to get k = 2. The inner for loop initiates j = 0. Go to the if statement, which says if (numList[j] = 0). Since numList[0] is not 0, skip the if statement. Increment j to get j = 1. Because numList[1] is not 0, skip the if statement. Increment j to get j = 2. As numList[2] is 0, execute the if statement, which says that count[k] = count[k] + 1, so count[0] = 0 + 1 = 1. Increment j to get j = 3. Since j > k, end the inner for loop and increment k to get k = 3. The inner for loop initiates j = 0. Go to the if statement, which says if (numList[j] = 0). Since numList[0] is not 0, skip the if statement. Increment j to get j = 1. Because numList[1] is not 0, skip the if statement. Increment j to get j = 2. As numList[2] is 0, execute the if statement, which says that count[k] = count[k] + 1, so count[3] = 0 + 1 = 1. Increment j to get j = 3. Since numList[3] is not 0, skip the if statement and increment j to get j = 3. Because j > k, end the inner for loop and increment k to get k = 4. The inner for loop initiates j = 0. Go to the if statement, which says if (numList[j] = 0). As numList[0] is not 0, skip the if statement. Increment j to get j = 1. Since numList[1] is not 0, skip the if statement. Increment j to get j = 2. Because numList[2] is 0, execute the if statement, which says that count[k] = count[k] + 1, so count[4] = 0 + 1 = 1. Increment j to get j = 3. Since numList[3] is not 0, skip the if statement and increment j to get j = 4. As numList[4] is 0, execute the if statement, which says that count[k] = count[k] + 1, so count[4] = 1 + 1 = 2. Increment j to get j = 5. Because j > k, end the inner for loop and increment k to get k = 5. The inner for loop initiates j = 0. Go to the if statement, which says if (numList[j] = 0). Since numList[0] is not 0, skip the if statement. Increment j to get j = 1. As numList[1] is not 0, skip the if statement. Increment j to get j = 2. Because numList[2] is 0, execute the if statement, which says that count[k] = count[k] + 1, so count[5] = 0 + 1 = 1. Increment j to get j = 3. Since numList[3] is not 0, skip the if statement and increment j to get j = 4. As numList[4] is 0, execute the if statement, which says that count[k] = count[k] + 1, so count[5] = 1 + 1 = 2. Increment j to get j = 5. Because numList[5] is 0, execute the if statement, which says that count[k] = count[k] + 1, so count[5] = 2 + 1 = 3. Increment j to get j = 6. Since j > k, end the inner for loop and increment k to get k = 6. The inner for loop initiates j = 0. Go to the if statement, which says if (numList[j] = 0). As numList[0] is not 0, skip the if statement. Increment j to get j = 1. Because numList[1] is not 0, skip the if statement. Increment j to get j = 2. Since numList[2] is 0, execute the if statement, which says that count[k] = count[k] + 1. This would attempt to execute count[6] = count [6] + 1. However, because the count has 6 elements, the highest index is 5, so this would throw an ArrayIndexOutOfBounds exception. Eliminate the choices that say Version 1 works as intended: (A), (B), and (C).

If Version 2 works as intended, the answer is (D); otherwise the answer is (E). Test Version 2. The for loop initiates `k = 0`. Go to the if statement, which says `if(numList[k] = 0)`. Since `numList[0]` is not 0, do not execute the if statement but instead execute the else, which says `count[k] = count[k - 1]`. This attempts to execute `count[0] = count[-1]`. However, since there are not negative indexes, this also causes an `ArrayIndexOutOfBoundsException`. Therefore, the answer is (E).

36. **C** Go through each choice one at a time.

Choice (A) correctly assigned `Bedrooms`, `Bathrooms`, `PetsAllowed`, and `Rent` to the class `Apartment`. However, making each of these four a class is unnecessary, since they each require only one value. Eliminate (A).

Choice (B) assigns the subclass `Apartment` to each of the classes `Bedroom`, `Bathroom`, `PetsAllowed`, and `Rent`. However, these four are characteristics of an apartment rather than an apartment being a characteristic of these four. Therefore, an `Apartment` class should contain these four attributes rather than the other way around. Eliminate (B).

Choice (C) is similar to (A) but `Bedrooms`, `Bathrooms`, `PetsAllowed`, and `Rent` are simple variables, which is a more minimal design. Keep this choice.

Choice (D) makes the five unrelated. These characteristics should be related as the number of bedrooms, the number of bathrooms, whether pets are allowed, and the rent are all characteristics of an apartment. Therefore, eliminate (D).

Choice (E) creates a chain of subclasses. This makes `Rent` a characteristic of whether pets are allowed, which is a characteristic of the number of bathrooms, which is a characteristic of the number of bedrooms. This is not correct, so eliminate (E).

Therefore, the correct answer is (C).

37. **C** If a method in a subclass has the same name as a method in a superclass, it must have exactly the same method heading. Statements I and III have different headings, but Statement II has the same. Therefore, only Statement II can be added. The correct answer is (C).

38. **A** The question asks for possible combinations of `max` and the number of executions of each of the marked statements. Look to see how, if at all, the three relate to each other. Statement A and Statement B are both contained within the for loop. However, Statement A is contained within an if statement in the for loop and Statement B is not. Therefore, for each iteration of the for loop, Statement B will be executed but Statement A may not be. Therefore, the number of executions of Statement A cannot exceed the number of executions of Statement B. In Combination II, the number of executions of A does exceed the number of executions of B, so eliminate any choice that includes Combination II: (C) and (E).

The value of max relates to the elements contained within the array set, but there does not seem to be a direct connection to the indexes, so there does not seem to be any connection between this value of the number of executions of the two marked statements. Test the two remaining combinations with particular examples to determine whether they are valid. To test Combination I, find a way for Statement A to be executed twice and Statement B to be executed three times. This means that the for loop has to be executed three times and the if condition would have to be false one time. To make sure the for loop is executed three times, keep the values in the set less than max and make sure that set.length = 3. To make sure that the if condition is false once, make sure that the value of m is greater than the value of set[k] exactly one time. Let max = 8 and set = {1, 2, 1}. Set m and count equal to 0. Enter the for loop, which sets k = 0. Since 0 is less than set.length, which is 3, and set[0] is less than max, execute the for loop. Since set[0], which is 1, is greater than or equal to m, which is 0, execute the if statement, which sets m equal to set[0], which is 1. Statement A is executed the first time. The if statement ends and Statement B is executed the first time. At the end of the for loop, increment k to get k = 1. Since 1 is less than set.length, which is 3, and set[1] is less than max, execute the for loop. Since set[1], which is 2, is greater than or equal to m, which is 1, execute the if statement, which sets m equal to set[1], which is 2. Statement A is executed for the second time. The if statement ends and Statement B is executed for the second time. At the end of the for loop, increment k to get k = 2. Since 2 is less than set.length, which is 3, and set[2] is less than max, execute the for loop. Since set[2], which is 1, is less than m, which is 1, do not execute the if statement. Skip to after the if statement, where Statement B is executed the third time. Increment k to get k = 3. Since k is not less than set.length, end the for loop. Thus, max = 8, Statement A is executed twice, and Statement B is executed three times, so Combination I is valid. Eliminate any choice that does not include Combination I: (B).

Now, attempt to find a valid instance of Combination III. In this case, the for loop has to be executed four times without the if condition ever being true. To make sure the for loop is executed four times, let set.length equal 4 with every value less than max. To make sure the if condition is always false, make sure the value of m is always greater than the value of set[k] for all k. However, m is initialized at 0 and the precondition indicates that set has no negative values. Since all non-negative values are greater than or equal to 0, the if condition would have to be true at least at the first execution of the for loop. Therefore, Combination III is not valid. Eliminate any choice that includes Combination III: (D). The correct answer is (A).

39. **D** The method is intended to insert an int at a given index, pushing ints to the right. In the returned array, indexes 0 through n - 1 should contain the same values as the indexes 0 through n - 1 of the original array, the index n should contain the value m, and the indexes n + 1 and above should contain the same values as the indexes n and above in the original array. Go through each of the choices.

Choice (A) changes the condition on the if statement to (k > n). The consequence on the if statement is to set temp[k] = arr[k]. The values should be copied to the same index only for indexes less than n, so eliminate (A).

Similarly, the value at index n in arr should be pushed to index n + 1 in the return array. Therefore, the inequality sign should not be changed to <=. Eliminate (B).

Choice (C) would not only place values at the wrong indexes but would also cause an `ArrayIndexOutOfBoundException`. When k = arr.length - 1, the command `temp[k] = arr[k + 1]` would call `arr[arr.length]`. Since indexes begin at 0, the last index of an array is always one less than the length of the array. Thus, the index equal to the length of the array is out of bounds. Eliminate (C).

Making the change in (D) would cause the int m to be placed at index n in the temp array. This is the intention of the method, so keep (D).

Choice (E) returns arr instead of temp. Since no changes are made directly to arr, the return of this method would be an unaltered copy of the original array. Since this is not intended, eliminate (E).

The correct answer is (D).

40. **E** The easiest way to solve this problem is to use DeMorgan's Law. This states that

```
!(p && q) is equivalent to !p || !q
```

Or, negating both sides

```
p && q is equivalent to !(!p || !q).
```

In this problem, set p to (X > Y) and q to (Y > Z).

```
!p becomes (X <= Y) and !q becomes (Y <= Z).
```

Finally, `!(!p || !q)` becomes `!((X <= Y) || (Y <= Z))`.

Therefore, (E) is correct.

Note that although (A) appears to be correct because it follows the transitive property of inequality, consider the two boolean equations after setting X to 6, Y to 8, and Z to 4.

(6 > 8) && (8 > 4) is false, but 6 > 4 is true.

Section II: Free Response Questions

1. (a)
```
public Screen(int  width, int height)
{
    numCols = width;
    data = new ArrayList<Pixel>[height];
    for (int k = 0; k < height; k++)
        data[k] = new ArrayList<Pixel>;
}
```

(b)
```
public Pixel pixelAt(int row, int col)

{
    ArrayList<Pixel> theRow = data[row];
    for (int k = 0; k < theRow.size; k++)
    {
        Pixel p = theRow.get(k);
        If (p.getCol() == col)
            return p;
    }
    return null;
}
```

(c)
```
public void pixelOn(int row, int col)

{
    Pixel newPx1 = new Pixel(row, col);
    Pixel p;
    ArrayList<Pixel> theRow = data[row];
    int index = 0;
    for (int k = 0; k < data[row].size(); k++)
        {
            if (col > data[row].get(k).getCol())
                index++;
        }
    data[row].add(index, p);
}
```

2. (a) Sample Answer # 1:

```
public int getTotalMarbles()
{
    int marbles = 0;
    for (int k = 0; k < sets.length(); k++)
    {
        marbles += sets.get(k).getNumber();
    }
    return marbles;
}
```

Sample Answer # 2:

```
public int getTotalMarbles()
{
    int marbles;
    for (int k : sets)
    {
        marbles = marbles + sets.get(k).getNumber();
    }
    return marbles;
}
```

The goal of the method is to return the sum of the total number of marbles and return 0 if there are no marbles. Begin by declaring an int type to store the total number of marbles counted thus far. In this case, we called it marbles. Give marbles initial value 0, since no marbles have been counted so far. Note that this is optional, since the default value on type int is 0. Now, create a for loop to go through each element in the ArrayList sets. To do this, use either a standard for loop or an enhanced-for loop. For the standard for loop, the first index is 0, so, in the for loop statement, initialize int k = 0, to represent the index of the ArrayList. Increase the index by 1 until the index is equal to the length of the ArrayList. (Note that to count the length, begin with one rather than 0, so the last array element has index length() – 1.) The for statement becomes (int k = 0; k < sets.length(); k++). To use an enhanced-for loop, simply use for (int k: sets). This automatically goes through each index of sets and calls each index k. Note that if sets is empty, sets.length() = 0, so the for loop will not be executed. In this case, the method will return the initial value of marbles, which is 0. This fulfills the requirement for that case. If the ArrayList is not empty, then for each index, the number of marbles in that index's MarbleSet should be added to marbles. To do this, execute either marbles = marbles + sets.get(k). getNumber() or the shortcut notation marbles += sets.get(k).getNumber(). Note that sets[k].getNumber() is not valid, since set[k] denotes an element of a simple array rather than an ArrayList. This is all that is needed of the for loop. Close the for loop, and return the value of marbles.

(b) Sample Answer # 1:

```
public int removeColor(String marbleCol)
{
  int num = 0;
  for (int k = 0; k < sets.length(); k++)
  {
     if (sets.get(k).getColor().equals(marbleCol))
     {
         num += sets.get(k).getNumber();
         sets.remove(k);
     }
  }
  return num;
}
```

Sample Answer # 2:

```
public int removeColor(String marbleCol)
{
  int num;
  for (int k : sets)
  {
     if (sets.get(k).getColor().equals(marbleCol))
     {
         num = num + sets.get(k).getNumber();
         sets.remove(k);
     }
  }
  return num;
}
```

Sample Answer # 3:

```
public int removeColor(String marbleCol)
{
  int num = 0;
  for (int k = 0; k < sets.length(); k++)
  {
    if (sets.get(k).getColor().equals(marbleCol))
    {
        num += sets.remove(k).getNumber();
    }
  }
  return num;
}
```

The method requires an integer return. Let the first statement of the method be to create this integer and the final be to return it. Call this integer num. Since no marbles have been counted yet, num can be initialized as int num = 0 or simply as int num since the default initial value of an int is 0. Now, go through each MarbleSet in the MarbleCollection using a for loop. This could be done using a standard for loop, for (int k = 0; k < sets.length(); k++). Remember that the index for an ArrayList begins with 0 but the length() is determined by counting beginning with 1, so the final element of the ArrayList is at index length() – 1. The following enhanced-for loop can also be used as shorthand: for (int k: sets). Action should be taken only in the event that the color of the MarbleSet matches marbleCol, so use an if statement. The condition should be sets.get(k).getColor().equals(marbleCol). Note that sets[k].getColor().equals(marbleCol) is not valid since sets[k] is the index for a simple array rather than an ArrayList. Therefore, the get method of the ArrayList class is needed. Also note that sets.get(k).getColor() == (marbleCol), since the == operator uses the Object definition, which requires that the two be the same Object rather than simply have the same information. Therefore, the equals method of the String class is needed. Should the if condition be met, two goals are to be met. The first is that the number of marbles in the set be added to num. This can be either the statement num = num + sets.get(k).getNumber() or the shortcut notation num += sets.get(k).getNumber(). The other goal is that the MarbleSet be removed. This can be done using the remove method of the ArrayList class with the statement sets.remove(k). Note that the remove method returns the removed element. Therefore, the two goals could also be done in one statement: num = num + sets.remove(k).getNumber() or num += sets.remove(k).getNumber(). Remember to close the if statement; then remember to close the for loop. Return num.

3. (a)
```
public class BinaryInt

{
    private ArrayList<int> digits;
    public BinaryInt()
    ( /* implementation not needed */ )
    public BinaryInt (int decimalValue)
    ( /* implementation not needed */ )
    public BinaryInt add (BinaryInt other)
    ( /* implementation not needed */ )
    public String toString()
    ( /* implementation not needed */ )
    public int compareTo(BinaryInt other)
    ( /* implementation not needed */ )


}
```

(b)
```
public BinaryInt(int decimalValue)
    {
        digits = new ArrayList<int>();
        while (decimalValue > 0)
        {
            digits.add(0, new Integer(decimalValue % 2));
            decimalValue / = 2;
        }
    }
```

(c)
```
public static void Test()
    {
        BinaryInt a1 =
            new BinaryInt(2314279623);
        BinaryInt a2 =
            new BinaryInt(3236550123);
        BinaryInt aSum = a1.add(a2);
        BinaryInt b1 =
            new BinaryInt(3412579010);
        BinaryInt b2 =
            new BinaryInt(2128250735);
        BinaryInt bSum = b1.add(b2);
        if (aSum.compareTo(bSum) > 0)
            System.out.print(aSum.toString());
        else
            System.out.print(bSum.toString());
    }
```

4.   Possible Solution # 1:

```
public class Parabola
{

    private int a;
    private int b;
    private int c;

    public Parabola(int a; int b; int c)
    {
        this.a = a;
        this.b = b;
        this.c = c;
    }

    public double getAxis()
    {
        return (double) (-1 * b / (2*a));
    }

    public boolean isOnGraph(int x, int y)
    {
        return (y == a*x*x + b*x + c);
    }
}
```

Possible Solution # 2:

```
public class Parabola
{

    private int a;
    private int b;
    private int c;

    public Parabola(int myA, int myB, int c)
    {
        a = myA;
        b = myB;
        c = myC;
    }

    public double getAxis()
    {
        int num = -1 * b;
        int den = 2 * a;
        double axis = (double)(num / den);
return axis;
    }

    public boolean isOnGraph(int x, int y)
    {
        int rightSide = a*x*x + b*x + c;
        boolean onGraph = (y == rightSide);
return (onGraph);
    }
}
```

The class should have three integer instance variables, a, b, and c. The constructor class has to take in three integer parameters to represent these instance variables. This can be done two different ways. One possible way is to call the parameter variables in the declaration something other than a, b, and c. When you do this, you can simply set the instance variables equal to the parameters, as shown in Possible Solution #2. This can also be accomplished by calling the parameter variables. However, in this case, in order to set the instance variables equal to the parameter, refer to the instance variables using the Keyword this, as shown in Possible Solution #1. Now define the getAxis method. This method needs no parameters but must return a double equal to $-b/2a$. Remember that the expression $-b/2a$ is not proper Java coding. To negative an integer, multiply it by -1, so $-b$ must be represented by -1 * b. Also, a Java complier would interpret 2a as an undeclared variable rather than 2 times a, so 2a must be represented by 2*a. Thus, $-b/2a$ must be represented in Java as (-1 * b / (2*a)). This can be done in one line, as in Possible Solution #1, or in several steps, as in Possible Solution #2. In either case, remember to cast the division of two integers as a double. Otherwise, the compiler will recognize this as integer division, which will drop a remainder and round down to the nearest integer rather than return a double. Now create the method isOnGraph. This must take two integer parameters, x and y, and return a boolean. It should return true if the values x and y satisfy the equation $y = ax^2 + bx + c$. Remember that raising a number to an exponent is the same as multiplying it by itself, so this can be rewritten as $y = axx + bx + c$. To test this in Java, use the boolean equals sign, ==, and the multiplication sign, *, to make the boolean statement y == a*x*x + b*x + c. This can be done in one line, as in Possible Solution #1, or in several steps, as in Possible Solution #2.

Glossary

Symbols

!= (is not equal to): a boolean operator placed between two variables that returns false if the two variables have the same value and true otherwise [Chapter 5]

&& (logical and): an operator placed between two boolean statements that returns true if both statements are true and false otherwise [Chapter 5]

! (logical not): a boolean operator placed before a boolean statement that returns the negation of the statement's value [Chapter 5]

|| (logical or): an operator placed between two boolean statements that returns false if both statements are false and true otherwise [Chapter 5]

A

abstraction: a declaration in a superclass that all subclasses must either override the superclass method or declare the subclass method as abstract [Chapter 11]

accessor methods: methods used to obtain a value from a data field [Chapter 7]

array: an ordered list of the same data type [Chapter 8]

ArrayIndexOutOfBoundsException: a run-time error caused by all calling of an index array that is either negative or greater than the highest index of the array [Chapter 8]

ArrayList object: an object of a type that is a subclass of List used on the AP Computer Science A Exam [Chapter 9]

assignment operator: a single equals sign ("=") indicating that an identifier should be assigned a particular value [Chapter 3]

B

base case: the indication that a recursive method should stop executing and return to each prior recursive call [Chapter 12]

binary: a system of 1's and 0's [Chapter 3]

binary search: a search of a sorted array that uses searches beginning in the middle and determines in which direction to sort [Chapter 9]

blocking: a series of statements grouped by { } that indicate a group of statements to be executed when a given condition is satisfied [Chapter 5]

boolean: a primitive data type that can have the value true or false [Chapter 3]

boolean operator ==: an operator that returns true if it is between two variables with the same value and false otherwise [Chapter 5]

C

casting: forcing a data type to be recognized by the compiler as another data type [Chapter 3]

character: a primitive data type representing any single text symbol, such as a letter, digit, space, or hyphen [Chapter 3]

class: a group of statements, including control structures, assembled into a single unit [Chapter 7]

columns: portions of 2D-arrays that are depicted vertically. These are the elements of each array with the same index. [Chapter 9]

commenting: including portions of the program that do not affect execution but are rather used to make notes for the programmer or for the user [Chapter 3]

compile-time error: a basic programming error identified by the interpreter during compiling [Chapter 3]

compiling: translating a programming language into binary code [Chapter 3]

compound condition: a complicated condition that includes at least one boolean operator [Chapter 5]

Computer Science: different aspects of computing, usually development [Chapter 3]

concatenation operator: a plus sign ("+") used between two strings indicating that the two string values be outputted next to each other [Chapter 3]

condition: a boolean statement used to determine flow control [Chapter 5]

conditional statement: a statement that is executed only if some other condition is met [Chapter 5]

constructor: a method in an object class used to build the object [Chapter 7]

D

decrement operator (--): a symbol used after a variable to decrease its value by 1 [Chapter 3]

double: a primitive data type for a number that can include decimals [Chapter 3]

driver class: a class that is created to control a larger program [Chapter 7]

dynamically sized: having the ability to change length and to insert and remove elements [Chapter 9]

E

enhanced-for loop: a for loop with a simplified call used to span an array [Chapter 8]

escape sequence: a small piece of coding beginning with a backslash to indicate special characters [Chapter 3]

F

flow control: indication of which lines of programming should be executed in which conditions [Chapter 5]

for loops: a loop with not only a condition but also an initializer and incrementer to control the truth value of the condition [Chapter 6]

full: all values of the array are assigned [Chapter 8]

H

header: the "title" of a method used to indicate its overall function [Chapter 7]

I

identifiers: names given to indicate data stored in memory [Chapter 3]

if: a reserved word in Java indicating the condition by which a statement will be executed [Chapter 5]

increment operator (++): a symbol used after a variable to increase its value by 1 [Chapter 3]

index numbers: integers, beginning with 0, used to indicate the order of the elements of an array [Chapter 8]

infinite loop: a programming error in which a loop never terminates because the condition is never false [Chapter 6]

inheritance: the quintessential way to create relationships between classes [Chapter 11]

inheritance hierarchy: the quantification of relationships between classes by using "parent" and "child" classes [Chapter 11]

initializer list: known values used to assign the initial values of all the elements of an array [Chapter 8]

in-line or short comments: comments preceded by two forward slashes ("//") indicating that the rest of the line of text will not be executed [Chapter 3]

insertion sort: a sorting algorithm in which smaller elements are inserted before larger elements [Chapter 9]

instance data/data fields: variables, listed immediately after the class heading, of an object that are accessible by all of the object's methods [Chapter 7]

integer: a primitive data type for positive numbers, negative numbers, or 0 with no fractions or decimals [Chapter 3]

interpreter: the part of the developer environment that enables the computer to understand the Java code [Chapter 3]

L

list object: an object form of an array with a dynamic size that can store multiple types of data [Chapter 9]

logical error: an error that lies in the desired output/purpose of the program rather than in the syntax of the code itself [Chapter 3]

long comments: comments that use ("/*") to indicate the beginning of the comment and ("*/") to indicate the end [Chapter 3]

loop: a portion of code that is to be executed repeatedly [Chapter 6]

M

merge sort: a sorting algorithm in which an array is divided and each half of the array is sorted and later merged into one array [Chapter 9]

methods: a group of code that performs a specific task [Chapter 7]

multiple inheritance: an illegal activity in Java in which a subclass inherits from more than one superclass [Chapter 11]

mutator methods: methods used to change the value of a data field [Chapter 7]

N

null: the default value of an object that has not yet been assigned a value [Chapter 8]

NullPointerException: a run-time error caused by calling an object with a null value [Chapter 8]

O

object class: a class that houses the "guts" of the methods that the driver class calls [Chapter 7]

overloading: using two methods with the same names but with different numbers and/or types of parameters [Chapter 7]

override (overridden): used a method in a subclass that possessed the same as a method in the superclass, causing the subclass method to be executed [Chapter 11]

P

parameters: what types of variables, if any, will be inputted to a method [Chapter 7]

planning: outlining the steps of a proposed program [Chapter 7]

polymorphism: the ability of a subclass object to also take the form as an object of its superclass [Chapter 11]

precedence: the order by which Java will execute mathematical operations, starting with parentheses, followed by multiplication and division from left to right, followed by addition and subtraction from left to right [Chapter 3]

primitive data: one of the most basic types of data in Java [Chapter 3]

programming style: a particular approach to using a programming language [Chapter 3]

R

recursion: a flow control structure in which a method calls itself [Chapters 9, 12]

recursive call: the command in which a method calls itself [Chapter 12]

return type: what type of data, if any, will be outputted by a method after its commands are executed [Chapter 7]

rows: the portions of 2D-arrays that are depicted horizontally and can be seen as their own arrays [Chapter 9]

run-time error: an error that occurs in the execution of the program [Chapter 3]

S

search algorithms: methods of finding a particular element in an array [Chapter 9]

selection sort: a sorting algorithm in which the lowest remaining element is swapped with the element at the lowest unsorted index [Chapter 9]

sequential search: a search of all the elements of an array in order until the desired element is found [Chapter 9]

short-circuited: the second condition of an and statement is skipped when the first condition is false, rendering the statement false [Chapter 6]

sorting algorithms: methods of ordering the elements within an array [Chapter 9]

source code: a .java file that defines a program's actions [Chapter 7]

span: using a loop to use or change all elements of an array [Chapter 8]

string literal (string): one or more characters combined in a single unit [Chapter 3]

strongly typed: characteristic of a language in which a variable will always keep its type until it is reassigned [Chapter 3]

subclass: a "child" class, with more specific forms of the superclass [Chapter 11]

superclass: a "parent" class, the most general form of a class hierarchy [Chapter 11]

super keyword: a keyword used to call an overridden method [Chapter 11]

T

truth value: the indication of whether a statement is true or false [Chapter 5]

typed ArrayList: an ArrayList that allows only one type of data to be stored [Chapter 9]

V

variable: an identifier associated with a particular value [Chapter 3]

W

while loop: a loop that cycles again and again while a condition is true [Chapter 6]

white space: empty space intended to enhance readability [Chapter 3]

Completely darken bubbles with a No. 2 pencil. If you make a mistake, be sure to erase mark completely. Erase all stray marks.

1.

YOUR NAME: _____
(Print)   Last   First   M.I.

SIGNATURE: _____ DATE: ___ / ___ / ___

HOME ADDRESS: _____
(Print)   Number and Street

_____
City   State   Zip Code

PHONE NO.: _____

IMPORTANT: Please fill in these boxes exactly as shown on the back cover of your test book.

2. TEST FORM

3. TEST CODE

4. REGISTRATION NUMBER

5. YOUR NAME

First 4 letters of last name				FIRST INIT	MID INIT

6. DATE OF BIRTH

Month		Day		Year	
◯ JAN					
◯ FEB	⓪	⓪	⓪	⓪	
◯ MAR	①	①	①	①	
◯ APR	②	②	②	②	
◯ MAY	③	③	③	③	
◯ JUN		④	④	④	
◯ JUL		⑤	⑤	⑤	
◯ AUG		⑥	⑥	⑥	
◯ SEP		⑦	⑦	⑦	
◯ OCT		⑧	⑧	⑧	
◯ NOV		⑨	⑨	⑨	
◯ DEC					

7. GENDER

◯ MALE
◯ FEMALE

The **Princeton Review**®

1. Ⓐ Ⓑ Ⓒ Ⓓ Ⓔ
2. Ⓐ Ⓑ Ⓒ Ⓓ Ⓔ
3. Ⓐ Ⓑ Ⓒ Ⓓ Ⓔ
4. Ⓐ Ⓑ Ⓒ Ⓓ Ⓔ
5. Ⓐ Ⓑ Ⓒ Ⓓ Ⓔ
6. Ⓐ Ⓑ Ⓒ Ⓓ Ⓔ
7. Ⓐ Ⓑ Ⓒ Ⓓ Ⓔ
8. Ⓐ Ⓑ Ⓒ Ⓓ Ⓔ
9. Ⓐ Ⓑ Ⓒ Ⓓ Ⓔ
10. Ⓐ Ⓑ Ⓒ Ⓓ Ⓔ

11. Ⓐ Ⓑ Ⓒ Ⓓ Ⓔ
12. Ⓐ Ⓑ Ⓒ Ⓓ Ⓔ
13. Ⓐ Ⓑ Ⓒ Ⓓ Ⓔ
14. Ⓐ Ⓑ Ⓒ Ⓓ Ⓔ
15. Ⓐ Ⓑ Ⓒ Ⓓ Ⓔ
16. Ⓐ Ⓑ Ⓒ Ⓓ Ⓔ
17. Ⓐ Ⓑ Ⓒ Ⓓ Ⓔ
18. Ⓐ Ⓑ Ⓒ Ⓓ Ⓔ
19. Ⓐ Ⓑ Ⓒ Ⓓ Ⓔ
20. Ⓐ Ⓑ Ⓒ Ⓓ Ⓔ

21. Ⓐ Ⓑ Ⓒ Ⓓ Ⓔ
22. Ⓐ Ⓑ Ⓒ Ⓓ Ⓔ
23. Ⓐ Ⓑ Ⓒ Ⓓ Ⓔ
24. Ⓐ Ⓑ Ⓒ Ⓓ Ⓔ
25. Ⓐ Ⓑ Ⓒ Ⓓ Ⓔ
26. Ⓐ Ⓑ Ⓒ Ⓓ Ⓔ
27. Ⓐ Ⓑ Ⓒ Ⓓ Ⓔ
28. Ⓐ Ⓑ Ⓒ Ⓓ Ⓔ
29. Ⓐ Ⓑ Ⓒ Ⓓ Ⓔ
30. Ⓐ Ⓑ Ⓒ Ⓓ Ⓔ

31. Ⓐ Ⓑ Ⓒ Ⓓ Ⓔ
32. Ⓐ Ⓑ Ⓒ Ⓓ Ⓔ
33. Ⓐ Ⓑ Ⓒ Ⓓ Ⓔ
34. Ⓐ Ⓑ Ⓒ Ⓓ Ⓔ
35. Ⓐ Ⓑ Ⓒ Ⓓ Ⓔ
36. Ⓐ Ⓑ Ⓒ Ⓓ Ⓔ
37. Ⓐ Ⓑ Ⓒ Ⓓ Ⓔ
38. Ⓐ Ⓑ Ⓒ Ⓓ Ⓔ
39. Ⓐ Ⓑ Ⓒ Ⓓ Ⓔ
40. Ⓐ Ⓑ Ⓒ Ⓓ Ⓔ

Completely darken bubbles with a No. 2 pencil. If you make a mistake, be sure to erase mark completely. Erase all stray marks.

1.

YOUR NAME: _____
(Print)
       Last   First   M.I.

SIGNATURE: _____   DATE: ___ / ___ / ___

HOME ADDRESS: _____
(Print)
               Number and Street

_____
   City   State   Zip Code

PHONE NO.: _____

IMPORTANT: Please fill in these boxes exactly as shown on the back cover of your test book.

2. TEST FORM

_____

6. DATE OF BIRTH

Month	Day		Year	
○ JAN				
○ FEB	⓪ ⓪		⓪ ⓪	
○ MAR	① ①		① ①	
○ APR	② ②		② ②	
○ MAY	③ ③		③ ③	
○ JUN	④		④	
○ JUL	⑤		⑤	
○ AUG	⑥		⑥	
○ SEP	⑦		⑦	
○ OCT	⑧		⑧	
○ NOV	⑨		⑨	
○ DEC				

3. TEST CODE   **4. REGISTRATION NUMBER**

⓪	Ⓐ	Ⓙ	⓪	⓪	⓪	⓪	⓪	⓪	⓪	⓪	⓪
①	Ⓑ	Ⓚ	①	①	①	①	①	①	①	①	①
②	Ⓒ	Ⓛ	②	②	②	②	②	②	②	②	②
③	Ⓓ	Ⓜ	③	③	③	③	③	③	③	③	③
④	Ⓔ	Ⓝ	④	④	④	④	④	④	④	④	④
⑤	Ⓕ	Ⓞ	⑤	⑤	⑤	⑤	⑤	⑤	⑤	⑤	⑤
⑥	Ⓖ	Ⓟ	⑥	⑥	⑥	⑥	⑥	⑥	⑥	⑥	⑥
⑦	Ⓗ	Ⓠ	⑦	⑦	⑦	⑦	⑦	⑦	⑦	⑦	⑦
⑧	Ⓘ	Ⓡ	⑧	⑧	⑧	⑧	⑧	⑧	⑧	⑧	⑧
⑨			⑨	⑨	⑨	⑨	⑨	⑨	⑨	⑨	⑨

7. GENDER
○ MALE
○ FEMALE

5. YOUR NAME

First 4 letters of last name				FIRST INIT	MID INIT
Ⓐ	Ⓐ	Ⓐ	Ⓐ	Ⓐ	Ⓐ
Ⓑ	Ⓑ	Ⓑ	Ⓑ	Ⓑ	Ⓑ
Ⓒ	Ⓒ	Ⓒ	Ⓒ	Ⓒ	Ⓒ
Ⓓ	Ⓓ	Ⓓ	Ⓓ	Ⓓ	Ⓓ
Ⓔ	Ⓔ	Ⓔ	Ⓔ	Ⓔ	Ⓔ
Ⓕ	Ⓕ	Ⓕ	Ⓕ	Ⓕ	Ⓕ
Ⓖ	Ⓖ	Ⓖ	Ⓖ	Ⓖ	Ⓖ
Ⓗ	Ⓗ	Ⓗ	Ⓗ	Ⓗ	Ⓗ
Ⓘ	Ⓘ	Ⓘ	Ⓘ	Ⓘ	Ⓘ
Ⓙ	Ⓙ	Ⓙ	Ⓙ	Ⓙ	Ⓙ
Ⓚ	Ⓚ	Ⓚ	Ⓚ	Ⓚ	Ⓚ
Ⓛ	Ⓛ	Ⓛ	Ⓛ	Ⓛ	Ⓛ
Ⓜ	Ⓜ	Ⓜ	Ⓜ	Ⓜ	Ⓜ
Ⓝ	Ⓝ	Ⓝ	Ⓝ	Ⓝ	Ⓝ
Ⓞ	Ⓞ	Ⓞ	Ⓞ	Ⓞ	Ⓞ
Ⓟ	Ⓟ	Ⓟ	Ⓟ	Ⓟ	Ⓟ
Ⓠ	Ⓠ	Ⓠ	Ⓠ	Ⓠ	Ⓠ
Ⓡ	Ⓡ	Ⓡ	Ⓡ	Ⓡ	Ⓡ
Ⓢ	Ⓢ	Ⓢ	Ⓢ	Ⓢ	Ⓢ
Ⓣ	Ⓣ	Ⓣ	Ⓣ	Ⓣ	Ⓣ
Ⓤ	Ⓤ	Ⓤ	Ⓤ	Ⓤ	Ⓤ
Ⓥ	Ⓥ	Ⓥ	Ⓥ	Ⓥ	Ⓥ
Ⓦ	Ⓦ	Ⓦ	Ⓦ	Ⓦ	Ⓦ
Ⓧ	Ⓧ	Ⓧ	Ⓧ	Ⓧ	Ⓧ
Ⓨ	Ⓨ	Ⓨ	Ⓨ	Ⓨ	Ⓨ
Ⓩ	Ⓩ	Ⓩ	Ⓩ	Ⓩ	Ⓩ

1. Ⓐ Ⓑ Ⓒ Ⓓ Ⓔ
2. Ⓐ Ⓑ Ⓒ Ⓓ Ⓔ
3. Ⓐ Ⓑ Ⓒ Ⓓ Ⓔ
4. Ⓐ Ⓑ Ⓒ Ⓓ Ⓔ
5. Ⓐ Ⓑ Ⓒ Ⓓ Ⓔ
6. Ⓐ Ⓑ Ⓒ Ⓓ Ⓔ
7. Ⓐ Ⓑ Ⓒ Ⓓ Ⓔ
8. Ⓐ Ⓑ Ⓒ Ⓓ Ⓔ
9. Ⓐ Ⓑ Ⓒ Ⓓ Ⓔ
10. Ⓐ Ⓑ Ⓒ Ⓓ Ⓔ

11. Ⓐ Ⓑ Ⓒ Ⓓ Ⓔ
12. Ⓐ Ⓑ Ⓒ Ⓓ Ⓔ
13. Ⓐ Ⓑ Ⓒ Ⓓ Ⓔ
14. Ⓐ Ⓑ Ⓒ Ⓓ Ⓔ
15. Ⓐ Ⓑ Ⓒ Ⓓ Ⓔ
16. Ⓐ Ⓑ Ⓒ Ⓓ Ⓔ
17. Ⓐ Ⓑ Ⓒ Ⓓ Ⓔ
18. Ⓐ Ⓑ Ⓒ Ⓓ Ⓔ
19. Ⓐ Ⓑ Ⓒ Ⓓ Ⓔ
20. Ⓐ Ⓑ Ⓒ Ⓓ Ⓔ

21. Ⓐ Ⓑ Ⓒ Ⓓ Ⓔ
22. Ⓐ Ⓑ Ⓒ Ⓓ Ⓔ
23. Ⓐ Ⓑ Ⓒ Ⓓ Ⓔ
24. Ⓐ Ⓑ Ⓒ Ⓓ Ⓔ
25. Ⓐ Ⓑ Ⓒ Ⓓ Ⓔ
26. Ⓐ Ⓑ Ⓒ Ⓓ Ⓔ
27. Ⓐ Ⓑ Ⓒ Ⓓ Ⓔ
28. Ⓐ Ⓑ Ⓒ Ⓓ Ⓔ
29. Ⓐ Ⓑ Ⓒ Ⓓ Ⓔ
30. Ⓐ Ⓑ Ⓒ Ⓓ Ⓔ

31. Ⓐ Ⓑ Ⓒ Ⓓ Ⓔ
32. Ⓐ Ⓑ Ⓒ Ⓓ Ⓔ
33. Ⓐ Ⓑ Ⓒ Ⓓ Ⓔ
34. Ⓐ Ⓑ Ⓒ Ⓓ Ⓔ
35. Ⓐ Ⓑ Ⓒ Ⓓ Ⓔ
36. Ⓐ Ⓑ Ⓒ Ⓓ Ⓔ
37. Ⓐ Ⓑ Ⓒ Ⓓ Ⓔ
38. Ⓐ Ⓑ Ⓒ Ⓓ Ⓔ
39. Ⓐ Ⓑ Ⓒ Ⓓ Ⓔ
40. Ⓐ Ⓑ Ⓒ Ⓓ Ⓔ

The Princeton Review®

Completely darken bubbles with a No. 2 pencil. If you make a mistake, be sure to erase mark completely. Erase all stray marks.

1.

YOUR NAME: _____
(Print)
         Last   First   M.I.

SIGNATURE: _____   DATE: ___ / ___ / ___

HOME ADDRESS: _____
(Print)
         Number and Street

_____
    City   State   Zip Code

PHONE NO.: _____

IMPORTANT: Please fill in these boxes exactly as shown on the back cover of your test book.

2. TEST FORM

_____

6. DATE OF BIRTH

Month	Day		Year	
◯ JAN				
◯ FEB	⓪	⓪	⓪	⓪
◯ MAR	①	①	①	①
◯ APR	②	②	②	②
◯ MAY	③	③	③	③
◯ JUN		④	④	④
◯ JUL		⑤	⑤	⑤
◯ AUG		⑥	⑥	⑥
◯ SEP		⑦	⑦	⑦
◯ OCT		⑧	⑧	⑧
◯ NOV		⑨	⑨	⑨
◯ DEC				

3. TEST CODE

⓪	Ⓐ	Ⓙ	⓪	⓪
①	Ⓑ	Ⓚ	①	①
②	Ⓒ	Ⓛ	②	②
③	Ⓓ	Ⓜ	③	③
④	Ⓔ	Ⓝ	④	④
⑤	Ⓕ	Ⓞ	⑤	⑤
⑥	Ⓖ	Ⓟ	⑥	⑥
⑦	Ⓗ	Ⓠ	⑦	⑦
⑧	Ⓘ	Ⓡ	⑧	⑧
⑨			⑨	⑨

4. REGISTRATION NUMBER

⓪	⓪	⓪	⓪	⓪	⓪	⓪
①	①	①	①	①	①	①
②	②	②	②	②	②	②
③	③	③	③	③	③	③
④	④	④	④	④	④	④
⑤	⑤	⑤	⑤	⑤	⑤	⑤
⑥	⑥	⑥	⑥	⑥	⑥	⑥
⑦	⑦	⑦	⑦	⑦	⑦	⑦
⑧	⑧	⑧	⑧	⑧	⑧	⑧
⑨	⑨	⑨	⑨	⑨	⑨	⑨

7. GENDER
◯ MALE
◯ FEMALE

The Princeton Review®

5. YOUR NAME

First 4 letters of last name				FIRST INIT	MID INIT
Ⓐ	Ⓐ	Ⓐ	Ⓐ	Ⓐ	Ⓐ
Ⓑ	Ⓑ	Ⓑ	Ⓑ	Ⓑ	Ⓑ
Ⓒ	Ⓒ	Ⓒ	Ⓒ	Ⓒ	Ⓒ
Ⓓ	Ⓓ	Ⓓ	Ⓓ	Ⓓ	Ⓓ
Ⓔ	Ⓔ	Ⓔ	Ⓔ	Ⓔ	Ⓔ
Ⓕ	Ⓕ	Ⓕ	Ⓕ	Ⓕ	Ⓕ
Ⓖ	Ⓖ	Ⓖ	Ⓖ	Ⓖ	Ⓖ
Ⓗ	Ⓗ	Ⓗ	Ⓗ	Ⓗ	Ⓗ
Ⓘ	Ⓘ	Ⓘ	Ⓘ	Ⓘ	Ⓘ
Ⓙ	Ⓙ	Ⓙ	Ⓙ	Ⓙ	Ⓙ
Ⓚ	Ⓚ	Ⓚ	Ⓚ	Ⓚ	Ⓚ
Ⓛ	Ⓛ	Ⓛ	Ⓛ	Ⓛ	Ⓛ
Ⓜ	Ⓜ	Ⓜ	Ⓜ	Ⓜ	Ⓜ
Ⓝ	Ⓝ	Ⓝ	Ⓝ	Ⓝ	Ⓝ
Ⓞ	Ⓞ	Ⓞ	Ⓞ	Ⓞ	Ⓞ
Ⓟ	Ⓟ	Ⓟ	Ⓟ	Ⓟ	Ⓟ
Ⓠ	Ⓠ	Ⓠ	Ⓠ	Ⓠ	Ⓠ
Ⓡ	Ⓡ	Ⓡ	Ⓡ	Ⓡ	Ⓡ
Ⓢ	Ⓢ	Ⓢ	Ⓢ	Ⓢ	Ⓢ
Ⓣ	Ⓣ	Ⓣ	Ⓣ	Ⓣ	Ⓣ
Ⓤ	Ⓤ	Ⓤ	Ⓤ	Ⓤ	Ⓤ
Ⓥ	Ⓥ	Ⓥ	Ⓥ	Ⓥ	Ⓥ
Ⓦ	Ⓦ	Ⓦ	Ⓦ	Ⓦ	Ⓦ
Ⓧ	Ⓧ	Ⓧ	Ⓧ	Ⓧ	Ⓧ
Ⓨ	Ⓨ	Ⓨ	Ⓨ	Ⓨ	Ⓨ
Ⓩ	Ⓩ	Ⓩ	Ⓩ	Ⓩ	Ⓩ

1. Ⓐ Ⓑ Ⓒ Ⓓ Ⓔ
2. Ⓐ Ⓑ Ⓒ Ⓓ Ⓔ
3. Ⓐ Ⓑ Ⓒ Ⓓ Ⓔ
4. Ⓐ Ⓑ Ⓒ Ⓓ Ⓔ
5. Ⓐ Ⓑ Ⓒ Ⓓ Ⓔ
6. Ⓐ Ⓑ Ⓒ Ⓓ Ⓔ
7. Ⓐ Ⓑ Ⓒ Ⓓ Ⓔ
8. Ⓐ Ⓑ Ⓒ Ⓓ Ⓔ
9. Ⓐ Ⓑ Ⓒ Ⓓ Ⓔ
10. Ⓐ Ⓑ Ⓒ Ⓓ Ⓔ

11. Ⓐ Ⓑ Ⓒ Ⓓ Ⓔ
12. Ⓐ Ⓑ Ⓒ Ⓓ Ⓔ
13. Ⓐ Ⓑ Ⓒ Ⓓ Ⓔ
14. Ⓐ Ⓑ Ⓒ Ⓓ Ⓔ
15. Ⓐ Ⓑ Ⓒ Ⓓ Ⓔ
16. Ⓐ Ⓑ Ⓒ Ⓓ Ⓔ
17. Ⓐ Ⓑ Ⓒ Ⓓ Ⓔ
18. Ⓐ Ⓑ Ⓒ Ⓓ Ⓔ
19. Ⓐ Ⓑ Ⓒ Ⓓ Ⓔ
20. Ⓐ Ⓑ Ⓒ Ⓓ Ⓔ

21. Ⓐ Ⓑ Ⓒ Ⓓ Ⓔ
22. Ⓐ Ⓑ Ⓒ Ⓓ Ⓔ
23. Ⓐ Ⓑ Ⓒ Ⓓ Ⓔ
24. Ⓐ Ⓑ Ⓒ Ⓓ Ⓔ
25. Ⓐ Ⓑ Ⓒ Ⓓ Ⓔ
26. Ⓐ Ⓑ Ⓒ Ⓓ Ⓔ
27. Ⓐ Ⓑ Ⓒ Ⓓ Ⓔ
28. Ⓐ Ⓑ Ⓒ Ⓓ Ⓔ
29. Ⓐ Ⓑ Ⓒ Ⓓ Ⓔ
30. Ⓐ Ⓑ Ⓒ Ⓓ Ⓔ

31. Ⓐ Ⓑ Ⓒ Ⓓ Ⓔ
32. Ⓐ Ⓑ Ⓒ Ⓓ Ⓔ
33. Ⓐ Ⓑ Ⓒ Ⓓ Ⓔ
34. Ⓐ Ⓑ Ⓒ Ⓓ Ⓔ
35. Ⓐ Ⓑ Ⓒ Ⓓ Ⓔ
36. Ⓐ Ⓑ Ⓒ Ⓓ Ⓔ
37. Ⓐ Ⓑ Ⓒ Ⓓ Ⓔ
38. Ⓐ Ⓑ Ⓒ Ⓓ Ⓔ
39. Ⓐ Ⓑ Ⓒ Ⓓ Ⓔ
40. Ⓐ Ⓑ Ⓒ Ⓓ Ⓔ

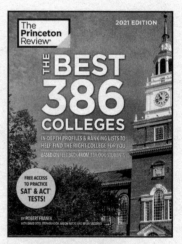